LIVING
ON
STAGE

LIVING ON STAGE

Acting from the Inside Out: A Practical Process

WALT WITCOVER

Back Stage Books, New York

Senior Editor: Mark Glubke
Cover Design: Eric Olson
Interior Design: Cheryl Viker
Production Manager: Hector Campbell

First published in 2004 by Back Stage Books,
an imprint of Watson-Guptill Publications,
a division of VNU Business Media, Inc.
770 Broadway , New York, NY 10003
www.watsonguptill.com

Library of Congress Control Number: 2004103242

ISBN: 0-8230-2832-1

Manufactured in the United States of America

First printing 2004

1 2 3 4 5 6 7 8 9 / 11 10 09 08 07 06 05 04

For JTB and RJH, in loving remembrance
of their lifelong devotion and support;
and to all those "Witcoverians"—my students,
past and present, who, together with my mentors,
Curt Conway, Herbert Berghof, and Lee Strasberg,
have taught me everything I know about
Living on Stage

Contents

ACKNOWLEDGEMENTS

This book would not have been written without the insistent assistance of my students, past and present, colleagues and friends. To all of them I am extremely indebted. Here I should like to acknowledge my special gratitude to:

My first collaborator, Priscilla O. Alexander, for her steadfast support and ever-ready ear, mind, heart, and helping hand throughout these sixty years;

My former student, stellar actress and respected author Barbara Barrie, for her encouragement and valuable advice in pursuing this project;

Devoted friends Jerry Stiller and Anne Meara, for over fifty years of loyal support and for Jerry's foreword to this work;

My editor at Back Stage Books, Mark Glubke, for his staunch encouragement and sound editorial advice;

My student and friend, Marty McDonough, for invaluable legal assistance on contracts;

Dramatists' Play Service, Inc. for permission to quote from *I am a Camera*, *Picnic* and *The Glass Menagerie*;

Leyna Gabriele and Peter Schlosser, former students and present colleagues, whose training of singers based on their work with me has in turn enriched my own work;

Rusty Wilson, Andrew Alburger, and Neil Stone, former students who first tested portions of this book as teachers in their own acting classes;

These students whose training sessions are recounted (under fictitious names) in the following pages: Jason Scott Campbell, Ed Farrell, Cybelle Gouverneur, Karl Jacob, Regina Kessler, Brendan McCarthy, Nadine Moody, Nicholas Psaltos, John Wallace, and Joyce Yao;

Former students who contributed tape-recorded interviews relating their experiences working with me and their application of my training on stage and screen, and to Regina Kessler, who arranged and conducted these interviews: Barbara Barrie, Prudence Barry, Robert Clohessy, Lenore Fuerstman, Leyna Gabriele, Tim Jerome, Tony Musante, Nancy Ponder, Peter Schlosser, and Patrizia von Brandenstein;

The Student Committee that solicited questionnaire responses detailing the influence of my training on subsequent professional work: Robert Clohessy, Ed Farrell, Lenore Fuerstman, Regina Kessler, Tony Musante, Nicholas Psaltos, Michael Stebbins, and Victoria Thompson;

The following students whose questionnaire responses proved most applicable: Lee Chamberlin, Alex Cord, Serge Delpierre, Carolyn Boston Geer, Luciano Guerriero, Carol Hebald, Helen Trowbridge Hoffman, Michael Hume, Annette Hunt, Robert Kerbeck, Bob Kiss, Valerie Lash, Al Markim, Bavat Marom, Marty McDonough, Craig Noble, D.J. O'Neill, Brett Reed, Lynne

Rogers, Bob Snively, Roseann Sheridan, Jacqueline Sydney, Susanne Traub, and JoAnn Wahl;

Authors Howard Greenfeld, Lynne Rogers, and Will Scheffer, the last two also former students, for their encouragement and professional advice;

And lastly—but also firstly—Regina Kessler and Michael Stebbins, devoted friends, for their steadfast persistence in getting me to write and continue writing these pages; for their constant encouragement and support; and for promoting this effort and pointing the way toward finding a publisher.

FOREWORD

I was waiting for action, which meant the four cameras and sound were in sync, and I would make my entrance. Just at that moment, someone shouted, "This is for America!" Welcome, Jerry Stiller, to the world of television shot before a live audience. I was in disarray. My concentration was gone. Patriotism had suddenly become an issue, and I wondered why I had ever decided to become an actor.

The momentary shock did not stop me from performing the scene. We did another take, and after checking the gate, the warm-up man shouted, "We're moving on!"

The studio audience applauded. Two-and-a-half hours later the show was in the can. No pick-ups, which meant we had done our work; in three weeks the edited show with music, commercials and promos would be aired—and it was for America.

At the beginning, there was just the dream of being on stage. Conquering the public's heart. Seeing my name on a marquee, living in the Dakota, eating at Sardi's, hobnobbing with the literati, going to parties, and getting into movies for free. I could never admit to my shallowness. I didn't dare. But it didn't stop me from trying to make it happen. The stage was the one place where a rich imagination and an out-of-control belief system could change my life. It was a perfect match for a profession that didn't have rules for a foolish but well-meaning kid who never learned structure.

Brought up in the Depression, when there were no jobs, dreams floated freely among the hardest hit—the poor. On the screen in movie houses, I could see larger-than-life actors laughing their way through life's travails. My kid's mind allowed me to leap up there on to the screen with Groucho, Chico and Harpo. I imagined myself a stowaway in the stateroom scene on board the ocean liner in *A Night at the Opera*. Little did I realize that one day Groucho Marx would invite Anne and myself to his home for dinner. So it only proves that the dream world and reality are sometimes not that far apart.

I had been performing in enough Broadway, off-Broadway, and regional theatre work to raise a family and even at times qualify for unemployment insurance. In the Sixties, my wife Anne Meara and I performed as a comedy team in coffeehouses and nightclubs across America and in Europe; we appeared on the Ed Sullivan show thirty times. And we wrote and recorded countless radio commercials.

All of this is a lead-in to my speaking about *Living on Stage*, the wonderful book by my friend, Walt Witcover. Having gone from the dream stage to falling in love with acting and knowing that show business was for me, I realized I had to convince someone that I could act. This is the gap I had to fill in. What the audience sees is not what's going on in the actor's mind. He is in a different

PART I

The Hazards of Acting

CHAPTER 1

The Acting Instrument

The new student stands hesitantly, apparently paralyzed, on the mottled carpet. He looks to me expectantly. Then to the easy chair I have just placed in the center of the carpet, facing me. And then back to me. Should he sit or remain standing? He wants me to tell him what to do. I keep my mouth tightly shut and merely stare at him. A confrontation? Perhaps. This is my first acting exercise.

We have already met, the new student and I. I interview him to find out why he sought me out as a possible acting teacher/coach. Usually it's word of mouth, from a book on New York acting teachers, or, more recently, from my web site on the Internet. I ask about his background, schooling, acting experience, and any previous training. I'm interested in his family, any history of performing or artistic activities in any relatives, his interests, physical condition, hang-ups, etc. And I share some of my background in theatre, acting, directing, and now teaching during the past fifty years. I explain my ideas about actor training, my commitment to process, my sequential approach, my starting from square one. We talk for perhaps forty minutes, getting acquainted. In that time, I ascertain whether I want him as a new student, and he finds out whether I am the teacher/coach to trust with this precious part of his life. We agree to work together. And we set up a convenient time to begin.

This young man is twenty-three. His only prior acting experience is in a student film at college—where he had five different majors and played sports. Now, a year out of college and marking time working in the family business, he is encouraged by his girlfriend to make a start at something he is really drawn to. That small experience of performing in a film has never been forgotten. It has precipitated a fervent desire to explore acting. Not yet on stage, in performance, in a play, but as a student. The young man is an athlete and knows the dangers of too much too soon. I like that—a clean slate for me to work with—and no rush for results. We have met just an hour-and-a-half ago, at noon, on his day off, when he could drive into mid-Manhattan from his suburban New Jersey home. And the outcome of our interview is an agreement to start working together, at first one session weekly. Now, after a lunch break, we are beginning here in my studio.

At first we do a few mild physical warm-ups, relaxing, continuing our conversation, continuing to get acquainted. He seems honest, relaxed, interested. He has agreed when I say that my training for the actor requires the Will—on his part to, come here regularly; the Willingness—to trust me and the various challenges I will throw at him; and the Understanding of what my training will bring. Though his conscious mind is the least valuable part of his acting equipment, like the door to this studio, it *is* the only way in. And while we both limber up, I mention some of the basic hazards that actors face.

"All performing artists—singers, dancers, musicians, mimes, clowns, and lion-tamers—share a common special problem. In contrast to 'creative artists'—such as painters, writers and composers, who may create when and where they choose, anywhere at anytime —the actor, like all other performers, must create on demand. He must do his thing at a special occasion. He performs where and when the audience comes, where and when the producer says "Curtain!" Where and when the camera rolls and the director calls "Action!" Where and when the actor hears his cue. All in public. The performer's work—the performance—is offered for the audience's approval or disapproval at the very moment it is made! Terrifying!"

After this ominous introduction, I ask him if he is ready for our first exercise. He feels fine—so let's go!

I get the armchair from the side of the studio and place it in the center of the carpet, facing front. I go to my desk, on the studio floor among the blue folding chairs, relics from the old Lindy's Restaurant, and a raised pew at the back, a relic from our Laboratory Theatre days at a Brooklyn Heights church. I now sit at my desk, take a fresh sheet of paper and a pencil, and turn to look at him. Not simply, as I have been looking at him until now—but with a new, more rapt attention. I stare—intently.

He doesn't know whether to sit or remain standing. This is new. Most students in this position get my unspoken message and immediately sit in the chair. But I welcome a variation. I enjoy this exercise. It reveals so much so quickly. He stands waiting, and after about twenty seconds, asks, "Should I sit or stand?"

I give no answer. I try not to move in any way. I merely write down what he has said. And return to staring at him. He starts to look around the studio—for help? Then back to me. After a few minutes—I want him to remember this moment—I decide to take pity on him.

"Yes, sit, if you like."

And he sits. Where he continues to look at me, waiting for my instruction. I wait, still staring, noting his every move and writing it on my paper. He begins to smile, tries to control it, then breaks out laughing. I smile. He turns serious.

"Should I do something?"

I make a motion of buttoning my lip. I will not speak. He straightens his face, ordering control. He fidgets, his hands opening and closing. When I focus on them, he stops. He shifts his position in the chair, his feet start tapping the carpet. When I look at them and make another note, he stops. He suddenly laughs again. And controls himself again. Now he looks for help all around the studio. Then back to me. And still he waits. Finally, it is enough. He has experienced what I intended. Now we can explore the purpose and the meaning of the exercise.

I ask him to try to tell me what he has felt during the preceding little confrontation. Confusion, nervousness, self-consciousness. And we compare those unwelcome feelings with what he had experienced earlier, during our interview in my office and while we were warming up on the carpet. Only when I had put the armchair for him in the center of the lighted carpet area that serves as a stage, and had retreated to my desk chair and begun staring at him in silence, did this unwelcome tension overtake him. Only when he had given up his ordinary volition, waited abjectly for my instruction, and looked for my guidance and approval. And he could now see that I had put him in the performing position—on stage—without anything to perform! And by staring at him in silence, I had put myself into the audience position—judging; and by writing, even that of a critic! By simply throwing him "on stage" without any preparation, I had led him into this unpleasant experience. Now I assure him that what he felt was quite appropriate. And his reactions were not nearly so extravagant as many a new student in this position. Some have become voluble, some hysterical, but all have been in some degree diminished, fractured, gone-to-pieces.

So I ask, what was the difference that led him into this most unpleasant state—after we had got on so well at our initial interview and in our first "warming up" together on the carpet. He hadn't felt at all uneasy and self-conscious then, had he? Not at all! But when I set the chair for him on the carpet and went to sit at my desk and looked intently at him and started taking notes, the climate seemed to change. The comfortable temperature of the studio seemed suddenly to get very hot—or very cold—in either case, most uncomfortable. Yet there were the same two people in this same studio—and the same actual temperature. Then, what was the difference?

"Well, you were there, and I was here."

"Yes, and what else was going on?"

"You stopped speaking."

"Yes, indeed. I shut up. Very difficult for me nowadays. What else?"

"You were staring at me."

"Indeed I was. Looking fixedly at you. Not as I had before, but much more intently. I focused on you."

"And you took notes."

"Yes, like a critic! But let's start with the primary differences. I came here and you stayed there. And by staring at you and shutting up, I made you feel that you were, well, how would you put it?"

"On the spot?"

"Yes. But we call that spot the stage. You were on stage, weren't you?"

"In a way, yes."

"And I stopped talking. As if I were in the audience at the theatre, I kept quiet. If you ever go to the Chinese or the Yiddish theatre, you'll discover quite a different kind of audience. It's more of a social occasion, so their attention is only occasionally on the stage—when the actor recites a famous speech, perhaps, or performs an unusual feat. Most of the time these more casual audiences are noisily visiting their friends. But I stared at you, didn't I?"

"Very much. It made me uncomfortable."

"Well, let me ask you. When you go on to the stage, would you like me *not* to look at you? At my watch, perhaps? Or for the nearest exit?"

"Oh, no. That wouldn't be so good."

"Not at all. So my staring comes with my being an audience. In fact, if I don't keep watching you intently, then you—the actor—will have failed. Agreed?"

"I guess so."

"Being stared at is not welcome very often in our culture. Particularly from someone we don't know, it makes us uncomfortable. Stare at some outlandishly dressed and made-up young person on the subway platform, and you'll often receive a menacing look in return that says, 'What are you staring at, Bud?' But being stared at comes with being an actor. Now let me ask you, while my attention was fixed on you, where was your own attention?"

"On you."

"Yes. But while we agree that the attention of the audience should be fixed on the actor, should the actor's attention be on the audience?"

"I don't think so. No."

"I agree. Ninety-five percent of the time, it should be on his fellow actors. The other times, when the actor plays a Narrator or Chorus, it may be on us out here. But your attention was not only on me; it was also on your own performance. You were wondering if I approved of what you were doing. What I wanted from you, and if you were doing enough. You were evaluating how well you were coming across. And that, plus watching me watch you, made you quite uncomfortable. And rightly so!"

Now with his unpleasant experience as evidence, we continue exploring more of the basic acting predicament. The hazards that afflict all actors, yesterday, today, tomorrow, on small stages or grand, live or on camera, before only a director or an audience of thousands. The actor must seem to be unaffected by those staring eyes demanding that he do something to earn our attention—that he interest, entertain, or inspire us. This obligation to please—to perform—is perhaps the first obstacle, the first paradox. Those actors we catch performing merely earn our disapproval. We honor only those actors who do not seem to be performing at all! Those who seem to be living when they are performing. And so we define where we are headed: Living on Stage, which is a very strange Paradox: Living, which is actually Performing, and Performing that looks like Living!

Do we ever hear it said that "Heifetz plays so well he isn't playing?" "Nureyev dances so well he isn't dancing?" Hardly. But, "Brando *is* the Godfather." "Streep *is* Sophie." "Fonda, or Tracy, or Pacino," or any admired, professional actor "acts so well he isn't acting!" A paradox, a paradox, a most ingenious paradox!

And the actor, in contrast to the musician, but in common with the singer and dancer, has only himself as his instrument. His voice and body, certainly, but also his mind, senses, emotions—his soul. His entire being is his instrument to be played upon by the author, the director, the composer, the conductor, the designers and the actor himself. And he must always seem to be not acting—not performing! As Harold Clurman puts it, he must tell "Lies Like Truth":

- To be in public and seem to be in private

- To repeat over and over again and have it seem always to be the very first time—unrehearsed, unanticipated, unknown

- To engender passionate concern for things, people, and ideas that do not matter to himself in the least

- And finally—to do what Hamlet calls the "monstrous" thing—to "force his soul" to create real physical and emotional responses to totally imaginary stimuli ("And all for nothing—for Hecuba!")

So we outline some of the major problems that lie in wait for the actor. And I explain that I have found that the best way to start tackling these problems is not to jump into the quicksand of "As If"—those parts of acting that usually first attract us to the stage. These demand a trained imagination and are foreign to our daily lives, appearing as kings and queens, heroes, villains, and fools, expressing passion in poetry, and trying to Be, to Show, and to Express.

I know all too well from my own experience what this often leads to: concern with How, and more tension. No. Not at all! If acting, "Living on Stage," is really living in the state of "I Am As If," then we must begin with the "I Am" part of acting—the living actor himself. And, as Stanislavsky maintains, he must come to the stage "continuing to live."

While what most often attracts us to acting is the "There and Then," it is a hazardous territory for the beginning actor. I have found that we must start with the "Here and Now." Only later can we begin to realize that acting is best approached as "I Am Here and Now—As If There And Then."

I continue. "For what we most look for in an actor is his ability to be Natural on stage. So I aim at this as my 'first base' in the game of acting. By 'Natural,' I mean the ability to live and behave on stage as truly, as effortlessly, as we do in life—offstage—in our better, most relaxed and least self-conscious moments. I mean to be true to ourselves. 'Second base' is to be Real. And to be Real, I mean to be true to the character in the situation in which the playwright puts him. This takes some doing, and we will come to this if you continue to 'stick around,' as I put it. For I think I can teach anyone who submits to my process to be Natural first and then to be Real. 'Third base' is to be 'Expressive.' This takes some talent, I'm afraid. And this means to reveal hitherto hidden facets of the character in new, freshly meaningful ways. And last—a 'Home Run!' By this, I mean a performance that is astonishing, unforgettable—the mark of those rare performances that linger long after, that really illuminate the play and provide those memorable experiences. But we must always follow the sequence. For now, let us focus on getting to first base—to learn to be Natural on stage. It is quite enough for a start."

To the second exercise. If time permits, and the student seems ready— clearly grasping my message—I may launch into this exercise immediately. Just as often, when I feel that the student has had enough input for one session, I will hold back and put off the second exercise for another session.

But this young man seems alert, again much more relaxed and "together." So I decide to move immediately to our second exercise: The Focus of Attention. This will offer a helping hand to the floundering, self-conscious, young would-be actor now at sea on an empty, perilous stage, and gasping for help.

I remove the pencils from the mug on my desk and hand it to this willing student. This mug was given to me years ago by one of my favorite students, now the Artistic Director of his own theatre out West. It is decorated with a stencil, rings of red apples, and yellow pencils and the phrase, "My Favorite Teacher." It is a true piece of kitsch, and I treasure it.

"Look at this," I ask him. "Explore it—and speak aloud whatever you discover."

It is a simple tangible object. Similar to other mugs he has often seen, but never, probably, has he seen this particular one. He takes it and examines it.

"Lots of apples. Lots of pencils. Inside full of inkspots. Smooth. Just an ordinary mug."

He sets it down, then looks to me for approval.

"That's it?"

He picks up the mug again.

I continue, "How many apples? How many pencils?"

He begins to count. He gives me a correct number and turns to me again, waiting for an evaluation. His look says, "Is that okay, teach?"

"Are all the apples alike? All the pencils?"

Again he looks. More closely.

"No. Some of the apples are different."

"In what way different?"

He really looks now.

"In fact, each apple is different."

"Really? In what ways are they different?"

He is studying the cup more intently. He relaxes further. And his focus of attention is sharpened. He is getting interested in the cup, in the problem of exploring, of searching.

He finds answers to my questions. And with each answer, he again looks to me—as if to say, "Is that okay? Is that what you want?"

I ask him to find three new things he hadn't yet noticed. His attention is challenged and he returns to examine the mug. And he gradually becomes more interested in the object.

When he gives me three answers, I ask for three more. And then three more again. Until I no longer have to prod him with questions, challenges. He is really looking, really searching, really involving himself in the exploration of my mug.

Finally, when I see that he has finally become involved, that he has forgotten to check me out, to see if I approve, I can call a halt to the exercise.

"Very good. You are now approaching the creative state."

"What? Looking at this mug!?"

"Exactly. When you were *really* looking. Each time I threw you a challenge—a question—your senses were exploring the mug. When you had found an answer, you came back to me with the implied question, 'Is that okay?' So our experiment shows us that a question, a problem, is of real value to the actor, drawing him further into his stage objects, into what Stanislavsky calls his 'Circle of Attention.' An answer, a solution, only leads him back to his audience with 'How am I doing?' Thus the first paradox for the actor: Questions are the answer! Problems are the solution! And human questions and problems can lead us into the creative state."

Later, my young actor will learn to develop an "Acting Score," a series of questions and problems discovered and arranged through improvisation and rehearsal in a role. Like an obstacle course, or any series of hurdles, these problems can be tackled each time he comes onto the stage in that role. And, if followed from scene to scene throughout the play, this Acting Score will stimulate him to find fresh, if similar, solutions at each performance. But for now, I continue.

"Stanislavsky was in the same position as you. He was a young actor, eager to be a popular leading man, who wanted to improve. He discovered that when he thought he was acting well, his audiences often did not agree, but when he thought that he wasn't so good, they were often more impressed. So he decided to ask the best actors of his day if they had some special insight into performing at their best. He sent out a questionnaire — 'When are you acting at your best?'"

"And they all replied, 'When I am in the creative state.'

"Another query: 'And what is that creative state?'

"Came the answer: 'When I am acting at my best.'

"Stanislavsky pondered. It seemed to him a little 'chicken-and-egg.' More research — years, in fact. And finally he discovered this remarkable truth: The creative state of the actor on the stage, while performing at his best, is nothing more nor less than the normal state of a human being offstage — not Performing — just Living!

"From this he drew this conclusion: To be fully alive on stage, free and in contact with our best impulses and talent, we must live as we live offstage. Though we are in a totally different climate, a totally different set of performing conditions, the same natural laws must apply.

I tell my student, "I don't know whether a fish, swimming happily in the water, sees the dry land, or the dry boat, as an alien climate. But I do know that when the fish is plopped out of the water and left on dry land, or in the dry fishing boat, eventually it gasps and dies. So it is with the actor. From his life, he looks at the stage, and it seems so similar to his own life. But when he comes to the stage unprepared, he gasps and seems 'to die.' While the stage appears to be just like life, with the same atmosphere, it is in fact violently different. And if unprepared, our actor will flounder and 'die' as well."

And I observe that when he was able to really examine my mug and get involved — and surprisingly, interested in it — he seemed to relax. His voice was more natural, more expressive. His entire being seemed much more at home — almost as if I weren't there, as if he were in private. The active focus of his attention to the mug had freed him from concern with my reactions, my evaluation, my approval. His "performing concern" had been replaced by a "human concern." A very important — in fact, essential — first step.

I declare that I have taken it as my job to acquaint him with the strange atmosphere of the stage, to introduce him to those alien waters. Then, in performance he will be able to swim as naturally as if he'd done it all his life. Together we will examine just what it means to "Live on Stage." We will explore together—I, as well as he, searching out the clues to this paradoxical state of being. For if I do not learn, he will not learn. And so we must recognize this most fundamental fact for the performer who wishes to live while performing: the actor must learn to replace his normal performing concerns with the human concerns—of himself today and of his character tomorrow.

I further observe that examining the mug is very similar to what babies do—without the will to focus, merely following their normal instincts—to look, listen, smell, touch, taste. They exercise their five senses, and this is healthy, constructive, an essential part of growing. So now the would-be actor must retrain these senses that have grown dull over the years. We must learn, all over again, to look, listen, touch, smell, and taste.

For the senses are the gateways to our experience, to our memories, to our imagination and to our inspiration. As the pianist must practice finger exercises at the keyboard and the dancer basic body movements at the *barre*, so the actor must exercise his senses, now with immediate experience, later with remembered and imagined stimuli. And so my young would-be actor-in-training has a clear start.

Before we part, I inform my student, now somewhat chastened and newly serious, of the next session's exercise. Of course he will continue exercising his five senses, and I advise him that we may well have a review of this "focus of attention" exercise with a different object. But for our next class, we will examine a Simple Familiar Task.

I explain that while I try to use as little jargon as possible, employing the simplest and shortest words, I must not explain too clearly what I mean. For then the student may perform the exercise too perfectly, and we will not learn as much. I must set traps for him—not so large that he will fall and break a leg, but small ones, so that he will stub a toe perhaps. I must lead him to discover that here is a basic acting problem that must be faced, and overcome, so that it will not remain to trip him up later on stage. So I only add that "simple" means not necessarily easy, but something that can be performed by will, not requiring talent or imagination; "familiar" means not new; and a "task" is something that wants or needs to be done. That is all.

I think that it has been a good session. He grasps my hand warmly, and we part. I think that his mind has been opened, and I am excited. Teaching an intelligent new student of potential ability is always a high for me. I cannot tell if this young man is talented. Not yet. But our technique exercises will help to reveal a talent—and nourish it—if it is there. Our exercises also will provide a strong defense against the damage of often-misguided teachers, coaches, and directors. I hope my training will develop good habits. Like any good training, it is meant to be habit-forming—healthy habits to nourish a young and eager acting instrument.

I look forward to our next session.

CHAPTER 2

Selecting and Accomplishing Stage Tasks

The day of our second class promises snow. In fact, New York City schools have been shut tightly and offices closed down in anticipation of the worst snowstorm of the year. I wonder if my student will cancel, for he drives in from New Jersey. But the storm swerves widely away from New York, merely dusting us with snowflakes, and my eager student arrives on the dot.

Again we warm up, facing each other on the studio carpet, doing simple stretches. I ask him how he felt after our first session a week ago. It made him think, he says. And it almost seems a complaint—as if he blames me.

"Good. That's my aim. I want to get you to question—to begin to look with fresh eyes, listen with fresh ears."

We review the focus of attention exercise—this time with another mug, a wild circus souvenir, tigers chasing around the cup, their tails forming the handle. Now there is no hint of a problem. He examines—searching, touching, smelling, sounding. He seems fascinated, completely involved with the object. I have to interrupt. Good!

"And did you bring the new exercise I challenged you with? The 'simple, familiar task?'" (I know he has—I could hardly miss the objects he has brought into the studio, but I play innocent.)

"I brought two. I'm not sure which one is right."

Last week I chose the exercises. The tasks were done for me. Now he is to choose the task. For himself as well as for the assigned problem. This is the next step in our training. But this is not only an acting exercise. This is also an actual piece of his life.

"Try them both. We'll see."

He reveals a wine jug full of pennies that he has brought with him. He finds an empty plastic pitcher from our prop shelves and sets it on the floor. Then, perching on the daybed at the side of the studio, he starts to pitch penny after penny at the pitcher, trying to lob them in. The first few go widely over the mark, but gradually he adjusts to the distance and his pennies now start to go into the pitcher. Indeed, he seems skilled.

"What are you doing?"

"Trying to get the pennies into the container."

"Why?"

"Well, we used to do it between classes, out in the back alley—to relax. It was our game. I thought it might fit the exercise."

"And does it? Are you able to toss the pennies here as well as you used to between classes?"

"I think so. Yes."

"Then you are continuing to Live on Stage. The tossing pennies may be a good task for our purpose—we have a clear control from your experience in life with it. And that's our main problem just now. It is basic to all our later work: to learn to focus attention away from performing concerns (what I think of your performance, or your own estimation of how well you're doing) and onto 'human' concerns (like getting the pennies into the pitcher). So—were you focused? Relaxed? Involved?"

"I think so."

"Of course you were. If you weren't, you couldn't have gotten the pennies into the pitcher."

"So I did it right?"

"Almost."

"What? But you just said—"

"Let's see your other task. Then I'll explain."

Now he brings a sack of paper penny-rolls and sits on the carpet with the jug of pennies. He upends the jug, spilling out a small mound of pennies. And he starts to fill the fifty-penny rolls. I observe him. He is again focused, relaxed, involved. But can I talk to him while he is filling the paper rolls without disturbing his concentration? Though I suspect he'll lose count, I think I'll try.

"What are you doing now?"

"Filling these rolls with pennies."

"So I see. And why?"

"Whenever my jug gets full, I have to roll pennies into these papers from the bank. Then I turn them in and get real money for them."

"And why are you doing it here and now?"

"It was time—the jug was almost full. And I thought it might be a good task—for the exercise."

"Are you able to continue doing it while we talk? Without losing count?"

"Oh, sure."

And in fact he is able to continue very well. I decide to wait. I sit and watch him as he continues. When the small pile in front of him has gone into the paper rolls, he pours out another mound and continues, this time first making ten piles of five pennies each. He has a method. And I decide I must watch and wait until he has finished this task. Until all the pennies are transferred from the wine jug into the paper rolls.

This takes about twenty-five minutes. While he continues transferring his pennies, I point out one of the reasons I now prefer this one-on-one training to the large classes I used to teach. How could I ever permit, nay, encourage, him to complete this task if ten, or twenty, or more students were waiting, eager to boot him offstage so that they could get on? There's no opportunity to take the necessary time in a classroom. Moreover, it's so boring—watching someone transfer pennies. "We get the idea, let's get on with it!" I can hear the other students groaning.

But that's exactly the point. The young actor starting basic training must be encouraged to have the same experience on the stage as he would off—in life. He must be given my permission to complete his task. More than my permission—my clear desire. When and where, if not here and now, will he ever find this permission and encouragement? When he begins performing, he is at the mercy of the author, the director, the audience—only those bits of life that are dramatic, interesting, important can be permitted on stage! But here and now, in this one-on-one training, my young would-be actor is led to experience this full completion of a simple, ordinary, often boring task on stage.

Furthermore, just because it is so boring, it must be encouraged. The actor must learn that he is not on stage to interest, entertain, or inspire the audience. That is the playwright's job. Or, if the author needs help in that department, the director is all too ready to provide assistance. It is quite enough for the beginning actor to be natural here today—and real on stage tomorrow. He must learn to continue to Live on Stage. And to be really alive, he must also very often permit himself to appear quite boring to any observer.

He finishes the task. There are now twenty-three rolls of pennies. He has eleven dollars and fifty cents for his effort—a well-earned reward. I question him again.

"And this task? Were you able to do it here as well as you might at home?"

"Yes. Maybe even better."

"What do you mean?"

"At home I sometimes get distracted, get up to stretch, turn on the TV."

"But here, then, in a way, you were *more* alive than at home?"

"I guess so. Yes."

"And why did you transfer the pennies from the jug to the paper rolls?"

"The jug was getting full. And I needed a little pocket-change."

"Not just because you used to do it at one time. Or because you thought it might be good for the exercise. You did it because you really needed and wanted to do it. You had a clear and present Why to support your What. It was an actual, necessary piece of your life."

And we could now see that the first task, tossing the pennies—while truly done and holding his attention for a time—was missing an important foundation. It had only one foot on the ground, so to speak: to serve as a good task to carry out my training exercise. Whereas the second task—rolling pennies—had two feet on the ground. It was a task necessary in his real life and, at the same time, a stage task so helpful in our training and developing our craft.

"Moreover, this task had the three essential ingredients that made it work so well for you."

"Three ingredients?"

"Yes. First is the desire, or need, to do the task. Second is the equipment necessary to do it. You had the pennies and the paper rolls. The third is enough time and space."

"And now you can see how bringing a piece of life to the stage means living More. For there will always be two of you on stage: you the actor and you the character. There are always two sets of tasks. One is for you the actor—to perform as best you can, carry out the desires of the author, director, composer, conductor, choreographer, so many others, not to mention yourself. Simultaneously, you are trying to fulfill the aims and needs of your character, trying to solve his problems. Today, here in the training studio, that character is you, yourself—as you are offstage, in life. Tomorrow, in performance, it becomes the character you play on stage.

"All too often, acting training starts with the Character—Who Am I? I know mine did—at college and in summer stock theatres. Even Uta Hagen, in her *Respect for Acting*, much of which I applaud, starts with that demand for the actor, 'Who am I?' I have found that concern to be very hazardous for the beginning actor. All too often, it encourages conventional images of character types. It sets up intellectual clichés that only tend to separate the actor from really continuing to Live on Stage. To inoculate against these lamentable habits that produce stereotypical results, I start with the actor's own persona, with his or her own life. This true foundation promises that my students will have no problem later with developing a fresh, believable character."

I point out that our first questions for the student actor must be the simplest, most fundamental in living: "What am I doing?" and "Why am I doing it?"— What and Why.

So this student has done very well. Remarkably well, considering that he has avoided many pernicious traps. These "pieces of living" tasks serve so quickly to reveal attitudes to acting that must be immediately addressed and, if need be, corrected. Often a student will give an idea or an indication of the task. He will do a pantomime, showing in gestures how he would perform the task if he had the actual objects, the desire or need, and the time and space to do it. This is clearly not Living on Stage, for it accomplishes nothing but informing us what he would do were he ever in that situation. It is a hypothetical task, at best. And it is audience-directed. The actor's attention is on his performance.

Another student will give a demonstration of a task; as the salesman of a new carrot peeler in Macy's basement, he will pare a carrot in his sales-pitch demonstration. This time the task is *actually* performed. But the purpose is again audience-directed; it is to win the interest of the customer, his approval and desire to buy the peeler. The aim is the transfer of the carrot peeler from the salesman to the customer and the transfer of money from the customer to the salesman, not the carrot peeled quickly with less waste or stress. Again, focus on an audience result—a successful performance.

Only the actual task, done for a real life purpose, and carried out on stage for a performing purpose as well, can fill the actor with the nourishment so essential to his beginning stage diet. A true What, supported by a life Why. Like a healthy plant or tree, the "What" is seen clearly above ground, while the "Why" is the supporting roots, often hidden in the earth below. Or, to change the analogy, the building soars proudly up high into the city sky; its foundations are buried deep in bedrock. One of the differences between Living on Stage and off is that in life we are not always aware of the "Why" that lies behind and supports every "What." A man and woman marry, and they constantly quarrel and make a miserable couple, but years later, when he dies and leaves her a fortune, we understand. One of the special rewards the theatre provides in its "two hours traffic" is to reveal the hidden "Whys" of human lives. For while the actor in life may not always be clear about his own motives, and the character he plays may similarly be unaware, the actor, before he steps on stage to perform, must develop a godlike insight. Unlike both himself in his own life and his character on stage, the actor must be almost supernaturally clear as to why his character does whatever he does!

We are getting close to discovering the essential ingredients of a reliably nourishing stage task. As well as the rewards such a task brings to the actor.

But that will best be left until next time. I must let today's session rever-
berate in my young student's head. For next time I only change one element of
the problem: he is to bring in a "simple *unfamiliar* task." This task may be more
difficult to select, I warn my student, but it will very likely prove somewhat
easier to perform.

Again he shakes my hand warmly as he leaves. I think we are making progress.

CHAPTER 3

"What and Why?"

An hour before his scheduled lesson the following week, my student telephones me. He is sick; an intestinal upheaval has incapacitated him. Can he reschedule his lesson?

Maybe at some evening later in the week?

"Of course," I say, though I am somewhat disappointed. "Let me get my calendar."

I discover that I am booked up. So we settle for next week.

As it happens, the next day another new student brings in another "Simple Familiar Task." This student seems to have had more trouble with this exercise, not yet realizing that it entails a true piece of his life. So I have suggested that he find a "chore"—something that he needs to do, that perhaps he has been avoiding, putting off. Probably it is nothing he would like to give precious time to. By bringing it here, "killing two birds" at once, he may "get even" with it.

He telephones me the morning before his next scheduled class. Not another sudden sick-call! No, he just wants to know if eating something can fulfill the task.

"I can't tell you. Why not try and find out?"

I must not give an answer. He must be willing to do it, fail if need be, and then learn.

That afternoon, he arrives promptly for our session. He brings a paper sack and a large cup of some drink. And as soon as we finish our warm-up exercises, and I have reviewed the progression of our previous exercises, relating each to the basic problem of "Living on Stage," now the floor is all his—for his "Chore." He grabs his bag of food, takes out two Big Macs wrapped in wax paper, opens the large orange drink, digs into the sack for fries, and starts bolting his food down as if he hadn't eaten in a week. I am concerned for his digestion. I hardly need another sick student!

"What are you doing?"

"Eating."

"So I see. Why so hurriedly? Are you starved?"

"I didn't eat much for lunch today. Too busy."

And he continues to munch, chew and gulp down his Big Macs, fries, and orange drink. As he eats, his gaze wanders, now on some inner thought, now around the studio, now to the bag of fries as he searches for more. Is he wondering if this supper will serve the acting exercise? I very much want him to find that out for himself. Finally he finishes. He finds the bag in which he brought his food, and he carefully cleans up the wrappers, his soiled napkin and the empty drink cup and deposits them on a side-table to be removed to the garbage bin after class. And he now turns to me.

I nod. "All done? Satisfied?"

"I think so."

I can see he's not sure if this eating fulfilled the problem of the exercise. "You're not sure? You got your food down—you didn't choke, your appetite was satisfied. So what's missing?"

"Something—I just can't say."

"I think I can. While you were eating, where was your attention?"

"On my food . . . and elsewhere."

"Exactly. Only when you had a problem did the task—eating your supper— engage your attention. When you were opening the sticky wrappings on the Big Macs, trying to get the lid off the orange drink, searching for enough fries in the bag—only when you had an Obstacle did the task engage your full attention. Eating itself does not usually occupy our minds—unless we're still so young that getting the spoon to the mouth is a problem. Or we're food critics analyzing the recipe. Or if we have just come from the dentist and can't chew on that side, or our right arm is in a sling, or the food is too hot or strange. We focus on whatever creates a problem. Otherwise, eating is generally an Activity, pursued with only part of our attention while we attend to something else—the television, the girl across the table, the newspaper, last night's dream, tomorrow's planning, or stimulating conversation. There is a place for Activities as well as Tasks on stage, as in life. They often exchange priorities from first to second or third place in our attention—usually spontaneously. The only thing that matters for us, on stage, is that we not confuse them—that we do not mistake an Activity for a Task. The Activity is a kind of accompaniment, supporting or contrapuntal, to the melody or prime theme, so to speak. If we mistakenly think we are engaged in a Task and are merely performing an Activity, the focus of our attention is starved, and performing concerns are sure to rush in to distract us and thus break our concentration."

"So my 'chore' is still unfulfilled?"

"I'm afraid so. But let me help you. Don't you have something that needs repairing? Or cleaning? Or rearranging?"

"Not that I can think of. Not here." But he looks around and sees his brief-case on the carpet a few feet away. He brings it over, opens it and starts to spill out its contents—a handful of notebooks and scraps of paper.

I observe, "Doesn't it need cleaning out?"

"I guess so. Only I never get around to it. I never seem to have the time."

"You do now. Go ahead."

And he does. He proceeds carefully to examine all the articles tumbled out from his briefcase. The notebooks, billfold, and cash are carefully put aside. The scraps of notes are examined and each in turn copied into the small note-book and then crunched into a pile for disposal. Some are crunched without being copied. He is very involved in this task. It occupies him completely. And he is doing it thoroughly. I sit and watch, silent. I am very pleased. He has found a true Simple Familiar Task at last.

Finally, he finishes. He takes the pile of crunched notes to my wastebasket and closes the briefcase. He turns to me with a broad smile on his face. I think he now knows he has won. He has lived a piece of his life here and now— on stage. He has had the experience; now we can examine the technical principle involved. In order later to devote himself to living a part of the life of his character, the actor must prepare here by first living a part of his own life. Here and now, and for as long as it takes, on stage. He must discover that while he is performing he is also living. Or, since he is Living on Stage, he is also performing.

Now he can go on to the next problem—the Simple Unfamiliar Task.

❊　❊　❊

For the next session, my student who called in sick comes bouncing in at eight in the evening, bright with anticipation, proclaiming he has brought his Unfamiliar Task!

After our physical warm-up, again I review the steps we have already trod: the experience of being launched onto the stage without anything to perform, and the ensuing discomfort. The solace of a simple object, that mug, on which to focus our attention. Then a Simple Familiar Task of his own— turning a collection of loose pennies into bankable fifty-cent rolls. The easy, relaxing accomplishment of a life-task supported by a life-purpose. Now to the next step—another life task brought here to the stage, this time, a new one—unfamiliar.

He confidently gets his overcoat and proceeds to unzip the lining.

"I'm going to sew a button," he announces "Something I've never done!"

I watch, fascinated, as he proceeds to do just that. First, finding the button and its proper location on the coat, then threading the needle—a challenging problem! But he persists, his concentration acute, and after some difficulty, he succeeds in this step. Then he fashions a knot at the end of the thread—had he observed his mother at this task? (He had indeed!) And now he applies himself to sewing the button carefully in place. This takes some time. He is careful, for he truly wants this button to remain firmly sewn. Finally he succeeds, figuring out how to finish off. He zips back the lining into the coat; he tries the coat on, proudly buttoning his newly-sewn button; and, smiling in triumph, he turns to exhibit the happy result to me. Victory!

I smile too. He has triumphed over the problem of the exercise. And we review what he has accomplished. Something new for himself that needed to be done. And it has served his acting problem very well indeed. So now I can confidently sum up the lesson, the exercise both experienced and learned. While an unfamiliar task opens us to the possibility of self-consciousness, that trap is counter-balanced by the need to pay extra attention to the new, unfamiliar problem. It demands increased focus and so strengthens the actor's circle of attention.

"Now we can dissect the ten essential elements of a good acting task. And the five rewards you thereby earn. First of all, as you performed this task— sewing that errant button on your coat—was it for you or for me?"

"For me."

"Exactly. Number one—it was yours. For you, or people in your life—not for me, or for an audience. Secondly, was there a clear purpose, a clear goal?"

"Certainly. To get it sewn to the coat."

"Third—was it possible?'

"Of course. I had the button and I had the coat."

"Also the needle and thread. And a little time and a little space. Next—was it sensible?"

"Why, yes, of course."

"You didn't have to wonder, 'Why am I doing this?' It was clearly logical, it obviously made sense to you—very important. And fifth—was there a clear sequence of steps?"

"I think so."

"Indeed. I counted twelve distinct steps." And I recount them for him. "A clear sequence that is logical is very reassuring. Next—number six. Was it here and now or there and then?"

"Here and now."

"In other words, it was right in front of you at this moment—not at home yesterday or tomorrow. It was immediate. Seventh—was it specific or general?"

"Very specific."

"Indeed, yes. Abstract or tangible?"

"Tangible."

"Quite. Later, of course, we will grapple with the many abstract ideas that plays are full of—love and hate, success, revenge, triumph and defeat. But these intangibles are hazardous for beginning actors. So we start with a button for a coat. Active or passive?"

"Active."

"Very. Though you didn't move from the chair, there was purposeful action. Essential. I remember an opera I saw that was full of crowds of people rushing from one side of the stage to the other. The director sought to create some action. But the only purposeful action I remember was between the scenes, when some stagehands moved a fireplace off from the forestage. It accomplished something, while all the rushing around of the chorus was merely busy—and therefore tedious. Busyness is no substitute for action.

"And finally—number ten—did it require attention?"

"Very much so."

"Essential for a rewarding stage task. Unless it holds your attention, you will flounder. I have found these ten ingredients to be extremely nourishing whenever we go on stage. Perhaps not all are essential all the time. But the more of these elements an actor has, the sturdier is his foundation, and the more secure he is. And the more secure he is, the freer he becomes.

"And now for the five rewards: Were you focused—occupied and involved?"

"Quite."

"Relaxed?"

"Why, yes, I think so."

"Very much so. A simple, truthful, logical task that can be performed at will relaxes us. Of course, the actor will also be asked to perform many tasks that require ordering the imagination—'As If' tasks that will often seem amazing. These require relaxation before we can begin to accomplish them. And so we come to them later in our training—in due time. Third—were you convinced?"

"Certainly."

"There was no question of why you were sewing that button. Everything you did served to bolster your sense of truth. Your belief in your stage life was unquestioned. Very helpful and most important. Fourth—were you encouraged?"

"I'm not quite sure what you mean."

"When we are focused, relaxed, and convinced of the truth of what we are doing, we are unconsciously encouraged to go further. Our unconscious creativity—our impulses—will arise to carry us forward, often far beyond what we had expected or planned. We discover creative, expressive behavior we might otherwise never have found. And fifth—finally—we are magically transported."

"Transported?"

"Offstage! While physically we remain on stage, of course, psychologically and artistically it is As If we are offstage. We are not preoccupied by our performing self, our inner critical eye and ear, or by the evaluation of our performance by the audience. For we are fully occupied in a truthful, logical, immediate and active confronting of a series of specific problems that engages our attention fully. We are truly Living on Stage. We are fully alive, trying to carry out logical character tasks for logical human purposes. We are fully focused, relaxed and involved, as we are in our better moments offstage, in life. That is what we mean when we say that an actor 'inhabits his character'—or seems 'not to be acting.' And we can achieve it through these simple exercises, for now, always in our own persona, but later, as the character we enact, by following clear, practical steps. We must learn to approach stage problems as we do in life, where we are not usually so aware of the ingredients or the process. In fact, only when something goes awry—physically or psychologically—do we examine what has been happening in our own lives. On the stage, however, we must know everything about our character's life—his motives and tasks, overt and hidden, conscious and unconscious—often much more than he may know himself. This chart of healthy ingredients and creative rewards, I've discovered, forms a clear springboard to Living on Stage.

**The Ten Vitamins that Provide Nourishment
for a Healthy Diet of Stage Tasks:**

1. It is Yours—for you or your character and people in your life—not for the author, director, or audience

2. It has a Clear Purpose or Goal

3. It is Possible to achieve

4. It is Sensible to pursue

5. It has a Clear Sequence of Steps

6. It is Immediate—here and now

7. It is Specific, not general

8. It is Tangible, not abstract

9. It is Active, not passive

10. It Requires Attention

The Five Rewards of a Good Stage task:

1. It Focuses, Occupies, Involves you

2. It Relaxes you

3. It Convinces you

4. It Encourages you — to go further

5. It Transports you — as if offstage

So in these five exercises, my young acting student has learned much. Now we are ready to turn a very important corner. He will begin to lie. To tell "Lies Like Truth." To add to his essential "I Am" the first essential grains of "As If."

But before we can turn that corner, I think that we must begin on a second major branch of the actor's training. By now, my student has acquired the ability to "continue to live" on stage — naturally and truthfully. He is able to maintain the common sense and what I call his "life logic" when he comes to the stage. He has begun to develop his all-important Sense of Truth. Now I turn his attention to the second essential area of the actor's work. It is that all-important ingredient that enables the actor to bring life to the playwright's character. It is his Personal Involvement.

PART II

**Personal
Involvement**

CHAPTER 4

Introduction to Analogy: Content before Form

Now that the task exercises can be more easily accomplished and analyzed, there remains enough class time to introduce the student to an equally essential new branch of our work. In succeeding classes, he will pursue this new sequence of exercises, while also continuing with my arrangement of Stanislavsky's "System of Physical Tasks."

This is a second major thrust, almost equal in importance to the first. It centers on Personal Involvement. Along with Communication and Selecting and Accomplishing Stage Tasks, it is one of the three main areas of my training—perhaps the three most important facets of the actor's work. I have begun with the Physical Tasks; they seem the most basic, clearest in idea and execution. We will focus on Communication as part of this new series of exercises in building a monologue directed to the audience, but our prime attention must now be focused on Personal Involvement.

By demanding Personal Involvement, I believe we imply that a fully satisfying acting performance demands more than the actor's conscious will, his understanding and commitment. It is not enough for the actor merely to speak the words intelligently and carry out the actions of his role; he must also be, somehow, "Convincing"; he must, in some not-so-obvious, seemingly magical way, be "Present." In order truly to Live on Stage, to "Inhabit" a character in thought and feeling, as well as in word and deed, we need to stimulate the active involvement of those parts of ourselves that are not usually subject to our wills. We seek not only actions, but also reactions—not only the actions of ordinary living, but the happenings—not only those things that in daily life we do to things or to others, but those that are done to us. We need, somehow, to reach those feelings we do not generate by conscious will power, but that are generally released, often despite ourselves, spontaneously. We need to engage our "Inner Instrument"—our senses and emotions, together with the spontaneous responses and impulses they stimulate. We need to find a path to emotional centers in ourselves that are akin to those of the characters we play—centers that will generate appropriate feelings and physical expression. If his acting is not to be conventional, merely a replaying of external, imitated clichés, each actor must find anew his own forms to suit the content of whatever role he plays. As Stanislavsky discovered in his own pioneering search for an organic process, each actor must find his own path to an inner structure that will give immediate, personal life to the text.

These intimate, very personal thoughts and feelings make up what we call a Subtext. It will be different for each actor; it may vary widely from the text; and it cannot—and must not—be written out as the text is, for it is constantly evolving. When each actor arrives at a Subtext through a training or rehearsal process, it will usually follow the same patterns in each performance. But, like human thought, or, indeed, anything in nature, it will never repeat precisely. My step-by-step process in working on a monologue leads the student to develop his own Subtext and thus learn both how to fashion one for himself and to apply it to any new text. As I have found that it generally takes three successive monologue exercises to instill a well-grounded approach, I have settled on three simple, modern monologues for this training. And while the process of leading a student through the steps of the first usually takes many weeks or, sometimes, months, by the time he tackles the third, it seems almost too easy. That work is usually done in a few steps, often in only four or five sessions. Finally, for subsequent monologues, for training, auditioning or performing, my actor may safely start, as most others usually do, with the text itself; but now he will know how to avoid the pitfalls of the immediate pull to the words and actions indicating character or emotion. He will immediately begin to construct his own Subtext and a personal Acting Score. He will be able to build a solid performing structure that will support him, free him, and lead him to channel his imagination and talent into more individual and expressive forms.

I have found an analogy that seems to explain my procedure more readily to our student embarking on this new path of starting "from the inside out"; for he will begin not with a given text (as is usually done with a monologue), but with my rough elements of a Subtext. I liken the journey of the role—what is first imagined by the playwright and then handed to the actor to bring to performance level—to that of the football in the course of a game. The conventional idea is that the playwright starts at the other end of the field, runs with the "ball" of his created character about halfway down the field, and then passes it to the actor. The actor is expected then to carry the "ball" down the rest of the field to the goalpost. Having made the character his own, he will then happily score. And this process may work quite well on occasion. But all too often, when the actor receives the text and then is told to "put some feeling into it," he is unable to make it his own. He is too close to the goalposts, as it were, without the prior preparation of his own instrument.

I have found it is much more helpful for the actor to start at the same end of the field as the playwright with some "football" of his own, which he can carry until he is ready to receive the author's "ball," his suggestion of the character. The actor's "ball" is some personal Analogy, which may not be at all outwardly similar to the author's story. Then, at the moment the playwright passes the "ball" of his text to the actor to continue the run to the goalposts, the actor is fully prepared and ready to make that "ball," that text, his own. He then carries it to victory during live performance. For unless the actor can infuse the work with his own living thoughts and feelings—his Subtext—the author's text will remain empty, conventional and lifeless. And the actor will not score!

Stanislavsky reminds us that our individual experience in life does not limit our ability to perform roles on stage to only characters very much like ourselves. Not at all. "Type-casting" does not exist for any artist. We don't have to have been born a Scottish king or queen to play Macbeth or his Lady. We have all had analogous feelings of envy—of another's looks, or job, or apartment, or success—even a desire to murder! Haven't we vowed to murder any fellow actor who lands the role we are dying to play? The seeds of all human emotions reside in each and every one of us. A performing artist—dancer, singer or actor—must find the seeds within himself that are kindred to those of the character he plans to perform. An analogy, I have found, is the surest way to guide the actor in bringing his own personal, essential life to each character he wants to bring to life on stage.

For our first monologue I have found an admirable selection. It is an introduction to a well-known and highly respected American classic—a play about a turning point in the author-narrator's personal, family, and professional life. The action passes some ten years previously in a city some distance off and covers some four or five months in its action. I do not tell my student what play we will be working on. I merely inform him that our first monologue is an introduction to a play about a turning point. Therefore, our first step is for him to think over his life and choose a turning point of his own to share with me at our next session. I will guide him from there.

I give a few guidelines. First, as we don't generally perceive a turning point when it is actually happening, and some distance in time is almost essential for this text, I suggest that the event chosen should be at least five years past.

Second, it should be personal, yet not so very intimate that the student would feel uncomfortable in sharing it with me. And in this respect, though by now I think I have already created a trusting environment in our sessions, just in case it needs to be spelled out, I assure my student that any information given here is privileged; it will not go beyond this studio. Lastly, if the turning point he chooses is a particularly painful one—a death, or separation, or major failure—I warn that the exercise will probably take many weeks. While he will not be talking about that painful event after our next session, he will be thinking about it throughout the weeks, or months, of this exercise. And I certainly don't want him coming to class dreading his having to review that painful part of his life at every session!

I deliberately withhold the name of the play or character, as well as the text of this monologue. I insist that only our process feed this work. Only by starting with similar raw material in the actor's own experience and then proceeding step-by-step in what might possibly have been the playwright's own process can the actor arrive at a Subtext. This Subtext will support the author's text, as our spine supports the rest of our body, and the sculptor's wire armature supports the clay, as he molds his vision into his art.

❁　❁　❁

At our next session, my student shares whatever turning point he has chosen with me. It may be the death of a parent, grandparent, sibling, friend, or pet; a parental divorce and subsequent distress; or a serious accident, a change in family fortunes, a move to another town or school, a first love affair—growing pains we all have experienced in one form or another. The student seems miraculously able to recall and recite innumerable details of these long-buried events. And often, with my prodding questions, as I seek ever more details, past wounds now elicit present pain. So I know we are on the right track.

Then, when my student has related the manifold elements of this turning-point—year, season, day, place, people, houses, schools, cars, sports, dates, events—all in evermore minute and precise detail, as those winding memory paths are retraced, I put him to the test.

"And while you were living through these events, what was happening on the front pages?"

"What do you mean?"

"Well, all you've been telling me were personal experiences. Hardly newsworthy. But at that time, can you remember any more important events?"

He looks blank. He searches his memory.

"For instance, who was president?"

"Carter? . . . No, Bush . . . Maybe Clinton?"

"Maybe you can remember some main events? Wars? Regional conflicts— social unrest? Violence? We've had a lot of that around the world, haven't we?

"Don't worry. I find this happens every time. Whenever we recall a period when we were deeply involved personally, it seems that all other events go out of focus. Whenever I see television footage of Kennedy's assassination, for instance, I think, 'How come I don't remember those images of that memorable event? I was around then, wasn't I?' But then I recall that 1963 found me deep in a year-long depression. But I can tell you exactly where I was some twenty years earlier, when I heard about Pearl Harbor, D-Day, Roosevelt's death, V-E and V-J days—those events were more vivid than any personal experience at the time."

My student is somewhat reassured. I continue.

"The reasons for this step-by-step process of building a monologue from the inside out, so to speak, are twofold. First, I mean to remind you of where you may seek the necessary raw materials for your work. The major resource is your life experience—in this case, the memories of that turning point. Another resource is what I call second-hand experience—your observation or research. As the social background of our personal turning points are usually dim or vague, we must do a little study in the library, or on the Internet, to sharpen our sense of those times. For the second purpose of our process is more immediate: the social background is an integral part of the specific monologue at hand."

So in the days before our next session, my student has a research assignment. He is to look up the social and economic climate in America at the time of his turning point; and he will also report on some of the violent events transpiring overseas. While his turning point may have taken only a day or two, or perhaps a week, or often longer periods up to a year, we settle on a season of three or four months as a reasonable time-frame for this research. He is to make notes of what he discovers on the Internet or at the library and bring his discoveries to share with me at our next class.

Of course, he will also bring in the next problem in his sequence of task exercises. And he is not displeased to find that our tree of knowledge, of acting craft, will now be growing in two main branches in each session.

❊　❊　❊

It is always a delight for me to see what astonishment my students bring to class when they discover the often shattering, memorable national and international events that were taking place at the time of their turning point. For a brief trip to the local library has revealed the "social background" to a personal trauma. And we realize afresh the value of digging into other times and places, other customs and ways of life, when we seek to live another life on stage—in our art, in our mixture of fact and fancy, in present performance.

"Excellent! Now we must move on to the next source of nourishing food for the hungry actor—where he is sure to find stimulating challenges to whet his creative appetite.

"After his life experience and his research, the third place where the actor finds inspiration is, of course, the input of our playwright. The actor is challenged by the outline of the role as written in the script; he is often excited by the dramatic or comedic opportunities our author offers him. But in this 'from the inside out' training process, I have found it best not to start with the actual text, as in the usual, more conventional approach. We will arrive at it before very long. But not the specific words as yet. Now I must only offer you the structure, a 'spine' of the text. So, here is a five-step outline of the monologue—the inner structure of this introduction. Remember that we are building toward an introduction to a play based on a turning point. So just imagine that you have fashioned such a play out of your own turning point, but, unlike our actual author, you will not have to write even a line! You need only try to frame an introduction to this hypothetical new play—an introduction based on this outline. And you will share it with me at our next session. Please do not write it out! Though you may refer to your notes. For now, record this five-step outline as I share it with you. All ready?"

And my student hurries to turn a fresh page in his notebook, pen in hand.

"First, what we might call 'an introduction to the introduction,' somewhat like a handle to a door. A first step in any good speech. I dare not clarify more right now, for I want to stimulate your own interpretation with my barest of clues. Only after I hear your attempt at this introductory part can I best offer more specific guidelines.

"Second, the gist of what you have brought in today—what we might call the 'social background.' This should describe the social and economic climate of the times here in America, as well as some of the violent happenings overseas. This section can be twice as long as the opening introduction.

"Third, what effect might the sources of the play in your memories have on the manner of its presentation? As a play not basically imagined, but constructed primarily of personal memories, it will appear, and sound, in certain special ways. I now ask for some of your suggestions as to how this fabric of memories will affect the production style of your play.

"Fourth is the cast of characters, starting with yourself. List all those who took part in your turning point and whom you may wish to include in the action of your play.

"Fifth and last is another character or element that doesn't actually appear on stage in the course of the action, but is represented by something that we do see or hear. And this other character or element should have some influence on the action of the play."

In this five-step breakdown I try to give enough clues to stimulate the actor's homework—yet not so many as to shape the form unduly. For our fourth source of inspiration is now brought into play—it is, of course, the actor's imagination. Like a bee sucking pollen from a variety of flowers to make its honey, the actor's imagination feeds on its first resource—his own life experience; its second resource—his observation, study, and research; and its third resource—the demands, challenges and opportunities presented by the playwright in the text. All of these the actor is to simmer in the crucible of his imagination. He must the try to shape his own introduction to his hypothetical turning point play according to my five-step outline for our next class. A new and more formidable challenge! I think my student is now seriously hooked. And I am just as eager to share in whatever new solutions he can offer for our next session.

※　※　※

Of course, the introduction that my student brings to our next class almost invariably confounds me; it is so very far from the actual text as I know it! I recycle the text in my mind, as I now try to offer further clues that might lead my student to rework his own incipient monologue closer to the size and shape of the as-yet-unrevealed text. While the student's first rough, five-step introduction is usually far from the text, as I continue to offer adjustments, and he continues to reshape his own introductory monologue, whatever he will present in our succeeding sessions marks a clear step forward. Now, perhaps for the first time, he begins to see the point of our unusual journey. And however far he now may swerve in size or content from the form of the text, I can always offer new clues for his progressive reshaping. For he now discovers that the fifth source of nourishment for the actor's inspiration and homework is this very sequential, step-by-step, trial-and-error Process itself.

At our next session, after listening to whatever five-step introduction my student has been able to formulate, I can suggest that the opening "introduction to the introduction" will present something of a paradox. A contrast between what he seems to be and what he really is—in something of a more imaginative expression of himself. I may even give an example of what I mean, using myself:

"As you see, I have a roll-book open on my desk; I've got a mug full of pencils to take notes. But I'm not your average teacher. He'll give you grades, passing or failing, and I'll only give you a challenge to exercise your imagination."

My student's domestic "social background" is often full of favorite movies, major sports events, and song hits; lists of all the famous people who died; and winners and losers in elections. I must ask for a reshaping that only describes the economic climate—the broad social fabric. When his reports of violence overseas ranges from North Ireland to Central America to West Africa or the Middle East, I now ask for selection; only one such area is to be mentioned. Finally, this storm of violence is to be contrasted with confused social events here at home. And lastly, he will give examples of three places that witnessed this domestic disturbance.

The attributes of his "memory play" are usually much too literal. He will often describe details of his setting—the house, yard, or school, or the weather and the popular music topping the charts. I remind him that our author assumes that the qualities of this "memory play" are those of all memory plays. This may seem a bit presumptuous, but, with a bit of poetic license, quite applicable.

My student's cast of characters often runs to a dozen or more; once opened, the paths to a significant memory soon become crowded. Parents, siblings, teachers, friends, relations, far and near—all may have played integral parts in the actual turning point. But now I point out that our budget will not support so large a cast. In fact, our author calls for only four. This doesn't mean that my student must reduce his cast to exactly four by our next session, but he must head in that direction, cutting down his list of characters to arrive eventually at that precise number. (Or, if in the unlikely case that he has listed only two or three characters, he will now have to enlarge his cast.) In addition, I may subsequently suggest that the last, or smaller group, is significantly different from the first, larger group, among which is the author himself. So he will please select accordingly and also tell in what ways that last character, or smaller group, is different. And what he, she, or they might also represent symbolically.

His fifth character or element will often turn out to be fairly abstract at first— God, spiritual values, or perhaps a work of art. In any case it is quite revealing, for it is the most imaginative element the student contributes. Now the challenge is to maintain the sense of whatever element he has selected, but for next time to rework it into a particular character—one who is absent, but still influential. And in the following steps, I ask my student to tell me more details about this final character. "Who was he or she? What did he or she do? What happened to him or her? And what was the last you heard—or might have heard—from that special person?"

All this now seems a great deal to assimilate. My student assiduously takes notes. I repeat and rephrase the various new clues. I try to be just specific enough—to give only enough help to stimulate the student's imagination to help bring him, in his own way and his own time, ever closer to our text. This fifth important element is always a trial-and-error process—as I think any truly creative process must be. I can only go by my own experience, and my best results have never been decided beforehand—only discovered, evolving through such a trial-and-error process. Whenever I was puzzled by a difficult dramatic problem, if I trusted this process, working through the doubt and confusion, it would eventually reveal the fresh discoveries that proved to be the right solution. And so now I try to bring my student to share, in his own time and on his own path, in his own discovery of a clear and rewarding creative process that he can learn to follow for himself.

As I give out progressive clues to the form of the text, and my student gradually shapes his introduction to his turning point play closer to this form, which so far I have kept from him, I will find a moment when I reveal the actual text.

This will come when I think he is ready. When I conclude that his format is close enough so that only the actual words of the playwright's own introduction can best chart the next steps, I will hand my student two sheets of text, copied out by myself, but with all stage directions omitted. Now the five-step structure and the size and shape of each paragraph will be clearly revealed. It is, as you might have guessed by now, Tennessee Williams' introduction to his *Glass Menagerie.*

> TOM: *Yes, I have tricks in my pocket—I have things up my sleeve. But I am the opposite of a stage magician. He gives you illusion that has the appearance of truth. I give you truth in the pleasant disguise of illusion.*
>
> *To begin with, I turn back time. I reverse it, to that quaint period, the thirties, when the huge middle class of America was matriculating in a school for the blind. Their eyes had failed them, or they had failed their eyes, and so they were having their fingers pressed forcibly down on the fiery Braille alphabet of a dissolving economy. In Spain there was revolution. Here there was only shouting and confusion. In Spain there was* Guernica. *Here there were labor disturbances, sometimes pretty violent, in otherwise peaceful cities such as Cleveland, Chicago, St. Louis. This is the social background of the play.*
>
> *The play is memory. Being a memory play, it is dimly lighted, it is sentimental, it is not realistic. In memory, everything seems to happen to music. That explains the fiddle in the wings.*
>
> *I am the narrator of the play and also a character in it. The other characters are my mother, Amanda, my sister, Laura, and a gentleman caller who appears in the final scenes. He is the most realistic character of the play, being an emissary from a world of reality that we were somehow set apart from. But having a poet's weakness for symbols, I am using this character also as a symbol. He is that long-delayed, but always expected something that which we live for.*
>
> *There is a fifth character in the play who doesn't appear other than in a larger-than-life-sized photograph hanging over the mantel. When you see the portrait of this grinning gentleman, please remember that this is our father, who left us a long time ago. He was a telephone man who fell in love with long distance. He gave up his job with the telephone company and skipped the light fantastic out of town. The last we heard of him was a picture postcard from the Pacific coast of Mexico, containing a message of two words— "Hello Goodbye"—and no address. I think the rest of the play will explain itself.*

If I have gauged the process wisely, the student will have a rewarding moment of happy revelation. For he now sees clearly where we have been heading, as his own introduction—his analogy—exactly parallels Tom's opening monologue. But I warn him that he is not to jump to these words. Instead, he is to continue the process we are engaged in and to use this actual text merely as a guide to the further shaping of his own introductory monologue. He is neither to embrace the text, nor consciously refrain from using any phrases that seem to him appropriate.

Some phrases may now seem entirely applicable to his own introduction. For example, "To begin with, I turn back time . . . This is the social background of the play . . . The play is memory . . . I am the narrator and also a character in it . . . I think the rest of the play will explain itself." These phrases are simple enough that if he finds them helpful in his own format, so much the better. He will use them—and welcome them—as he refines his own introduction. He is still introducing his own play about his own turning point. He will later arrive at a point where everything but the proper nouns will be Mr. Williams'—only the stage magician, the Depression, Spain, Guernica, the "otherwise peaceful cities," and the characters remain as yet to come. But now our author has magically been transformed from a feared, demanding taskmaster to a welcome friend—he says it so much better!

❊   ❊   ❊

Our process progresses as my student continues to reshape his introduction ever closer to the text. But now I can throw out an additional new challenge. This will explore a new avenue for the actor's creativity. I want to move him out of his chair, as he shares his introduction with me, and stimulate him to expressive action. But he must learn to find his own way. I can only suggest that he is ready for a new form of stage communication—the language of purposeful behavior. He has already been following this path in his exercises with physical tasks, but now he is to find his own clues in the text itself. For our next class, I merely ask him to explore a new dimension: he is to try to "Activate the Intention" of the monologue. I give no more clues than this. Whatever he will attempt, we can only learn.

But, before I introduce the next sequence of problems in developing this introduction to a play, I must return to our sequence of Physical Tasks. These have been proceeding concurrently with the development of our initial monologue. So here I must now revert to our sixth exercise: the first doses of imagination, of lies, must mix with the facts of the actor's presence to arrive at that strange and wonderful mixture—a Stage Truth.

PART III

"Lies
Like
Truth"

CHAPTER FIVE

"I Am—As If"

At our next session, usually the fifth in my private training process, my eager new student arrives with a baby in tow for his next exercise in this "System of Physical Tasks." Or so it seems—a life-sized baby doll, fully dressed—and an ensemble of baby accoutrements. He proudly announces,

"I have a very unfamiliar task!"

I am somewhat afraid that he does. So I try to calm him down, as we warm up in our stretch exercises that help reduce any tension—both on his part and my own. For a tense actor—or teacher—is like a piano with the lid to the keyboard closed. No matter how well prepared, how inspired the student or the teacher may be, his instrument just will not sound. So it is for any actor—or dancer, singer, musician, or athlete. Tension is the performer's number one enemy. No matter how talented, how trained, or how ready the performer may be, only a relaxed instrument can perform well. In the actor, physical tension will inhibit not only what has been rehearsed and learned, but also, certainly, any fresh imaginative or true emotional flow. And imagination and emotional flow are what our training is all about. As Stanislavsky evolved his System to discover and forge a path "from the Conscious to the Unconscious," so all our exercises, our "Methods," our processes are designed to tap and release the creativity of the actor—to build the conditions that will permit and encourage his talent to find fresh expression.

And now for our new exercise: another Unfamiliar Task—but this time for a totally unreal, imaginary reason. A lie. An actual What supported by a made-up, fictional Why. I introduce the student to the actor's imaginary life with but this teaspoon of fiction. After having worked solely with actualities until this new problem, assiduously establishing the facts of the living actor, himself, here and now, I use the next exercise to prepare the student for his contemplated existence both in and out of his imagination. This is an unfamiliar task that is half fact, half fiction—an imaginary, unreal justification supporting an actually new, unfamiliar task: I Am—As If. It is this unique combination of Fact and Fancy that are the essential ingredients of good acting: The actual living actor, actually thinking, feeling, and doing—As If he were embroiled in a totally imaginary set of circumstances. This is, in a nutshell, the true paradox of acting!

Now my eager student brings his baby doll to the carpet. He unrolls a baby blanket and takes out the package of a new diaper. He announces, somewhat sheepishly, "My girlfriend told me she was pregnant. And as I don't believe in abortion, I decided to marry her and have the baby. And since I'll have to learn to change a diaper, I thought I'd better start now. So here I go. I've never, ever done this before."

And he does proceed to do just that. Laying the baby doll on the carpet, he proceeds, with some difficulty, to undress it. He then opens the diaper package, figures out how the diaper unfolds, manages to get it on the "infant," and then puts the clothes back on.

I have realized that my student is attending to the letter of the exercise. He prides himself on being able to meet any challenge that anyone throws at him. But I sense a separation between his fervent intentions and his belief in his subsequent actions. So I begin to question him.

"What's your girlfriend's name? How old is she? How long have you been going together? When did she tell you this? Where? How did she find out? Were you surprised? Do you think it was an accident? Or by design, on her part perhaps? Did you tell your parents? Had you planned to marry? What about her folks? Is she working? When is the baby due?" Etc., etc.

As he answers my questions, thinking hard to make a sensible justification for his task, I can sense my student getting more and more serious. He is beginning to believe in his "As If"—his fiction, his imaginary Why, his lie. And he now pays closer attention to his task; the doll takes on more of an actual baby's reality to him. He seems more and more to be living in the situation he has created.

And so he has mixed fact and fancy to arrive at a Stage Truth. All artistic truths are mixtures, in ever-varying proportions, of fact and fancy. And the actor must justify his fiction with solid, specific bits of an alibi. I liken his problem to that of the ice-skater who sees the birds skittering all over the newly frozen lake near the Plaza in Central Park at the first freeze of winter. It may look frozen solid—the birds have no difficulty in scampering all over it—but let our skater try, and he is sure to break through the thin ice and fall into the icy water below. That ice is not thick enough to support him.

So it is with the actor. The playwright may give him enough details to bolster his belief in the play. But to perform it—actually to Live in the Given Circumstances—the actor depends upon layers of justification. He needs to fashion details that have the ring of truth and that will justify his actions. Thus can he successfully support himself when he moves to behave in his character's situation.

* * *

My eager student arrives promptly for our next exercise. I think he enjoys meeting the challenges of these tasks. And now he comes triumphantly carrying not only a shopping bag crammed with hidden objects, but an ironing board, which he manages to deposit in the green room with a wicked grin. I am aware of my contradictory feelings: I am pleased at his preparation, but also a bit guilty that he has transported this rather cumbersome object.

"We do have some household equipment. Look through our props, or ask me. I believe there is an ironing board."

"No problem." I see that he wanted to come fully prepared.

So—after our stretching and relaxing warm-up, reviewing our lessons and hearing any news on his home front, I retreat to my desk. He sets up his ironing board and fetches an iron and a rumpled white shirt from his shopping bag. He stretches the shirt out on the board and looks about for an outlet for the iron. Evidently he is on a mission—he seems pressed himself to get this shirt pressed.

"You want an outlet? Look there—behind the daybed on the wall over there."

He connects the iron and brings the ironing board closer to the bed. He seems to know what he wants to do and yet is somewhat tentative about the exact procedure. As he tests the iron for heat, he tries to find the best place on the board to stretch out the rumpled shirt. He seems seriously occupied with a serious problem.

"I've got to get this shirt ironed for the Senator. He needs it for this evening, and none of the laundries would promise it by five. And it's the only white shirt he brought."

I sense a story here. "The Senator? For this evening? Why are you responsible?"

"State Senator Smith. One of our four. I've been apprenticing on his staff since the first of the year, and tonight he's speaking in our town hall. So I've got to get his stuff ready or else!" He is ironing the back of the shirt in broad strokes.

"I didn't know you were working in politics. And do you know how to iron?"

"Part of my family obligations. And no—I've never had to iron. Just seen my Mom do it." He is trying to arrange the front of the shirt so it lies flat. "I borrowed our iron and ironing board. At least it was washed." He seems confused by the buttons; he presses around them and then turns to the sleeves, flattening them with determined sweeps of the iron. He holds up the shirt to assess his work. There are still wrinkles. He tries to press them out.

Finally he appears satisfied. Though hardly a perfect job, it will do. He starts to fold the shirt, but hesitates—what will happen to the pressing?

I am moved to offer help. "I think there are some wire hangers on the coat-rack outside. You're welcome to use one."

Grateful for even this small favor, he fetches a hanger and carefully drapes his shirt on it. And now he can hang it proudly on the hat rack. He turns to me, ready for my verdict.

And together we examine the exercise—the problem, the conception and the execution. It posits a Seemingly Unfamiliar Task with both the action and its justification lies. Here we explore those total "Lies Like Truth." In actuality, he has done quite a bit of ironing, a required part of his boarding school regimen. And to prove his ironing skills, he fetches another rumpled shirt and proceeds to iron it. But now, he remembers to fill the iron with the necessary steam-making water. And now there is no hesitation—the collar first, then efficiently the front panels, the back, the sleeves, the cuffs. This is an excellent demonstration of the actual fact behind the fictional stage truth. And no, he is not apprenticing on the staff of his state Senator Smith. Though there are such training positions for young apprentices in politics, there is no Senator Smith in New Jersey at present, only two state senators, and no such meeting at the town hall this evening. But a school friend actually did serve in such a position at one time. So a net made up of bits of actual and imaginary circumstances was woven to support and justify the fictional approach to the task. And the task carried out As If actually unfamiliar. When clearly it was actually very familiar indeed. And the shirt is indeed his own.

Very good. Was I convinced? I think so, increasingly as he filled in his circumstances. Was he convinced? He thinks so—more and more as he acted on the imaginary Why to carry out the imaginary What. Like a snowball rolling down the snowy hillside, the fictional task performed for a fictional reason acquires greater truth as it is performed under those imaginary circumstances. The more specific, detailed, and plausible his imaginary justification, the more the actor believes in the situation, and the more fully he will commit himself to trying to resolve his character's problem. Similarly, the more he involves himself in carrying out his problem-solving tasks, the more he will believe in their purpose. Finally, real feelings now arise in response to his imaginary Why and What. He is indeed behaving As If in imaginary Given Circumstances. He is in the Creative State. He is truly Living on Stage.

We are now ready, I tell him, to do a wrap on this first series of exercises. It sums up our initial work on the What and Why, our starting from "I Am" and proceeding to the first bits of "As If." For next class, he is to bring in two tasks, related to each other if possible: one Actually Unfamiliar and one Seemingly Unfamiliar. Both are to be performed for imaginary reasons. And, if properly carried out, I will not be able to tell the actually unfamiliar from the seemingly unfamiliar—the fact from the fiction. Fact and Fiction must seem to be indistinguishable on stage. The actor must learn to tell "Lies Like Truth" and to make a habit of it. Like every good training regimen, this series of exercises is designed to become habit-forming. So all my willing student need do is "stick around." (My mantra and perennial answer to many a student's question!)

We part again. Again, I think we are both encouraged.

❊   ❊   ❊

Our next session brings a double-header. Today a fact and a fiction are to be explored in tandem: one actually unfamiliar task and one seemingly unfamiliar task, both justified by fictitious reasons. And the most intent observer should be unable to tell the fact from the fiction—both should seem equally true. Such is our "stage truth." Moreover, the particulars of the recipe, the varying amounts of each kind of ingredient, this must remain the actor's own private formula. No one need know. And when the most intimate and pungent ingredients are used, no one should know what they actually are but the actor himself.

My eager student arrives in a rush to perform these tasks. He immediately sprawls on the carpet with a large shopping bag and removes a brand-new telephone device. I am not at all sure what it is—part household dial phone, part transportable cell-phone? And all locked in that impenetrable, clear plastic armor. As he boldly attacks the plastic cover, my student explains.

"I just picked this up for my sister. She needs a new phone in her new dorm at school. I thought it would be a good back-to-school present for her."

He has broken through the plastic cover to let the phone set tumble out on the rug. Now he studies the printed folder that also falls from the package— evidently some instructions.

"You're not familiar with this equipment?"

"Not at all. It's the latest model."

He is intent on the sheet of instructions, comparing parts of the equipment with the step-by-step guidelines as he proceeds to construct a functioning state-of-the-art telephone that is home-based, yet also transportable.

Confidently he proceeds with his task. Evidently, he has had some experience assembling similar new electronic devices. Though this particular device seems new, it does not faze him. And indeed, in another few minutes, it is successfully assembled. Voilà!

I am somewhat impressed with his skill. "All finished? It'll work now?"

"Oh, yes, I'm pretty sure." And he immediately dives into the shopping bag for another article. He pulls out a necktie. "I'll test it at the party tonight."

"Party?"

"To celebrate my sister's return to college and her new dorm. The family wants to show our appreciation. It'll be a surprise for her—and a celebration. She's finally growing up!"

And he proceeds to attempt to tie this necktie. It seems clear that he is quite unfamiliar with this task.

"You seem strangely unfamiliar with this tie. You don't know how to tie it?"

He embarrassedly admits, "Yeah, my Dad always tied them for me. At graduation—and for our yearly company meetings. Only now I've got to go directly from here. He won't get there 'til late.

"I can't believe you never learned to tie a tie. When I was your age—and younger—we always wore them. In the Depression, men wore them even on bread lines."

"Well, we missed out."

He is tying and retying the tie, carefully reviewing the left-over-right formula he has memorized. But the ends never seem to match—either too long or too short. He persists, and finally his efforts are rewarded—the tie is now quite well made. Success at last! He grins in triumph.

"So now you can go to the party—with a phone ready to install and a tie properly tied. Two unfamiliar tasks that you managed to accomplish. Or are they? In actual fact? Let's investigate just what is actually going on here."

We analyze the exercise. The bits of fact—a sister returning to college next term, plans for a new phone, a possible party, and many company meetings in the past. He has rearranged all to support the fiction of a new dorm celebration this evening and a first time tying a tie. And yes, he has tied many a tie, while this is indeed his first encounter with this particular phone. To prove the actual fact behind the imagined fiction, he now ties another tie perfectly, with an admirably familiar skill. While applauding his skill in giving artistic truth to an actual lie, I must now confess that I guessed that tying the tie was the lie—not from the odds of common experience so much as the giveaway of his hands' familiarity. They seemed to know how to "over and under" with the wide end of the tie more than would seem plausible if it were actually a new experience. And we are brought to realize that while our imagination knows we are only pretending, our muscles have habits acquired over the years. They too must be told to behave "As If" in the imaginary circumstances, or they will give us away. And what the audience sees may well contradict what it hears — a cardinal sin that will undermine any performance. So, while the actor welcomes the necessary muscular memory of the athlete, dancer, or musician in a good deal of his training and rehearsal, the built-in Anticipation of muscular memory is an ever-present hazard. For an acting performance must always strive to create what William Gillette so aptly identified as "The Illusion of the First Time."

Still, my eager student has gobbled up these first exercises with a healthy appetite. It is clear that he is now ready to move forward — to another level.

I outline our next move — like a knight on a chessboard, both forward and to the right. Until now, we have been focusing on the first two major questions for the actor: What? and Why? They seem to be the most immediate and clearest, the closest to our conscious daily lives. But now we come to two other questions, perhaps even more basic: Where? and When? Or, in our stage parlance, what we call "Given Circumstances." Offstage, in life, we exist at every moment in a specific time and place, in actual circumstances. On stage, our characters live in the times and places, in the circumstances dictated or given by the playwright. Thus the actor must learn to live in two sets of circumstances at once. While in fact he is always Here and Now, in the theatre, on the set or on location, performing a rehearsed role for an audience, the character he plays is always There and Then, living out the life of the drama for the "two hours traffic of our stage."

So our next exercise will be a first exploration of this circumstantial hazard: how to live here and now As If there and then. And I will not permit my student to gorge himself on the "junk food" that we were offered in this respect — those high dramatic moments of passion. In the external training we suffered through at college or summer theatres when I began, we were encouraged to jump right into richly dramatic speeches of royalty, knaves, heroes, and fools — living in far-off realms and ages ago in poetically charged critical speeches of high tragedy or low comedy. No — my student's first ventures into this most important direction are very humble indeed. He is merely to bring in a "Familiar Time and Place." My student is to select a moment from his own life and try to relive it here at our next session in a semblance of his own space. That is all.

But a few guidelines will help. The moment he selects must be recent and ordinary. It must not be unusual, in any time of crisis, or facing any stressful decision — a quite unmemorable moment, in fact. While not necessarily a literal reproduction, the moment should be taken from actual experience, preferably some time in the past two weeks. He can be home or in the office, for example—some place where he is generally unobserved, indoors, relaxed, and alone. And occupied with? Well, that we shall discover!

My hungry student leaves to digest this new problem. Again, we are progressing with all deliberate speed. And with encouraging signs of positive forward movement.

CHAPTER SIX

"Where and When?"

At our next session, my effervescent student arrives with no shopping bags whatsoever. I am quite surprised but try to control my reaction. He immediately pulls the armchair to the carpet, where he seats himself, apparently very pleased. And he proceeds to tell me, "Last Monday, I was cleaning up my room and I discovered this letter-opener my sister had lost. I knew it was hers, as she had complained to me about losing it. So as I cleaned up the room, I made a particular effort to save this letter opener for her. It took me some time, but I was able to do it pretty well. The room is all straightened up now."

And he sits back, quite satisfied with himself, the letter-opener still fast in his hands. I wait.

"So what are you going to do?"

"What do you mean? I cleaned up the room."

"And so the exercise is—what?"

"Cleaning up the room."

"Oh, so you're just going to tell me about it?"

He is nonplussed. I continue: "For the last few sessions you have been carrying out a variety of stage tasks—familiar and unfamiliar, actual and imaginary, with apparently a good grasp of the various principles involved. Now you just sit and tell me what happened in your room last Monday evening. Is this a forward movement in our acting?"

Immediately, he jumps up. A light has dawned.

"Can I get some stuff from my truck? I'll only be a few minutes."

"Of course. Whatever you like." I'm pleased that now he seems to understand. He rushes out and down the elevator. I sit patiently. He returns in seven minutes with an overstuffed shopping bag. He takes out a number of shirts, socks, and other articles of clothing, and scatters them about the carpet. Then he proceeds to gather up his clothes, folding each and carefully making a pile of orderly clothing. He is immediately involved in his task.

"So what are you doing now?"

"Straightening my room."

"Why?"

"My Mom said I better do it or else."

"I see. And where are you?"

"In my room. At home."

"When?"

"Last Monday evening—about 9:00."

"Last Monday? Or today?"

He seems confused. He ponders my conundrum. I think I must shed some light.

"Offstage, in life, we are Now in actuality, in our outer life; we may also be Then in our memories, hopes, plans, or imagination, our inner life. One of the most interesting and essential differences between Living on Stage and off is that on stage we are *both* Here and Now and *also* There and Then. So while it may be Tuesday afternoon in actuality here in the Studio, artistically it is also last Monday at 9 p.m., in your room at home."

He seems to understand. And he continues to straighten up "his room."

"Where were you at 8:00?"

"At work. I had a late customer."

"And did you have dinner?"

"I ate a sandwich at the store about 7:30."

"And are you alone now at home?"

"No. My Mom is downstairs watching her TV, and my Dad is upstairs watching his."

"And after you clean up your room, do you have any plans?"

"Join one of them and see what's on." And he continues his task.

Finally he is finished—neat piles of shirts, socks, and other clothing on the edge of the carpet. He stands in some confusion. He doesn't know what to do.

"Yes? And now, what?"

"I've finished my task."

"And that means your life is finished?"

"Oh. Well—no. I guess I'll go down and watch some TV." And he moves to the door.

I am pleased. He seems to have found out where we are heading with this exercise.

So now we can analyze the problems this "familiar time and place" presents. It poses a challenge to the student to imagine a very clear set of Given Circumstances that can simply begin to move the actor into living here and now As If there and then. I do not send him to Elsinore or Verona or to some more interesting past. Those removes bring in many additional problems, best left to later. It is enough to be in mid-Manhattan and a New Jersey suburb with but a week's time in between to experience and understand the very important technical principle involved.

"Offstage, in life, we live in one set of circumstances; we may also remember, dream, plan, or imagine another. But on stage we live simultaneously in two sets of circumstances: the actual one of the actor performing and the imagined one of our character living. That created set of circumstances in our imaginations becomes our reality when we act on stage."

He grabs his notebooks and starts writing. He wants to get this idea down while it's still warm. And I think we have met and begun to conquer another essential step in laying a basic foundation for Living on Stage.

I feel confident that I can now challenge him with our next exercise: another "Familiar Time and Place," but this time with two kinds of tasks—one Planned and one Unplanned.

He seems alarmed. "How can I prepare an unplanned task?"

"That's what we'll try to discover." He may have several tasks in these circumstances, of course, but there must be at least one of each kind. And I carefully refrain from explaining what I may mean by "Planned" and "Unplanned." He must find these out for himself—or with my help at our next session.

❊　　❊　　❊

At our next session, my student appears with a confident grin and a full briefcase slung over his shoulder. He immediately sets up a desk and chair, opens his briefcase, and scatters papers and notebooks around the desk. He also places a prop telephone on a corner of the desk. And he sets to work with some of the papers on the desk.

After a few moments I interrogate him. "What are you up to now?"

"Figuring out the costs. I'm just back from measuring for a new carpet. I have to decide how much to charge for the dimensions of that room." And he is deep in his calculations.

"Where are you?"

"In my office."

"When?"

"Yesterday afternoon, around four o'clock."

"Yesterday?"

"I mean today. Yes, today—Monday."

As it is actually Tuesday, I smile. He has caught on.

Suddenly the phone rings. Not the prop phone he has placed on his desk, but the cell-phone in his pocket. He takes it out and answers it.

"Yes? . . . no, not yet . . . I'm figuring it out now . . . later : . . I'll be home and let you know then." He hangs up and glances at me in apology. "My father." And he continues his paper work. Then he lifts the prop phone and proceeds to dial and hold a conversation with someone he imagines is on the other end of the line. But now he speaks without listening; he talks about measurements and problems with the particular space. He hangs up and immediately dials another supposed customer. After another supposed one-sided "conversation," he hangs up, arranges his papers, puts a few into the briefcase, and heads off-stage. He turns to me, both pleased and also somewhat confused. He is finished. Or is he?

Now we can discuss the exercise. Again it occurred in a Familiar Time and Place: at his office, yesterday afternoon, in the course of his daily work routine. All seems true, logical, grounded in a specific, familiar place and a specific, familiar time. Only the telephone calls were distinctly different. And, while I acknowledge that his tasks of figuring out costs for square feet of carpet were truly done, I must draw his attention to the various telephone calls. One, the first, from his father, was so clearly true, and the others, from and to his customers, were equally clearly *performed*, or what we call "Indicated." He immediately acknowledges the difference. The first, from his father on his own cell-phone was an actual call; the other two were imaginary and thus merely acted.

I am impressed, I tell him, that he was able to take the actual call without breaking out of his created time and place, answering his caller, actually here in the studio on Tuesday, yet also, as it were, taking it in his office at work on Monday. Aside from his glancing up and explaining to me, it was an excellent example of living both Here and Now *and* There and Then. At the same time, the calls he created were so obviously contrived, "performed" with a simulated truth that failed to ring true. We discuss this clear difference and agree that responding to imaginary calls is a new kind of technical problem for him. I urge him not to tackle this problem at this time. Later, when we have done some sensory work with imaginary objects, seeing, touching and hearing, this kind of acting problem will be solved without difficulty. But for the present, I urge him to note the difference between the calls—to remember the actual listening to his father's voice and his own true replies, and his one-sided dialogue without any true listening on the prop phone. It is an excellent lesson, and he understands at once.

But he has dealt with the given problem—planned and "unplanned" events in a set of given circumstances. In life, we have either planned or unplanned tasks. On stage, we have another kind—a Seemingly Unplanned Task. In rehearsal, everything becomes well planned for the actor. But for the character he plays, so many events and tasks must seem to be unplanned, no matter how often they have actually occurred for the actor. He must learn to deal with one of our fundamental acting problems: "The Illusion of the First Time." And it is this that he must address for our next lesson: Three kinds of tasks in another familiar time and place. Planned, Seemingly Unplanned, and Actually Unplanned. And the two kinds of unplanned tasks must appear indistinguishable.

He seems bewildered. "How can I plan an unplanned task? I can't ask my father to call again during our next session!"

That is exactly the problem. I assure him he will find the answer.

❀   ❀   ❀

Apparently he has found an answer by our next session, for he enters confidently with a golf bag full of clubs over his shoulder. He immediately sets up a chair on the carpet, leans his bag of clubs against it, and goes to get a bowl of water. He needs to clean his clubs, he explains, having just come back from a round of golf with his father and friend. And no, he didn't win; he actually scored the highest. Now it is about 5:30 in the afternoon of this Sunday, and he will make amends by committing himself to a thorough cleansing job here in the garage. These are precious golf clubs, he explains, inherited from his father, and now among his prized possessions.

From a pocket of his golf bag he extracts an old towel and a small abrasive, which he finds difficult to release from its container. Dipping first the towel and then the abrasive in the water, he carefully cleans each of the clubs, stacking them in turn along the armchair. On the fifth club he notices what appears to be a spot of dirt embedded in the head of the iron. He goes to the pocket in the bag again and finds a tee, which he now uses as a chisel or file-point to loosen the packed dirt before removing it with the wet rag.

Again, he arranges the cleaned club leaning on the chair in the neatest of rows. The clubs threaten to fall, but he quickly rearranges them more safely. He comes to the drivers—three massively headed clubs, each head wrapped in a protective sleeve. More rubbing with the abrasive, more using the tee to dig up packed dirt, more wiping with the damp rag. Finally, all the clubs are cleaned. He starts to stack them carefully in the bag, realizes he has misjudged the correct pocket for these first clubs, and rearranges them in another slot. Great care, great concern—he is clearly devoted to the game and most respectful of his tools. Finally, the task is done, and he can stack the golf bag with the cleaned set of clubs in the corner, ready for the next round on the links.

Is the exercise accomplished? Has he solved his problem? Yes, I can begin, there were clearly a number of what we would called "unplanned tasks." Engaged fully in the obviously planned task—cleaning his clubs—he appeared to encounter a variety of unexpected obstacles that led to new, apparently unplanned tasks. I enumerate the number I observed, carefully refraining from distinguishing between those that would appear to be actually and those seemingly unplanned. For almost all the tasks were actually unplanned. Only two of them, and I was able to identify one immediately, were contrived to appear As If unplanned—that is, seemingly spontaneously chosen. As a good deal of the actor's stage life is spent trying to make many planned tasks appear to be unplanned, this is an important problem to explore and conquer.

I could readily identify his using the tee as a cleaning aid as something contrived—seemingly unplanned. And my student agrees. "Somehow I didn't believe in it myself. But why?"

"In life, when we go off in an unplanned direction, it is in response to a fresh obstacle. We perceive the new problem, then search for a solution, hit on one and proceed to follow it. There is a clear sequence of events, however swiftly we may go through it. Here, your new problem led you directly into the golf bag for the tee. It then clearly registered as something either planned or a familiar solution to a familiar problem. Your anticipation of the result led you immediately to the solution. You failed to 'cross the bridge,' as we say—a not-uncommon problem."

We are led to examine again the perennial acting hazard of Anticipation. The better the play, the director's contribution, the actor's performance, the more this trap looms for all actors. Only in improvisational theatre are we freed from this lure of the planned result. Once read, or decided upon, much less rehearsed or performed, the perils of Anticipation are as much a part of a repeated performance as the undertow is to the ocean. It is an occupational hazard and must be recognized as such. Only then can we successfully learn to guard against its life-threatening pull and train ourselves to avoid it.

For many years I sought to find an alternative word to "Anticipate." "Don't anticipate" was the feeble best I could manage. It only dug us more deeply into anticipation. Finally I realized that "Anticipate Something Else" could solve the problem. And so it has proved. What Stanislavsky calls "The Flow of the Day" and the point of Lee Strasberg's question, "What would you do if the scene didn't take place?" (in the character's situation, or course), I now call a "Lifeline." I think it implies what both these master teachers imply, and it also suggests how very supportive it can be for the actor. Succeeding exercises will clarify this technique.

My student's other Seemingly Unplanned task turns out to be picking up and rearranging the falling golf clubs. And we both agree that his actual fear of their actually falling stopped him from permitting any perceptible fall. Again, that Anticipation!

But he has met the challenge of the exercise, and, while not surmounting it fully, he has been led to understand fully both the perils and the practical solutions to the ever-present acting hazard it presents. Half the problems of the actor, I believe, come from being insufficiently Private in Public; another half come from Anticipation. The third half—yes, in acting, three halves make a whole!—comes from insufficient Personal Involvement.

We will continue to encounter all of these hazards as we forge ahead. And though I seem to be more confident than my student, he may now proceed to our next exercises. These will aim to reinforce the very valuable actor's habit of setting up the concrete, specific circumstances of a familiar time and place for himself. No matter what information the playwright or director may provide in this area, the actor must always add additional details as well. For it is most important for the actor to develop his Sense of Truth, to learn that it must constantly be fed, satisfied, nourished. The playwright will give the actor some crumbs of imaginary truths, but to Live on Stage, much less grow in performance, the actor must add so much more!

I hope these exercises will also develop his skill in living through both actual and imaginary combinations of familiar and unfamiliar and planned and unplanned tasks. He must learn to combine actual truths and imaginary lies to create what we call "Stage Truths." So now I challenge him with a first combination.

"For our next session—another Familiar Time and Place. But this time, it may be at some future time—within the next week or two. Again, an ordinary moment, nothing critical, that might very possibly lie ahead for you. And in that time and place, three kinds of tasks: one both planned and familiar; the next, planned and seemingly unfamiliar. And the third, familiar and seemingly unplanned. You may have other tasks, of course, but at least one of each of these three kinds. All clear?"

My student seems wary. "I think so . . . maybe . . . I'll see."

"That's all we want. Until next week, then?" And we part. Full-speed ahead, with attendant—and appropriate—trepidation.

❖　❖　❖

Our next session starts in a rush. My student seems unusually excited, as he empties a sack of clothing, spreading shirts, trousers, underwear, socks, and shoes about the floor. He is immediately engaged in sorting and folding this clothing and then selecting the items to pack in a copious backpack. It seems that he is preparing for a very special weekend; a good friend is getting married, and a final bachelor fling will mean a weekend in Princeton, with a special skydiving party on Saturday morning. An unusual, though perhaps appropriate, flying farewell to bachelorhood!

Now he is in his room at home on the very morning of that weekend to come—8:30 Friday (actually three days hence); he is due to start picking up his fellow-skydivers in half an hour. He is fully focused on his problems and engaged in solving them.

I note his planned and familiar task as he sorts and folds his clothing. I note his planned and unfamiliar task as he tries to select the necessary articles for this first venture in skydiving. And I note several unplanned and familiar tasks, as he rearranges his clothing in the backpack, removing rolled up shirts and pants to repack his shoes on the bottom. He packs and then decides to leave some CDs at home. Finally, he jots down some notes on additional articles he must collect. He finishes with a backpack stuffed full, and, eager to be on his way, he heads out the door.

Indeed, yes! My student hardly needs my congratulations. I can tell that he knows he has done it well. He is properly excited. He has lived through a possible future event while manipulating my arbitrary combination of tasks. All the "unplanned" and "unfamiliar" are contrived, created lies. Bits of his life— actual and imaginary, past and future—were rearranged to support this scenario and to create a Stage Truth. And his own justification led him to live through the sequence of physical problems on stage with full conviction and attendant excitement. It was almost as if we were both actually going off for a weekend of skydiving!

I am very gratified. We examine the principles underlying the exercise that my student has apparently absorbed. We appreciate again the actor's need to bring bits from his own life, as well as from his imagination, to the Given Circumstances of the playwright. And we confirm that on stage we can live Here and Now and also There and Then at the same time and in the same space!

And so I know that we are ready to move on to another level. My student is ready for a new challenge, a new dimension in his developing craft: Interaction with another actor. This will introduce our fifth major question: With Whom? But to maintain the fairly even flow of these progressively mounting acting obstacles, the new element must remain a surprise. Only now I must contrive to bring two students, at about the same level of training, together to our next session—a challenge in logistics for myself!

But again, before we plunge directly into this next sequence of task exercises that will bring the actor into interaction with a partner—to actual scenes from a play, I must revert to my sequence of building a monologue. For, like this trunk of our growing tree of technique, our own "System of Physical Tasks," an essential branch of the actor's craft has also been growing at the same time. This is his developing personal involvement, his building a viable subtext that brings life to an author's text.

PART IV

**Activating
the
Intention**

CHAPTER 7

Finding an Intention

What does it mean to "Activate the Intention" of a monologue? I hope that during the days before his next class, this challenge will germinate in my student's imagination and lead to his discovery of some kind of action, some kind of purposeful physical behavior. This challenge may present something of a problem at first, for we have not yet spoken of Intentions at all. But he has been following them all through his task exercises, whether he has realized it or not. I want him to discover what I mean for himself and to interpret my phrase in the simplest, most practical way. And, most of all, I want him to find that in trying to activate an Inner Intention, he will stimulate a most creative part of his instrument.

At our next session, my student at first confesses his confusion.

"Don't I have to find an intention somewhere before I can activate it?"

"I think you'll find that your intention is there already—in the heart of the text. Simply put, when you speak your monologue, what are you doing?"

"I'm trying to introduce my imaginary play about my turning point."

"Yes, of course. But while you are 'introducing' your play in words, what are you really doing? How can you express what you're trying to accomplish—your goal or objective—in a more active way?"

"Well, I'm getting the audience ready to understand my play."

"Yes, but how can you say that more actively?"

"I'm preparing them for the play?"

"Exactly. You're preparing—not only the audience, but also perhaps yourself and your stage equipment. Preparing is an excellent word, and one capable of so many possibilities. Remember Stanislavsky's first book on his System— *An Actor Prepares.* You might say that all of our training is preparing to perform.

So we might conclude that our Intention in this monologue is 'to prepare for the play.' Does that sound right?"

"Certainly."

"So that's what I want you to try to do. Explore a possible preparation for your play. Don't worry if it's not perfect—it will change many times as we go on. Whatever you come up with, we'll be heading in the right direction. Try this physical intention now to accompany your monologue. Or, if you prefer, you can just explore the active preparing without speaking."

"All right—I think I've got it."

He proceeds with his Subtext version of the monologue, and, as he speaks, he fetches a stool, then a chair, a ladder and a small bench, and places them strategically around the stage area. He seems at once more purposeful, and his monologue, while still personal, is now more closely attuned to the form of the text. Progress! But what is he accomplishing with these physical tasks?

"What are you doing?"

"Trying to prepare."

"Prepare for what?"

"My play."

"And what are those pieces of furniture meant to suggest?"

"I really couldn't say. Just some stage set-up, I guess. But it felt much better to be doing something."

"Yes, indeed, doing something purposeful almost always helps. But suppose we try to find a specific focus for your physical life—not just some general physical task. Where does the first scene of your play take place?"

"In my parents' house."

"Which room?"

"I don't know . . . oh, yes—my bedroom."

"And how are you dressed?"

"Dressed? Well . . . I suppose in my robe and slippers."

"You mean not as you are now?"

"No, but when the play begins."

I continue, trying to get him to perceive the two different roles he will be playing. "Then now you are—who?"

"The narrator?"

"Exactly. And when your play begins?"

"The character?"

"Indeed, yes. So now you have two concrete goals to pursue. One is for your Narrator self, who is preparing for the play to come; and the other is for your character self, who will take over, so to speak, when the play in your memory begins. Two specific tasks to perform—two expressive ways in which you might activate your Intention. Right?

"Only when you know your destination can you more readily find your way. When you start your introduction, as the Narrator, you are here and now—perhaps coming to the bare stage. And when you finish—when 'the rest of the play will explain itself'—you are ready to become the character. You are prepared to appear as you were back at the time of your turning point, and the stage is set for the first scene. Of course, in an actual production, you might have all sorts of helpers, but for now you alone are director, as well as author and main actor. So just let your imagination be guided by this goal: find out how, while you prepare us with your words—by activating the inner Intention—you may also prepare outwardly and physically for your play. I am encouraging you to use your imagination, as well as your physical tasks, and whatever stage furniture, props and pieces of costume, sound, and lighting you may find helpful. In short, as Hamlet advises us, try "to suit the action to the word."

And he leaves with a stimulating new problem imbedded in his imagination. A challenge that I hope will be both nourishing and rewarding. For the physical preparing—activating this intention while the words are spoken—is akin to the pianist's left hand accompanying his right. Or the cello and piano accompanying the violin. Or the brasses accompanying the strings and woodwinds, the orchestra accompanying the soloists and chorus. A tapestry of complementary harmony and counterpoint can be created that weaves its way to a common aim—a unified voyage toward the artistic destination.

All too often, this creative extension of the actor's talent is left unexplored or deemed the province of the director. But in my own directing, I have found that my most valuable resource is the actor's creativity. So, in my training of actors, I try to stimulate this most vigorous branch of the actor's talent and imagination. I seek to make activating an inner intention an integral, habitual part of my student's preparation—of his growing craft—and thus a most rewarding element of his rehearsal technique.

❊   ❊   ❊

At our next session, my student arrives with a much more evident purpose. Now, as he introduces his play, in words much more closely connected to the form, size, and shape, of our playwright's text, he proceeds to set up his bedroom with a few pieces of stage furniture, and then to dress himself in his bathrobe and slippers. He has actually prepared for the opening scene of his play, while at the same time speaking his introduction. And his Subtext has become more meaningful—the physical tasks and objects have somehow made his introduction more immediate, more personal. He discovers the additional value of accompanying his Subtext and text with a logical sequence of personally relevant objects and tasks.

But while he has advanced in purposeful physical action, and his introduction is indeed closer in form to our text, his communication with me—his audience—has faltered. In focusing on a new element—actively pursuing his intention—he has lost ground in his communication. This is quite expected. We cannot march forward equally on all fronts; every additional new element may precipitate a temporary loss in others. So now he must find out Why he is speaking to me—his audience—and what he actually seeks from me: my attention, my interest, my understanding, and my sympathy. This prologue to his play, as most overtures to any performance, is meant to make his audience want to attend to his drama, to touch and involve that "intimate stranger" who is the ideal audience for every artist.

This is quite enough for this session. He has made significant progress. In succeeding sessions, he will continue to hone his text until it embodies practically all the playwright's words, while at the same time maintaining his communication with me. Eventually, he will be ready to forego speaking out his own specifics of time, place, and characters, and finally use the entire text. At the same time, he will gradually adjust his sequence of preparatory physical tasks to the five-step format of the text: first, an opening to engage my attention; next, a reminder of another time in the past—perhaps setting up the furniture; third, a suggestion of the effect of memory on the presentation—perhaps lighting, maybe music, maybe properties. Fourth, as he introduces the main characters, perhaps his own change of clothing, with particular objects for his "mother" and "sister"; and finally, the object representing the absent "father" put in its special place. As he is still physically preparing for his own play, speaking the author's text will present something of a dichotomy. But his subtextual connection with his own memories and research will be further solidified.

Finally he is ready to prepare for our author's play: to transport us to the alley apartment in St. Louis in the mid-1930s, to introduce Amanda and Laura and himself as Tom. Now he is to read the first scene of *The Glass Menagerie* and find that it takes place around a midday Sunday dinner in winter. And he will surely come up with a preparation for that opening after-church meal. He may set the table, provide specific "Mother" and "Sister" objects, and find certain articles of clothing with which to enter into that world. He is now actually preparing for Mr. Williams' play—and, still in his Subtext, he is connecting with his own, personally-motivating memories. Our process has gradually brought him to our Narrator's text and tasks, which are animated with personal feeling from his own analogy. Now it seems almost inevitable that he is both Here and Now and progressively There and Then—as himself at first and then "becoming" Tom. Now he is truly Living on Stage.

When my students arrive at this destination, invariably they are surprised, as well as rewarded, by the seeming ease and inevitability of this wedding of word, thought, and action. It now seems "organic"—as if it grew naturally, hardly fought through in our step-by-step, often laborious, process. But we can now see that such a seemingly inevitable, organic welding of thought, word, and action, is the product of a clear, conscious series of steps—from personal actor-analogy, through intimate memories, some historical research, and a play-wright's structure to character word and deed.

CHAPTER 8

Essential Elements

While the structure of my first monologue is built around a turning point in the narrator's life, I do not imply that we must always start from some such past event in the actor's own life. In fact, while I continue to hone this analogy-to-text process in each of the next two monologues I ask my students to prepare, I now focus on what I call the "Essential Elements." To start the creative process in each of these next monologues, I try to extract the few basic human ingredients that will send the actor into action. These are primarily a simple situation and a simple intention.

For my second monologue, once again I will not reveal the actual circumstances behind the text. Not at all. For these specific circumstances are of little immediate use in forging a connection between the student and the spine of the monologue. And I am confident that the student will find his own way toward discovering an apt analogy and follow the inside out path to an organic performance. It matters not whether the text is intended for a man or a woman. When the specifics of each are translated into the universal, human Elements, we can all connect with the circumstances, problems, and needs of all these characters. Indeed, I am continually surprised at how readily every one of my actors-in-training can make immediate personal connections to these varied pieces. When I communicate the basic elements of circumstances and intentions, and the actor finds his own personal analogy, he is invariably able to enter immediately into the essential situation and problems of each. And I find that while our first monologue may have taken many weeks, or even months, to prepare, each succeeding scene will take much less time—until it may be only three or four sessions in all for the third monologue. Starting with "I Am" and gradually proceeding toward the "As If" will again prove to be a solidly rewarding route. So now I merely suggest.

"Ready for our next monologue? This one is a soliloquy—speaking not to me as audience, but to yourself. The basic elements I offer to challenge your imagination, as well as your growing acting technique, are these: You are alone in your room, trying to solve some creative problem. You are having difficulties. And you speak your thoughts aloud. That's all."

"That's it?"

My student is somewhat confused. But I remind him, "We can all relate to these elements. We have all tried to create alone—to compose, or play an instrument, write, draw, or dance, or work out an acting problem—and suffered creative blockage. We have all tried to find a way through. The only element that we may not have experienced often is the speaking aloud of our thoughts. But aren't these elements enough to challenge you into exploring a not-unfamiliar moment from your own life?"

So at our next session, my student will set up a specific familiar time and place where he can feel at home—a simple technical problem he has already mastered in our physical task exercises. There and then—and here and now—he will proceed to put his attention to some creative problem: drawing or singing, playing the guitar or writing, for example. And he will start to reveal his thoughts in a spoken "free association."

This last challenge usually proves most difficult. For speaking our thoughts aloud is not a normal act for most of us. On the contrary, we have been trained to "think before we speak!" Spontaneous revelation of our intimate thoughts is often daunting. One of the differences between our own lives and those of characters in a play is that stage characters speak their thoughts aloud, in soliloquies, much more readily and fluently than we ourselves do in our daily lives. For those of us who have had the experience of free-associating on a psychiatrist's couch, it will be familiar. But I also remind my student, "Don't you unconsciously burst out into words whenever something goes wrong? A sudden curse or two when the door slams on your finger? Or, while you're scraping the carrots, don't you frequently remember and shout out the perfect put-down you couldn't think of when you wanted one an hour before? We all find our thoughts spontaneously erupting into speech on such odd occasions—somewhat like islands of sound rising abruptly from the silent ocean floor. Now it becomes our task to encourage in speech the expression of the march of unspoken thoughts that are always continuing in our minds."

I begin with a flow of vocal sound, rising and falling as we stretch and move. Then an urge to mumble, to open our voices to a stream of unintelligible sounds, until finally we can more easily give voice to our thoughts as they arise. By encouraging this free flow of voiced feelings, the actor soon becomes comfortable enough to let his thoughts move from a mumbling sound into continuous speech. When thus properly and gradually approached, voicing thoughts never remains a problem.

❀ ❀ ❀

Our next session finds my student preparing a semblance of his own room. He begins voicing his thoughts as he sets about to solve his own creative problem. He is trying to shape a new song, and his frustration mounts as he struggles with his inspiration and subsequent failure of satisfactory execution. He evidently knows this problem from experience, and now he has little difficulty in living through this struggle here on stage. He has clearly understood the assignment, for he is just as clearly trying to carry it out and to resolve his creative problem.

So now I can share some more of the specific elements of this monologue. He is a writer, trying to report on some violence he has just observed on the streets. But he wants to shape not merely a factual report, but something more imaginative. After all, he calls himself a writer, not a journalist. He recalls a successful author he admires who suffered similar creative pangs and used some personal technique to prod his inspiration. He tries this technique—and finds that it fails to solve his problem.

❀ ❀ ❀

With this new input, my student tries again. He is living closer to the situation of my text. So I can offer further clues to the sequence of events. He is in some foreign city, trying to survive while intending to write; this time the admired writer's secret is to prod his imagination with a personal mantra, reciting his own name. But when our young writer attempts this mantra for himself, it only leads at first to a fantasy of success and then a realization of his own actual abysmal lack of success. Finally, from somewhere, somehow, he finally finds the inspiration that enables him to write a couple of imaginative sentences that do at last satisfy.

Now, after my student enacts an improvised moment on the circumstances I have suggested, it is comparatively simple for him to move to some foreign place, to replace the creative task he has chosen with writing, and to try to report on some violence in the streets. Thus, in gradual stages, the basic elements are adjusted from the actor's own analogies toward the specifics of time and place— the "given circumstances"—of the character in the author's situation.

❀ ❀ ❀

In our next session, when my student is able to assimilate these new challenges and live through this problem in the sequence of events I have suggested, all the while speaking his thoughts aloud, he is at the threshold of our author's text. It is time to share it with him. We are working on Chris's opening soliloquy from van Druten's *I am a Camera*:

CHRISTOPHER: *"In the last few days, there has been a lot of Nazi rioting in the streets, here in Berlin. They are getting bolder, more arrogant." No, that's all wrong. That's not the right way to start. It's sheer journalism. I must explain who it is who is telling all this—a typical beachcomber of the big city. He comes to Berlin for the weekend, stays on, runs out of money, starts giving English lessons. Now he sits in a rented room, waiting for something to happen—something that will help him understand what his life is all about. When Lord Tennyson wanted to write a poem, they say he used to put himself into a mystic trance by just repeating his own name. Alfred Tennyson. Christoper Isherwood. Christopher Isherwood. Christopher Isherwood. I like the sound of my name. "Alone among the writers of his generation, Christopher Isherwood can be said to have achieved true greatness."*

"Shut up, idiot. The only book I ever published got five reviews, all bad, and sold two hundred and thirty-three copies to date. And I haven't even started this new one, though I've been here six months already . . . Well, you're going to start now, this minute. You're not leaving this chair until you do. Write "Chapter One." Good. Now begin. Create something. Anything. "I am a camera, with its shutter open, quite passive. Some day all of this will have to be developed, carefully printed, fixed."

And again, my student is agreeably surprised to find how very close he is to the text itself. It only remains to do a little research on the growing Nazi threat in 1930s Germany, to substitute Tennyson for his own role model, and the final discovery of "I am a camera with its shutter open." Again, my student has been brought to "inhabit his character", and in much fewer steps than it took for our first monologue.

The two "discovered" new elements—Lord Tennyson, the role model who's unblocking technique he suddenly remembers, and the final, fresh resolution to his problem (the inspiration that leads him to that imaginative metaphor of "I am a camera")—that are often sticking points. For they do present a very specific new acting problem. Here we encounter that "discovery" on the part of the character that the actor has already known from the text and must now seem to discover, as if for the first time. This is an all-too-prevalent problem that lies in wait for all actors in every role: that underlying acting problem of Anticipation, which will entangle the actor and keep him from creating the all-important "Illusion of the First Time." The *I am a Camera* monologue throws out this challenge most clearly. Indeed, it is one of the reasons I find this selection so useful in my training.

When I focus my student's attention on this new problem, he searches for clues that will seem to reveal something that he already knows, but that now, and at each performance, will be newly discovered by his character. I try to offer some hints.

"Haven't you done a series of 'seemingly unplanned tasks' in our technique exercises? These 'discoveries' are quite similar—merely 'seemingly unplanned, or unexpected events.' Moreover, whenever we make a discovery, or seem to get a new idea, it is usually triggered by some immediate sensory perception. Something we see, hear, touch, smell, or taste will summon up an association—either remembered or discovered. So, explore what you can set up that will lead you—here and now, not just when you worked at home—to both Tennyson and the figurative image of the camera with its shutter open."

It is enough. For, if not immediately, sooner or later, my student will find a book or a poem that will lead him to our poet, and some sequence of objects that will lead him to his comparison of himself to a camera. I do not mind if it is merely a literal camera—at this point in our training, the technical process is much more important than his imaginative creativity. And in the very next session, or two at the most, my student should be able to live through this monologue truly and logically. His own analogy and his research provide a firm subtext as he speaks aloud his thoughts—the text—and follows a sequence of logical physical tasks, "discovering" these two new ideas as he seeks to achieve his goals.

While both my first and second monologue assignments were intended for male characters, my female students have found no difficulty in working on them successfully, in each case making the circumstances her own. As "Tom" she can relate to a dependent afflicted sister and an overbearing mother; as "Christine" she can try to write from her immediate experiences in pre-Nazi Berlin. In both these instances, when I initially focus on the human elements, sex hardly matters. For my third monologue, I use one intended for a female character: Georgina's opening monologue from Elmer Rice's *Dream Girl*. As written, she wakes up, bemoans her depressed state, considers psychotherapy, rejects it, and continues through a lengthy self-analysis, both outer and inner, as she daydreams, listens to the radio, all the while performing her morning routine: she showers, brushes her teeth, makes up, gets dressed, and leaves for another day. I have eliminated the radio and the other voices that our heroine imagines conversing with. But again, I withhold all this for the time being and give my student only the barest elements:

"Now for our third monologue. This one should be a snap—no problem at all. The three essential elements are these: You are preparing for your day. You are trying to resolve both personal and professional problems. And you are speaking your thoughts aloud."

Notice, I do not say: "You are in bed, waking up. You are depressed and frustrated, in love with your brother-in-law. You are a would-be writer who works in a bookshop. You have submitted your novel and been rejected by all but the last publisher. And you have a date for lunch with a sexy guy you're not sure you should encourage." Nor do I list a sequence of morning grooming tasks or specifics, such as showering, finding a scary gray hair, admiring your legs, or wondering if you're normal, still a virgin at twenty-four. In no way can these specifics help the student at this point. On the contrary, the more specific are the demands, the less likely the student will be able to connect—to get personally involved. And the more likely he is to rush to conventional forms, to clichés of indicated concern. We all have, have had, and will have problems we constantly try to resolve, and we all prepare for each new day. Specifying what personal and professional problems the student focuses on and tries to resolve, or detailing in what order he should tackle the morning tasks can only divert the student, or any actor for that matter, from the immediate personal involvement he is fully capable of. In short, insisting on textual fidelity too soon only makes the text more out of reach! The task of bringing the text alive—or bringing life to the text—is only made more difficult! Connecting with the Spirit of the monologue is very much more helpful now than trying to connect with the Letter.

❊　❊　❊

In response to my initial challenge of these three basic elements, the student will bring into our next session an improvisation that invariably includes physical tasks of some dressing and grooming, as well as his mulling over personal and work problems. These are often boy or girl friend frustrations and career ups and downs; these elements are always ready. "Chris" or "Christine", having gotten used to speaking inner thoughts aloud in our previous monologue, no longer have trouble being candid.

So it is no problem now for me to begin asking for adjustments—fresh challenges that will bring the actor's sequence of inner and outer tasks closer to the size and shape of the text. For example:

"Very good. Now let me throw you a few more specifics: You live at home and work in a mundane job to support your artistic ambitions. Your personal problem is that you're in love with the wrong person. And your professional problem is that you've submitted your work, so far unrecognized, and been turned down by all but the last possible employer. You've also got a lunch date with someone who may or may not be helpful, may or may not be interested in you sexually, and whom you may or may not want to encourage."

❊　❊　❊

This leads to a second improvisation that begins to have the shape of the monologue.

Now I can add the elements of introspection and physical self-examination, the constant self-appraisal to find strong and weak points, the daydreaming of success, the mother's nagging, and even writing as the artistic activity.

Again, this new set of challenges is easily met. And so at only the third attempt at this selection, the student is usually quite prepared to accept the text. While considerably longer and more convoluted than my first two monologues, my student's "acting muscles" have been toned up and strengthened so that this monologue is assimilated in what seems to be no time at all. The student will readily perceive the new demands—a prescribed sequence; correlation of inner problems and outer tasks; and references to specifics of the ancient 1950s: Dorothy Parker, Schrafft's, virginity at twenty-four. He will now know how to respond to them intelligently. His technique is now fully able to meet and conquer all the challenges in what seems now a very brief, step-by-step process.

And the student cannot help but perceive that he has surely grown in craft—in perception of problems, as well as technical skill in resolving them. More and more, the student finds it easier, and more welcoming, in each new selection, to follow this inside out, I Am to As If, Spirit before Letter, Sequential, Step-by-Step Process to Living on Stage.

In succeeding monologues, I will be able immediately to assign the text itself. For I am confident that now the student will find his own way toward discovering an apt analogy and then will follow our path through an organic process. Starting with I Am and gradually going toward the As If constantly proves to be a most reliable and practical, solidly rewarding route. By following this path, the student actor learns how to look for and extract the essential, basic "human elements" inherent in the specific character and circumstantial details—the spirit behind the letter of the text. And these "human elements" will always permit and encourage him to find useful and relevant personal analogies.

Finally, the repertoire of monologues will grow more challenging—new characters, foreign and classic material, Shakespearean invocations and soliloquies, sonnets and "arias." This route, this technical process, practiced and almost perfected, continues to prove increasingly supportive and rewarding as the student actor stretches his talent and technique to bring new life to ever more luxuriant branches of dramatic and poetic foliage.

PART V

**First Work
with a
Partner:
Scenic
Exercises**

CHAPTER 9

Encounters in Structured Circumstances

"Scene Study" has long been the mainstay of professional acting training in New York. Whatever introductory classes may be offered in technique exercises, the students much prefer to join a "scene class." And just as often without any prior preparation. To the young acting student, "Technique" classes imply work, while a "Scene" class promises fun. What a trap for the unwary young actor!

Upon enrolling, scene class students are met with a variety of approaches, depending on the habits of individual teachers. Curt Conway, my first acting teacher, had trained with the Group Theater in the 1930s. He suggested scenes from the modern repertoire—from Chekhov and Ibsen through American plays of the 1920s and '30s. And he would assign the two students for each scene. Herbert Berghof, my next acting teacher, would ask,

"Who wants to do a difficult scene?"

And as my hand shot up, he would send me, together with whatever hapless other student offered himself, to such esoteric fare as Moliere's *Misanthrope* or Lorca's *Doña Rosita.* It appeared that Herbert liked unusual and challenging scenic material. Lee Strasberg, my third—and last—acting teacher at first offered no guidelines whatsoever. We chose partners and whatever material we liked. I remember bringing to his scene classes rich twosomes from Strindberg's *Miss Julie*, Shaw's *Androcles and the Lion*, William Inge's *Come Back, Little Sheba*, and scenes arranged from *Huckleberry Finn* and D.H. Lawrence's *Sons and Lovers.* Only much later, at his sessions of the Actors' Studio, was I to hear him reiterate, over and over, his mantra, "Choose a simple scene!" But he never elaborated.

Stella Adler, always the leading lady of the Group Theater, continued to assign those seminal scenes from Odets' first explosive drama, *Waiting for Lefty*. Sanford Meisner, another Group alumnus, always led off with his "repetition" dialogue; only second year students were permitted scenes from actual plays. Robert ("Bobby") Lewis, another Group alumnus and co-founder, with Elia Kazan and Cheryl Crawford, of the Actors Studio, would throw his students climactic confrontation scenes from modern or classic plays. And his rationale, it would appear, was in his dismissive, "Who wants to do simple scenes!"

Uta Hagen maintained copious lists of scenes she had amassed over the years; she would study the two students waiting at her desk, delve into her lists, and choose what she determined appropriate for each pair of students (whom she may have paired together or who may have signaled their desire to work together). Other teachers at the HB Studio would hand out lists of suggested, as well as prohibited, scenes to their students. Often the prohibitions appeared to stem from scenes the teacher had seen once too often and so were found to be boring. Imagine a piano teacher proscribing the scale of D-major, say, or Beethoven's *Für Elise*, from her students' lessons, because after hearing it so often she now found it boring!

Rarely, if ever, was the scenic material chosen with due regard to appropriate material for the students' level of training or skill. There seemed to be no alphabet of scenes—no guidelines to suggest any appropriate sequence of stage interactions.

Thus paired up, the students search out the specified texts, or choose whatever may strike their fancies, at the Drama Book Shop, at their local branch of the public library, or at a neighborhood book store that caters to the classes at various acting studios around the corner. The two students then meet at each other's apartments, or at a coffee shop, or in the park, and "rehearse" the scene together. Usually this involves reciting the dialogue for maximum effect, directing each other, and offering each other suggestions intended to help themselves or impress their teacher and fellow students. The partners proceed to memorize their lines, they "practice" together, and then they perform the scene in the next class. The teacher—and often the other students—offer comments and criticism; and the student performers then revel in the success, or bemoan the failure, of their performance. The results are often directly related to the stage-worthiness of the material. For all too often, the scene is chosen to make an impression—dramatic, comic, shocking—a scenic hit. It is rarely chosen to help the actor hone his craft with appropriate challenges for his level of training.

It has been my painful experience that this approach generally leads to greater anticipation and a concern for a preconceived, usually conventional result. I had been a party to this regimen not only in my own training, but in the first classes I taught as a young acting teacher. But the jump to performing, the playing for results that seemed inherent in this approach, continued to bother me — though I was hardly aware of the specific causes of the problem at that time. But when Herbert asked me to join the faculty of his HB Studio, after teaching my own private classes for six years, I decided to entitle my scene classes "Scene Technique" in order to emphasize the process-rather-than-product approach on which I hoped to focus.

I also rearranged a two-person dialogue from my college years that I had been experimenting with in my private classes. Now I assigned it as my first scenic exercise to two students who would chose to work together, or whom I would pair off together. This dialogue could take myriad shapes, depending totally on the three scenic elements I would assign each pair of students. These were the Relationship, the Circumstances, and the Intentions of the two participants. I would ask my beginning scene students to prepare two different scenes with this short dialogue, each scene embodying two different combinations of these three ingredients. And I would hand them this dialogue, typed without any stage directions whatsoever. It was also, quite deliberately, without any punctuation. For punctuation, I had discovered, is often the subtlest form of stage directions:

A. Well

B. Well I'm here

A. So I see

B. Yes

A. Well

B. Is that all you can say

A. What do you want me to say

B. Nothing

A. Nothing

B. You don't trust me

A. It's not that

B. Then what

A. Never mind

B. Stop it

A. What

B. That

A. I can't

B. Try

A. This is hopeless

B. What's the matter

A. I don't know

B. You don't know

A. No

B. Then go

A. I will

The students would perform this exercise at the next class. Two different scenes with the same dialogue, in two very different times and places, with two different relationships and two different sets of intentions. And usually this little scene, with the actors contributing the specific dramatic ingredients, left us impressed with the value and the power of the actors' own contributions. But no matter how effective the two different scenes with the same dialogue would be, almost invariably, the "sandwich" scene, as I called it—the meat of spontaneous change of furniture and properties between the two slices of bread of the rehearsed scenes—would prove the most natural, the most true. Because this scenic changeover, this simple stage preparation was not rehearsed or "performed," it was the only "scene" not done to impress the class and myself. And so this exercise quickly brought home to us all the difference between true, living behavior that was simple and purposeful, and that "Acting" which was fashioned to be interesting—dramatic or comic—to make a hit, to score.

Now I also recalled the many occasions in the Actors Studio when Lee Strasberg would shout in frustration at the Hollywood stars who had flocked there, parched for his fount of wisdom whenever they had a few weeks release from the Los Angeles desert, "Choose a simple scene!"

It became as much a mantra as his "RELAX!" Finally, I understood that these actors, no matter how successful or dedicated, had not an inkling of what Lee meant. How could they choose a "simple scene," when their aim was always to make a star impression? So I gradually realized that I would have to choose the scenes for my actors-in-training. By trial-and-error, as I had found everything else worth knowing in acting, directing, and teaching, I discovered just what a "simple scene" was. Moreover, I found out why it was so helpful—nay, essential—in a solid training process. Like a Bach *Two-Part Invention* for the young pianist, it is a necessary bridge from the elementary scales and arpeggios of Basic Technique to the music of melody, harmony, and rhythm of Scenes. And few young performers will seek out such training pieces. Don't we all want, most of all, "to make music"—and so express our passions in terms of our art?

Today I can readily find and assign a "simple scene," for I well know its ingredients: It is a scene of modern life to which the student actors can readily relate from their own experience; it is couched in contemporary prose, with no great dramatic or comedic climaxes. It presents clear, accessible relationships and circumstances, with easily understood and familiar intentions. In short, it is a scene in which, when the actor places himself in his character's—or an analogous—situation, he can usually trust his own responses and impulses to be "right."

During my twenty-five years teaching at the HB Studio, I managed, with the "Well" scene and also, gradually, with the subsequent scenes I would assign, to fashion a diet of basic scenic material for my students. However, I still sensed in my students that pull toward performing that comes with knowing and starting with the text, then rehearsing on their own outside of class, and finally bringing the results to the next class as to a theater. When I became the Acting Mentor for the Class of 1981 in the BFA Theatre Program at the State University of New York College at Purchase, I was charged with fashioning the entire four-year acting training for that Company, "Purchase Six." So I tried to formulate a more process-oriented entrance to scene work. I would ask for improvisations on the scenic situation and sometimes "prior life" exercises to explore relationships and circumstances. But I still began with assigning the text. Not until much later was I to realize that even knowing the name of the play, much less the text of the scene, was an inherent pull toward playing character images or scenic results!

I continued my search for a more seamless transition from technique exercises, usually with the individual actor working alone, to the interaction that scene work requires. At the University of Maryland's Baltimore County campus, some time after my Purchase years, I continued to explore possible connections. But only after I had left UMBC, in my private studio in downtown Baltimore, was I first able to fashion the bridge I had been seeking. I learned to lead my small group of very willing, mature students from their solitary exercises—at first with simple objects and tasks, and then with simple circumstances—into a natural progression that would evolve into working with a partner. I developed "Scenic Exercises" that I continue to find most fruitful. They form a solid bridge from individual task exercises to working on scenes with a partner. And I have discovered several valuable guidelines.

I allow no outside rehearsing together. There is individual preparation, on individual elements, but all the work with the partner is done in class. The name of the scene, as well as the text itself, is withheld from the students. And so, with no preconceptions of scenic results possible, a fresh scenic form is evolved out of content. With my gradual input, the "scenic partners" progress to the very verge of the text. At which point, finally, I am happy to hand out the text itself, for they are now ready to accept and embody the author's words. Now they come to the text with their Relationship, Circumstances, and Intentions fully developed. Thus, they are well armed to resist the pull towards anticipated, stereotypical images of conventional scenic results.

And so—two students, Will and Frank, have independently arrived at this turning point in their training. They have been studying privately, and separately, with me for several months. Now they are ready for this new direction. I think that they will prove to be compatible. I have asked them both to arrive at my studio—unbeknownst to each other—at the same hour. We meet and get acquainted as we warm up together on the carpet. Then they settle down, Will sprawling on the daybed by the door and Frank perched on the raised pew at the rear. I sense that they are expecting me to call on each in turn to perform his assigned exercise. It is a reprise of the "familiar time and place with three tasks: planned, seemingly unplanned, and actually unplanned."

I ask Frank to go first. He sets up a chair and table—a corner workshop in his design offices. He starts to work on an art project, his radio turned to a classical music station. I can see he is involved, fully engaged in his task. So I turn to Will and ask him to do his exercise. Will is somewhat surprised, but agreeably sets up his own space a good distance away from Frank—the better to maintain his privacy. Sensing this will not help my exercise, I indicate to Will that he is to work further on stage, thus possibly encroaching on Frank's space. Puzzled, but agreeable, Will obliges. He is "at home," and he begins to prepare supper for himself and his girlfriend. Now Frank's hammering and radio are filling the studio, but Will studiously ignores the sound—he is determined not to hear. Meanwhile, Frank, crossing to the prop shelves to get some water, pointedly ignores Will. He is just as determined not to see. The two actors try to continue their individual tasks, but their studied avoidance of each other is taking its toll. I decide to intercede.

"Frank—where are you?"

"At my art studio. This morning."

"And who's with you there?"

"Er—no one."

"You're sure? You didn't go around someone on your way to get the water?"

"Well, I tried to . . ."

"Avoid Will. Yes, that was quite clear. But he's quite unavoidable, isn't he? And Will—where are you?"

"At home. Waiting for Sally—about six o'clock.

"And who was with you?"

"No one, at first. Then, I think I saw Frank. Yes, I know I heard him."

"But did you allow yourself to acknowledge him? In your kitchen while you were expecting Sally?"

"I didn't think I was supposed to."

"Of course. Because you hadn't invited him. And Frank, did you allow yourself to acknowledge Will? Even though he isn't usually at your studio, preparing supper?"

"I thought you were testing my privacy."

"Not this time. I was actually testing your willingness to accept the unforeseen, the actually unplanned, in fact."

And so we can examine this exercise—and the actor's unconscious preconceptions that it aims to challenge. Yes, we often need to maintain our public privacy on stage when the actor may hear or see things that his character doesn't. But here I am more concerned with the actor learning to accept the unexpected—when it intrudes on his sight or hearing—as we do in life. If he were actually in his studio, I tell Frank, he would never ignore Will. He might be surprised to see him in so unusual a spot, but he would never ignore him. Similarly, I think Will would never deny Frank's presence, surprising as it might be to see him so at home in Sally's kitchen. Only the preconception of the actor puts such blinders around him. And these preconceptions can only lessens his normal abilities to live truthfully on stage—to perceive and respond spontaneously, as we do offstage, in life.

"But how can we continue our tasks and live our lives in our familiar time and place with such new intrusions?" Their objections rise in chorus.

"Well, let's see. Let's try it again. And find out what might happen if you acknowledge what your senses clearly tell you. This time, you begin, Will."

Will resumes preparing for his supper with Sally. Frank watches, waiting, confused. But when I suggest he go on stage to perform his exercise, he proceeds manfully. He goes to his worktable, but now greets Will as he goes. They immediately relax. And they get acquainted; continuing their tasks, they find out quite a bit about each other and why each appears to be a surprise visitor to the other. They maneuver round this problem and manage to stay clear of the verbal traps. And their tasks develop easily as their confidence and freedom grow. I see that the lesson is being understood—and learned.

"Excellent! Where are you, Will? And you, Frank? And when?"

And we discover that each has been able to maintain his own "given circumstances"—and yet also acknowledge and accept the highly unexpected, even highly improbable. As in life, we adapt to unexpected occurrences, so on stage, when our stage lives are usually so programmed, we can also continue to live and adjust to the unexpected. We need not ignore, the first trap of this challenge; nor need we fall out of our own circumstances and jump into our partner's—if he seems more positive. And neither do we need to challenge our partner's time and place, provoking a fight, or seek to dramatize and embroider the "scene." We can learn—and here, my apt students clearly are learning—to live with the outrageously unexpected, while continuing to maintain our own circumstances. In short, to Adjust. And I hear again Lee Strasberg in my memory, insisting so often, long before I was able fully to understand, much less to appreciate, that "Whatever happens to you on stage is also happening to your character!"

Once this is fully acknowledged and applied, it is a jungle of monkeys off our backs! Finally, we can understand that while in life, offstage, we are in one set of actual circumstances (though we may wish, dream, or remember another in our minds), on stage we always live in two: As characters, we live in the imagined time and space of the "given circumstances" of our play; and as actors, we are performing in the actual space and time of the studio, sound-stage or theater. Now, with this new discovery—that each actor may also Live on Stage imaginatively in circumstances of his own—we find that we are able to maintain further, often innumerable and contradictory sets of circumstances. Thus, in our stage art, in the imaginary made manifest in acting terms, do we create and live in an impossible world—a mix of manifold imaginary circum-stances—a magical truth!

For our next exercise, I now assign a much simpler problem. Both Will and Frank will inhabit a common place and time; again familiar, and again with three tasks. One will be planned and familiar, one planned and seemingly unfa-miliar, and one familiar and seemingly unplanned. One of the tasks is to be shared in common, while the other two are to be done separately. They are to discuss and agree on the time and place and the one task they are to share. But they are not to rehearse, nor reveal to each other what separate tasks each will undertake. Finally, they do not actually have to have been together in the agreed-upon space. A plausible space-time for such an encounter will serve the exercise quite well.

❊   ❊   ❊

At our next session, this exercise proves to be no problem at all. They have chosen to be in my kitchen, preparing for a student gathering. They are cele-brating Will's being cast in a new film. They set the table and start to prepare separate dishes—peeling artichokes and practicing making various cocktails. I can easily pick out the planned-familiar, the planned-seemingly-unfamiliar, and the familiar-seemingly-unplanned tasks. Though anyone unaware of the exercise would hardly notice these tasks as such. All the while they are con-versing naturally, continuing to get acquainted. It is a simple, structured improvisation with the full ring of truth—logical, specific and purposeful. They are not performing, but Living on Stage. Still in their own personas, but completely involved and behaving in the "given circumstances"—Here and Now *as if* There and Then. They are truly communicating—truly interacting in a most convincing manner. I have no need to admonish them, with long-remembered strictures—

"Relate to your partner! Listen to him! Don't anticipate!"

All of these stage traps are easily avoided. The actors are not here to play a scene, but to pursue a number of tasks in a logically structured situation culled from their own lives. And these tasks were both "actor tasks"—my arbitrary assignments, and "character tasks"—what each chose to try to do, both separately and together, in the imagined circumstances. They had no "How," which a text inevitably suggests; no dialogue to try to remember; no stage directions as to specific moments of behavior; no image of the scene in result terms. Thus unencumbered, they were free to Live on Stage rather than perform. After the exercise, I am careful to spell out just what has helped them to really Live on Stage. For I want them to remember this experience—and to fix in their memories the ingredients and processes that have led them to this simple, honest interaction.

I am very pleased; it is time to move on. Now we can prepare for their next exercise—a move into the next dimension, the Fifth Major Acting Question: "With Whom?" In other words, their Relationship. Until now, I have kept my students from any attempt at another character; it is vital that until now, they are acting solely in their own personae, with their own actual relationship. The only imaginary elements are those of "Where and When?" and "What and Why?" I now introduce this next dimension with one new imaginary element. Again, they are to choose a familiar time and place with three tasks: planned and seemingly unfamiliar; familiar and seemingly unplanned; and both seemingly unplanned and seemingly unfamiliar. But the new element will be an Imaginary Secret. Will and Frank are each to imagine about the other an intriguing secret, one that begs for a decision to be made, one that is kinetic—dynamic. It must not be revealed. But if properly chosen, this imaginary secret will begin to effect a change in their actual relationship.

And so, until our next session. Their interest mounts apace!

❄ ❄ ❄

At our next class, I can see that both students are stimulated by this new problem. They set this "scenic exercise" at the gym; they are working out together. They have no difficulty at all with carrying out the assigned tasks. But their secrets hardly seem to matter to them. I suspect that they may be forgotten. For I can perceive very little inner consideration or effect of this supposedly important private information on their outer behavior. Though I am not to know their imaginary secrets, if they are truly planted and of sufficient import, something hidden will be suggested. I will not fail to see they are pre-occupied with something other than what they say and do.

We discuss the problem, and we find that their secrets have not been sufficiently challenging. Will had imagined that he'd mentioned Frank's new CD to someone at a record label who might be interested in producing and marketing it. And Frank had imagined that he found out something about Will's girlfriend that boded no good for him. I can see that both secrets were too general and of too little import to occupy their imaginations. I explain that now the challenge must be to invest these, or similar secrets, with greater immediacy. They must matter more; they must demand attention and possible action.

❊ ❊ ❊

For our next interaction, I also raise the stakes in my structure. I require all four of the kinds of tasks we have been exploring: planned and familiar, planned and seemingly unfamiliar, familiar and seemingly unplanned, and seemingly unplanned and seemingly unfamiliar. And the sole shared task will involve a different category on the part of each partner, leaving with another task to be performed separately. Now this four-task interaction is clearly more fraught; I can see that they have something on their minds, something not yet spoken. Will, we discover later, has chosen as his imaginary secret that he is considering asking me to assign him another scene partner—he finds working with Frank too frustrating. And Frank's secret "information" about Will's girlfriend is now much more threatening. And this time, it is clear that there is an unspoken Subtext coloring their conversation, their behavior, and, indeed, their relationship.

It is time to explore a wholly different, imagined relationship.

Again I will not ask either of my students to veer from his own persona. Instead, I ask them to relate to their partner as if he were someone else in their own lives—someone meaningful. It may be someone old or young, man or woman, relative, friend, enemy, teacher, boss—whomever. But it must remain a secret. To permit the interaction, I also request that proper names be avoided. For the structure, I merely suggest that they choose a common time and place and two or three tasks, from any category. And I add that I think they will find it helpful if they each settle on their secret relationships before agreeing on the time, place and circumstances. This is clearly an unusual new challenge, and I can see their imaginations begin to warm up.

❊ ❊ ❊

At our next session, as their interaction proceeds, I find myself wondering if they truly understood the exercise. For their behavior is fairly similar to their previous work. Will seems to want to have some more fun and brings some "weed" to share with Frank, and Frank treats Will with a similar friendliness. Are they truly imagining different relationships at all? After the exercise, we find that Will has related to Frank as his college roommate, someone with whom he did in fact share such moderately illicit moments; while Frank has related to Will as his kid brother. I can see the true application of each of these relationships; but I suggest that they are overly close to their own actual relationship, as acting class scene partners. For our next exercise, I urge them to risk a further imaginative leap—to try someone of a different age or sex, an authority figure, or a resented figure—to raise the stakes of the interaction. I am reminded of just such an interaction in my Baltimore studio that raised the hackles of the entire class, between two students whose work had not yet seemed particularly compelling. It turned out that each had imagined the other as a particular estranged sibling; and this interaction immediately brought out such strong claims, such resentments, and such a depth of feeling that everyone was amazed—the students in the exercise most of all.

❧   ❧   ❧

And now our next session brings just such an interaction. To spur more vivid responses to one another, I suggest to Will and Frank that each relate to the other as to someone he would not like to be alone with. The relationship is immediately charged—unspoken resentments seem to fill the air. Will and Frank are now barely speaking; they avoid each other, and any necessary interaction is accompanied by curt, wounding monosyllables. Impressed by the richly heightened coloring of their scene, I impulsively call out another suggestion, "Now change your relationship to each other! This time, to someone you respect very much!"

And again, their interaction takes on a completely different color. The vivid turnabout is again unmistakable. As they finish their tasks in this newly respectful relationship, I think it is time to examine the ingredients that have proved to have so potent an effect.

For the person they chose not to have to interact with, Will immediately related to Frank as to his former girlfriend; while Frank, in turn, related to Will as his former boss. And to bring a highly respected relationship to their interaction, Will chose myself, and Frank his voice teacher. Thus, having both demonstrated and felt the power of this means of heightening relationships, my "scenic partners" are now very ready to move into my next scenic interaction. Now, and seemingly inevitably, they will be working on an actual Scene from an actual Play.

CHAPTER 10

First Work on Simple Scenes: Improvising upon Scenic Elements

We begin not with a poetic, highly charged classic, or a far-out, contemporary avant-garde assault, or even a traditional scene of climactic confrontation. No. This first scene must be a clearly accessible encounter between characters relatively close to our actors' experience. Their circumstances, relationship, and manner of speech should be fairly familiar, and they are pursuing simple intentions that are clear and consciously chosen.

I have paved the way for just this next step. As in our monologue work, I will not start with the text of the scene, but with the Scenic Elements: A set of Circumstances, Tasks, or an Intention, and, now, a specific Relationship. Moreover, these first scenic exercises will not aim toward the actual scene in the play, but towards a possible, or even probable, part of the "prior life" of these two characters that is suggested in the text of the entire play. These events might have happened before the play begins, or before the scene in question. Finally, I phrase these elements in such a way that each of the actors may interpret them in terms of his own actual experience. For this particular scene, I have chosen a possible "prior life" interaction between Tom and Jim, well before they come to dinner at the Wingfield apartment in the second act of *The Glass Menagerie*. I offer a few clues:

"The setting is to be a place of work; the time during a workday. The relationship is between two co-workers, one in a somewhat superior position and the other somewhat inferior. And their intentions are to try to perform their respective jobs so as to maintain or better their positions.

"And to enable both of you to use your own experience, we will do the scenic exercise twice. You will exchange roles, thus providing each of you, in turn, the opportunity to specify the workspace and to play the 'superior' role."

To smooth the transition from improvised scenic exercises to work on an actual scene from an actual play, I may not even mention that we are starting to explore a scene from a play. But if I do, I certainly do not reveal which scene from which play by which author. They will find out soon enough. I am trying to prevent the possibility of my students having any image of a scenic result from possibly having seen prior performances. (And, as the scene in question is from *The Glass Menagerie*, there have been many!)

* * *

At our next session, Will sets up the office in the swimming pool where he had been head lifeguard back in his hometown in the Midwest. He casts Frank as a new lifeguard under his supervision. And they improvise very well indeed; Will knows his job and merely instructs Frank. It is not very close to Tom and Jim's relationship in the play, but now I merely observe and begin to discover what I need to adjust in my next instructions. Whatever occurs, this improvised interaction cannot ever be "wrong." So long as it is true to the actors' relationship and circumstances, it can only tell me what new adjustments I must suggest to bring the work ever closer to the play. Frank, in his turn, sets the scene in his art studio with Will as a new employee. As Will had before him, Frank gives instructions and tasks for a newcomer. It is now very clear to me what adjustments must be made.

So, for our next session, I offer some clues for further adjustments: It is not the first day on the job. Indeed they have been working together for some time. The "superior" is not directly over the "inferior." Both have blue-collar jobs, but the one is more of a laborer and the other does more clerical work. And I will also move the location to a wholesale warehouse where goods are shipped to retailers. But I am careful still to leave specifying the particular kind of warehouse to my actors.

* * *

With these new adjustments, my actors readily improvise new tasks, again exchanging roles in turn. They are again living easily, conversing freely, carrying out their tasks with a will. And now I clearly see I need a new adjustment to bring them still closer to their characters in this as-yet-unrevealed scene. I must share ever more necessary clues. And now to an essential element that I have refrained from mentioning: that of Character. But I am confident that my actors at this stage will not fall into the "Character-Image Trap" they might have, had I begun with this element. Moreover, the characters we are moving toward are clearly not very far from recognizable parts of themselves or their friends. Jim, the shipping-clerk, is a gregarious, popular, "regular" guy, aiming to move up into the front-office of the warehouse; while Tom, the laborer, is a would-be poet, a loner, who suffers through these workdays to support his mother and sister, while he dreams of—and secretly plans for—his day of escape.

I point out that we have elements of both the extrovert and introvert inside ourselves. At times we are more fully social, and just as often we may be equally secretive and solitary. In playing a stage role, the actor draws on that part of himself, as well as his own life experience that, in whatever degree, connects with the "spine" of his character.

❊ ❊ ❊

So, at our fourth improvisation on this prior life of Tom and Jim from *The Glass Menagerie*—I can safely reveal these facts at this time—the results are quite different.

My actors have no difficulty with my new adjustments. Clearly they have both lived in the "Jim role" as much as the "Tom role." Both actors are artists and both have also had to spend time in the workaday world. Now I can move them much closer to the actual scene in the play. The scene will still be at the warehouse, for it is there that the "precipitating event" takes place. We learn in the final scene of Act I that at some time during that Thursday workday at the warehouse Tom has invited Jim to come home to dinner the next evening. We encounter them on stage in Act II, arriving at the Wingfield apartment; and their relationship and intentions are revealed in the ensuing scene on the fire escape, when both young men share previously hidden secrets with one another.

This is a very strange event, given the prior relationship of these two co-workers. They are not friends; they actually know very little about each other. Indeed, they rarely converse at all. Unfortunately, we seldom see this element revealed in conventional productions of the play. And then I can tell that the actors (and director) have gone directly to the interaction written in the text without ever having explored the prior life that establishes their relationship and makes this scene so unusual. Nor have the actors found the specific spring-boards that makes this particular scene happen here and now, at this precise point in the lives of these two young men. The author (and the director, we trust) will know why this scene must happen at this point in the play; but it is the actor who must discover and reveal why it happens just at this point in his character's life.

So now I share two vital pieces of information. Their boss has observed Tom slacking off on the job and has told Jim that Tom may be fired if he doesn't shape up. And Tom has finally decided to agree to his mother's entreaties of several months ago—that he should invite some "nice young man" to dinner to meet his reclusive sister Laura. As Tom informs his mother of Jim's imminent visit just the evening before the visit itself, his invitation appears to be a very recent decision on Tom's part. What precipitates this sudden change in Tom? And why? These vital questions are stimulating challenges for the actor's creative energies.

My actors are challenged to prepare to incorporate an inner problem. "Jim" has memories of the "secrets" improvisation of previous class sessions; while "Tom" will investigate using some personal, perhaps also secret, motivation of his own, while he searches the play for helpful clues.

❊ ❊ ❊

At our next class, I see that my latest input controls my actors' work inordinately. With a clear objective, they seem to forget their relationship and their warehouse tasks. Their jumping to a scenic obligation has almost obliterated the relationship and the working lives they have built up in previous sessions. The actor's knowing what the scene wants and his eager desire to fulfill those wants are clear acting traps—a subtle snare of Anticipation. But now I only need to point this out, to remind my actors of their relationship, of the working tasks necessary in the circumstances, and the devious paths both Tom and Jim must have followed before deciding to act on the new information.

In addition, now I will indicate another route to solving this problem: I suggest that each of the actors speaks his thoughts aloud. Both have already done this in their earlier private exercises and in at least two of the monologues—soliloquies, really—that we have worked on. To maintain the necessary privacy for such free expression of Subtext, I add that the partner will "not hear" such spoken thoughts. He will respond only to dialogue addressed to him. This may sound a bit odd at first, but I know that my actors will discover that it is a convention easily followed in practice. It also addresses a major acting hazard. This is that all-too-familiar problem that arises when the actor knows the entire play and thus much more than his character might. But in the guise of his character, that actor must only *seem* to know, or act upon, whatever knowledge his character might reasonably be expected to have.

❊ ❊ ❊

With this new adjustment, the interaction is much more logical, true both to the working day routine and the new inner problems our actor-characters have made their own. Jim, not yet able to reveal the whole truth, hints at Tom's need to pay more attention to his work. And Tom offers his invitation to dinner the following evening, which surprises Jim but which he is pleased to accept. It is clearly the right time to reveal the text and move the event to the time and place of the scene on stage: a Friday evening in May at the Wingfield apartment.

So I hand the actors the text of the scene—typed with only the dialogue, eliminating all stage directions. I begin, just after Laura rushes off to the kitchen, with Jim's speech, "What's the matter?" And I ask my actors not to learn the words, or even obligate themselves to the shape of the scene. I ask them just to improvise as they have been doing, but now using all the new information about their Relationships, Circumstances, and Intentions the text reveals. It will be a rough paraphrase.

❊   ❊   ❊

At our next session, I am chagrined to get just that: a paraphrase of the dialogue of the scene. Gone and forgotten are the truthful ebb and flow of conversation and work. Now, in both versions of the scene, as "Tom" and "Jim" switch roles in turn, they both just sit and talk. Somehow, lifting their interaction from a place where they were clearly at home with clear sequences of tasks to occupy them, and taking them to a living room space in which neither appears at all "at home" is a wrench. It is clear to me that "Tom"—in turn, Will and then Frank—must first find his own spaces in this family apartment, spaces that are private, maybe even secret; while "Jim"—in turn, Frank and then Will—must specify what habits and concerns a young man seeking to acquire "social poise" would occupy himself with on such a special, social evening. Again it is clear that the inherent Anticipation that comes with barely a reading of the scene has swamped the fuller, more expressive tasks and concerns that would give the scene the texture of the occasion, as well as the surprises and the depths it truly reveals.

So for our next session, I suggest two separate exercises: for "Tom" a private moment of free solitude in which to explore his own special, even secret, places in this small apartment, places where he may hide his books, manuscripts, whatever. This exercise is meant to encourage "Tom" to begin to live in this space. And for "Jim," a similar private moment of preparing for a social occasion—to find what objects fill his pockets, pockets that he later describes to Laura as "a regular drug store."

❊   ❊   ❊

Our next class puts us back on track. The four individual improvisations, each exploring some prior time with character-based concerns, have enriched my actors' work. But I perceive that a new element must be incorporated before the events of the scene can truly transpire. Although Jim has an immediate problem, helping Tom keep his job, Tom has a much more enticing problem—to affect his escape. Now, with the tantalizing, recently-received Merchant Marine membership card, Tom can envisage his escape from the warehouse and this apartment as happening "soon." And so one more exercise for "Tom"—when he receives his liberating card and plans to invite Jim to dinner.

❊ ❊ ❊

Now all the elements are in place. At our next session, the scene is performed admirably. Both actors seem fully alive, fully inhabiting their varying points of view, as both "Tom" and "Jim" in turn reveal their secrets to each other and encounter such varying responses. The dialogue follows the text, not always the precise words, yet in form and sequence extremely close. Textual fidelity, as well as timing and staging, may best be left to a director. The actor's work is largely done when he has made the circumstances, relationships and intentions of his character his own. He must not concern himself with *how* they may best be revealed—it is for the director now to shape, edit, polish.

And so I congratulate my actors and immediately assign them the elements of another scene.

My second "simple scene" is again from a modern play with accessible characters and situations. A scene fairly early in the play, when the stakes have yet to mount to dramatic or comedic heights. A scene that the student actors can readily relate to—if not from their own actual experience, then from others they may have observed in their families, friends or communities. A scene in which the characters express themselves in modern, idiomatic, conversational speech. And most important, it is a scene in which, when the actors have put themselves into their character's circumstances, their own impulses will be reliable, trustworthy and "right." For one of the most valuable lessons I can offer my acting students is an essential reward of these scenic sessions—and that is learning to Trust Oneself.

Again, I will suggest a set of Essential Elements: Circumstances, Relationships, and Intentions. These Elements will provide the springboard for improvisations evolved out of the actors' own analogies. Again, I will ask my students, in turn, to alternate the roles they are undertaking as part of the process. And then, with my gradual adjustment of the elements, when the interaction approaches the shape of the scene, only then will I reveal the actual text. This process, from analogy and Subtext to textual fidelity, gets progressively easier and faster. As in the similar work the students have already done in their first monologues, the process is designed to become a habit.

I unabashedly avow that my training, like most accepted training regimens, is indeed meant to be "habit-forming." After three scenes approached in this manner, I am now confident that in succeeding scene work the student can safely begin with the actual text. He will be able to analyze the text himself and develop his own necessary analogies, Subtext, and gradual adjustments. This process, "from the inside out," will have become a familiar and useful approach. In whatever new variations new material may suggest, with the greater challenges that come with larger roles to flesh out on stage or in films, it will continue to serve my actors as a firm, dependable process in tackling new and progressively more demanding—and more rewarding—acting problems.

CHAPTER 11

Reprise: Encounters from Another Perspective

When I turned seven years old and begged my mother for piano lessons, she found a teacher who would give a cut-rate "group class" for my older brother and myself. While I soon managed to oust my brother from our "class," I was all but defeated by the unpleasant surprise that came with this victory; I would have to endure hours of painful practice before I ever hoped to play! What kept me going through the dark clouds of awful scales and required finger exercises were those peeping rays of sunshine, that promise of those melodies waiting at the back of my elementary music books. Such "pieces," soon to be mine, were clearly to be my reward at the summit of this uphill path to piano playing.

Much later, I discovered that the path to dancing was similarly stressful, but also clear and sequential. Having only what dance floor skills remained from those Friday evenings at Miss Rigby's sessions in foxtrot, waltz, and rumba during high school years, I was a complete tyro in our "Dance for Actors" workouts at the American Theater Wing after the War. But Kathleen O'Brien's clear sequence of physical stretches, followed by a basic vocabulary of jumps, leaps and hops, were followed by the simple routines we could master by the close of each class. They were our reward. And more complex dance sequences were to be ours by the end of the semester. In music and dance, as in most other performing crafts, "A" led to "B," "B" to "C," and so on.

But in acting classes—such a variety of starting places! Such confusion of sequence in any alphabet of training, much less practice! And such pervasive inability to distinguish the cart from the horse!

Thus, throughout my years of teaching acting, I have constantly sought to identify basic acting problems more clearly and arrange them in a more appropriate sequence of mounting difficulty. I discovered that eighty percent of the solution lay in a more precise definition of the problem. And, after years of frustration, I found I was able to devise clear, accessible, sequential solutions to these perennial problems for my actors-in-training.

One of the most frustrating, universal acting problems I faced as I tried to find a more logical and helpful sequence has been the transition from working alone on basic technique exercises to working together with a partner on scenes. These two fundamental branches of actor training were approached, and continue to be approached, like two completely different subjects.

I was only to discover the missing link much later, in my own classes, through many years of trial-and-error and on-the-job-training. As the series of exercises described in the previous chapter is perhaps the most innovative training sequence I have yet devised, I think it deserves another look—from another perspective.

Here, then, and in the next chapter, is a record of similar problems and similar solutions. What follows, from a different perspective, are those steps with which I now lead my students from training in individual physical task exercises to interacting with a partner. And then to "Scenic Exercises" that lead to performing scenes from a contemporary play "from the inside out"— or from the elements to the text. And so, a similar sequence of problems with a similar sequence of practical solutions—but now with two young women as our heroines!

Today I have arranged for two of my female students to meet for their first interaction exercise. Lynne has already done the familiar-time-and-place exercises with various problems built on the planned, unplanned and unfamiliar tasks; while Gaby has just arrived at this point in her training. I have wanted to start Lynne working with a partner for some weeks, and I have found Gaby to be unusually adept in understanding and performing my exercises: something tells me the "casting" will be right. I think they will work well together; so now I have asked Gaby to come an hour after Lynne, and Lynne to stay forty minutes after her usual private session for this first partnering exercise. And I have asked each of them to prepare, in addition to her other work, the familiar-time-and-place with planned, seemingly unplanned, and actually unplanned tasks. Both know that I am preparing some kind of interaction between them, and they have been trying to find out what this new "partnering" might entail.

"Stick around!" and "You'll find out!" are the only clues I give to this important turn in my training process. My students are conditioned to be brave.

They meet as scheduled, and we do a few warm-ups as they get acquainted. They are about the same age, late twenties; I sense that they both are a bit apprehensive, as well as both curious and eager. I ask Gaby to go first. She sets up the elements of her room—the sofa and a box or two as end- and coffee-tables, and then gets the sewing materials she has brought with her. She removes her boots, settles comfortably on the sofa, and proceeds to put her attention to repairing a tear in a pillowcase. She has some difficulty untangling the thread, but then threads her needle and focuses on her sewing quite calmly and purposefully. Lynne and I observe her intently. When she has repaired the pillowcase, Gaby notices a hole in one of her stockings; she takes it off, explores it, and decides to repair it also. Which she then proceeds to do, again quite calmly. At this point I suggest to Lynne that she should set up and begin her own exercise.

While she seems a little hesitant about intruding on Gaby's sewing, Lynne dutifully carries her bag of props to the table on the other side of the carpet, brings a chair, and proceeds to unwrap some fresh vegetables, a knife, and some plastic kitchen bags. But first, she also removes her boots. She focuses intently on her work as she scrapes each stalk of asparagus, cuts each into three-inch pieces, and then proceeds to attack the other vegetables. Her work makes some noise, but Gaby studiously ignores her, as if she weren't there. And Lynne resolutely ignores Gaby, involving herself completely in her dinner preparations. I decide to interject.

"Gaby, what are you doing?"

"Repairing a hole in my stocking."

"So I see. And where are you?"

"In my room. Thursday evening."

"And who is there with you?"

"Why, no one."

"Are you sure? Didn't you hear someone cutting up vegetables?"

"Well—yes. But I thought I wasn't supposed to notice."

"So I observed. And Lynne, where are you?"

"In my kitchen, preparing dinner for Chris. Friday evening."

"And who is there with you?"

"Uh—no one. That is—I'm not sure."

"You didn't notice Gaby sewing over there?"

"Well—yes. But I thought I wasn't supposed to see her."

"Exactly. Because you didn't expect to see her. But if you were actually at home and you noticed Gaby, for some unknown reason sewing on a bench in your kitchen, would you ignore her?"

"Well, maybe not . . . I'm not sure."

"I hardly think so. And Gaby, if you heard someone cutting vegetables in your apartment, would you continue to avoid acknowledging her?"

"Why, no, but I thought—I mean, I thought we weren't supposed to. In all my previous exercises, you taught me not to acknowledge you when you spoke to me."

"Of course. But I am here, beyond the fourth wall, so to speak. Lynne is there, on the carpet in your space. A bit different, isn't it?"

"Yes, but—but—I guess I'm confused."

"Good. I want you to recognize that I'm throwing a new problem at you. You might call it 'the arrival of an unexpected guest.' On stage, of course, quite often the actor must not acknowledge things of which she may be quite aware, but her character cannot be; but now I'm drawing our attention to a different problem. At home, if either of you became aware of each other in your space, you would hardly ignore her. I don't know exactly what each of you would do, but you certainly would not deny her presence. How you respond is up to you, but if you are to remain alive and convincing, some response seems to me to be essential. Which brings up an interesting problem inherent in the actor's attempts at Living on Stage.

"In a conventional rehearsal process, the actors are programmed to expect just what they (and the director, of course) have planned and rehearsed. This not only leads to Anticipation, but it often reduces us to being less alive than we are offstage. You've all seen the chair that falls over on stage, or the papers dropping from the desk—and the actor resolutely ignoring the mishap, pretending it didn't happen. Because it wasn't planned to happen. Of course, when the actor pretends not to notice, her character doesn't notice also. Which then appears quite strange, as we in the audience *do* notice. And so all faith in the reality of the stage event is lost—that "suspension of disbelief" we bring with us to a play evaporates! The audience then can see nothing else *but* the fallen chair or papers and wonders why the characters don't see it as well.

"Last evening I attended an opera, very impressive for the most part, but full of similar unnatural behavior. At one point in this classic epic, the commander commanded his men to 'Go! Get going!'—and the men just stood there. In life they would have been court-martialed on the spot, but here they knew that their commander had a few more phrases to sing. And since they were programmed to go only after he'd finished—after all, he was the star of the evening—they didn't dare make a move until he'd sung all his prepared verses. And I wondered if I was the only one to wince at the unreality of it all.

"In this exercise, I deliberately draw your attention to the actually unplanned event. I saw very well your various tasks, planned and unplanned. You took off your boots, Gaby—I think actually unplanned. You took out your sewing—

and that appeared planned. Then you had difficulty untangling the thread—also apparently unplanned, but I couldn't say whether actually or seemingly. Finally, you noticed the hole in your stocking and proceeded to sew it—seemingly unplanned. Am I right?"

"Why, yes. And untangling the thread was actually unplanned."

"Good. And you, Lynne—you also took off your boots—actually unplanned? You found you had to fasten the shopping bag to the table to collect the asparagus peelings, seemingly unplanned?—and continued preparing the vegetables for dinner, all planned. Right?"

"Yes, but fastening the bag was actually unplanned. I'd never done it before and there was no garbage pail."

"Excellent. So you were able to adjust to a new obstacle and continue to live truly. It helps that this interaction is what I call a "Structured Improvisation." By that I mean that you deliberately, but separately, chose circumstances: Where and When, Why you are there, and What you start out to accomplish. But you have not chosen *How* you will behave, nor *With Whom*. As you have not rehearsed it, you have no image of how it should go, and therefore are freed from the perils of Anticipation. You only expected that each of you would be alone on stage. But now I'd like you to continue, and if you become aware of each other—if you see or hear each other, don't try to ignore that unexpected presence. Permit yourselves to acknowledge the unexpected—and find out what happens. Try to keep in mind what my mentor, Lee Strasberg, repeatedly admonished us: "Whatever happens to you on stage is also happening to your character!""

(Of course, by "Character" at this stage of my training, I do not mean that role suggested by the playwright that the actor undertakes to impersonate in performance. That problem will properly be addressed later. Now the "Character" of my student is herself offstage, in life, and, in the present exercises, As If in her own home.)

That's all the instruction I give. Only to free these normal young women from the abnormal prisons into which they had locked themselves—of ignoring another unplanned, unexpected presence. They proceed to continue their lives: Gaby in her bedroom on Thursday evening, and Lynne in her kitchen on Friday afternoon. Yet, both are also here in the studio, also occupying the same space at the same time.

Lynne is curious about Gaby's sewing and sneaks a furtive look in her direction. Gaby notices the glass of water on Lynne's table, rises, and goes to Lynne.

"May I have this, if you don't want it?"

"Certainly," Lynne answers. Gaby takes a drink from the glass and brings it with her as she goes back to her sofa.

"What are you sewing?" Lynne asks.

"My stocking. I just noticed a hole. What are you doing?"

"Preparing dinner for Chris. He likes his asparagus all cut up."

"So do I." Gaby finishes her sewing. She puts her sewing kit away, and goes to get her songbook. "Well, I'd better study my score." And she proceeds to do just that, settling back on the sofa with her music.

Again I decide to interject. "What are you thinking, Lynne?"

"I wonder how she got here. And how long she's going to stay."

"And if you have enough for dinner if she just stays on. She's in your kitchen, isn't she?"

"Yes, we have an open kitchen."

"And Gaby, is she in your bedroom?"

"Well, in another part of the apartment. But it connects with my room."

"So you are each able now to accept each other's presence, and to bring that other into your own circumstances. Excellent. That is just what we do in life. We *adjust* to the unforeseen and bring the unexpected into our own circumstances, no matter how unusual or unwelcome. And so we find we can live through the programmed events of the stage and also accept and incorporate the unplanned and unexpected. Thus we can remain fully alive and only benefit from the new, the actually unplanned event. Indeed, good actors will welcome such fresh stimuli, as parched desert wanderers welcome an oasis—the fresh water of an actually fresh element can only revive our tired bodies and jaded spirits with the tonic of new problems."

I think they are now somewhat relieved. They have met and coped with this surprise interaction; they have understood and resolved the acting problem I had set for this first interaction session. Their reward has been freedom from obvious falseness and a training experience that should remain part of their craft, to remind them always to "live in the moment" when Living on Stage. It is time to move on.

"The following exercise will be much easier. For our next session, I will ask you both to agree on one and the same 'familiar time and place.' It need not be a space you both have actually occupied, nor need you spend actual time there. A plausible such occasion will serve quite well. In this familiar-space-and-time, you'll set up at least three tasks—one planned and familiar, one planned and seemingly unfamiliar, and the third familiar and seemingly unplanned. You will share at least one of these tasks and do at least one separately. I encourage you to agree on the circumstances—the time and place—as well as the one task that you will try to do together. This might well be the problem that brings you both to this place and time. But do not let each other know which tasks you will attempt individually. These must remain private. The usual sharing of unnecessary information between partners in a scene-class leads to a lamentable condition I call 'Partneritis.' It merely increases the dangers of destructive Anticipation!

Please avoid it. And as you move forward in these 'partnering exercises,' keep in mind that you are still yourselves, with the relationship you actually have. You both study with me, now at about the same step in the training, you've just met, and you're going to work on 'partnering' together. The important element of 'With Whom?'—something other than your actual relationship—still lies ahead of us, still around the corner. Exchange phone numbers, agree on the Where and When, the Why, and the task you share—but no rehearsing!"

❊   ❊   ❊

At our next session, I can tell that both my students are bringing a pleasant anticipation to this new exercise. I think they are pleased to be working together. They proceed to set up a semblance of a kitchen, and Lynne arranges a shelf of condiments and some foodstuffs. She seems quite at home.

Gaby leaves the studio and a moment later knocks at the door. Lynne answers and they greet each other warmly. It is evidently a meeting to which both have looked forward. Gaby has brought a bunch of tulips, wrapped in plastic, which Lynne is delighted to accept. She finds a pitcher, looks into it, and then deposits the bunch of flowers without removing any of the plastic wrappings. I am curious and make a note. They then proceed to prepare a dinner—new to Gaby, which Lynne has evidently arranged to introduce her new friend to a new oriental recipe. Lynne fills a jar with chopped beef and hands Gaby a bowl of chopped onions, instructing her to mix with the beef. Gaby proceeds to do so, with a knife, gingerly, until Lynne shakes some drops of the condiments into the beef mixture and then provides Gaby with a set of chopsticks with which to accomplishing the mixing more efficiently. As Gaby continues the mixing, Lynne unwraps a package of thin rounds of dough. She shows Gaby how to spread a teaspoonful of the meat and onion mix in the center of each round, fold the sides together, moistening them with a bit of water, and crimp the top of what has become a dumpling. Together, they spread the dumplings on a paper towel; and now, assured that Gaby is able to make them properly, Lynne goes to set the table for dinner. I have seen many tasks, and the girls are conversing while working most freely and comfortably. It is enough. I can interject.

"Have you completed your tasks?"

"Why, yes." Lynne is apparently surprised. "I hadn't really noticed."

"Fine. I know you can continue quite easily, but I think we can stop here. It's quite enough."

And I proceed to enumerate the various tasks they have undertaken—preparing a dinner, Lynne instructing Gaby, and the various categories of tasks they have so easily accomplished. Both girls seem a bit surprised that it has all been so easy. Because it was grounded in a simple, specific logic, I explain—

and quite within their own experience. And yes, Gaby in fact does know how to make these dumplings—her naïvete and need to be instructed was a fine example of a "seemingly unfamiliar, though planned" task.

But I must now draw their attention to the "familiar but seemingly unplanned" task that seems to have tripped up Lynne.

"Lynne—do you usually leave the plastic wrap on a bunch of flowers when you deposit them in a vase?"

Lynne blushes. "No, not usually . . . but I saw the water in the vase was dirty, and I didn't want to set the tulips in dirty water."

"And why didn't you get fresh water?"

"Well, there's none here in the studio."

"But you know there is in the kitchenette outside."

"Yes—but I didn't think I should leave the room."

"Why not?"

"Well, I—I don't know. At home, I know I would have gone and changed the water."

"But here you had not expected to have such an obstacle, and you hadn't planned for it to happen. Though it was just such a familiar, unplanned task that the exercise explores. Without realizing it, you locked yourself into the Anticipation that robs the actor of her free will and normal logical behavior on stage."

It is a good lesson. For again we are made to realize that we must continue to fight against the unnatural limitations that too often we bring with us when we try to Live on Stage—even in such a free-form "Structured Improvisation" as this interaction exercise.

By exploring such limitations, we can learn to bring the freedom of offstage life to the planned life on stage—now in this improvised exercise, later in the much more rigid forms of the scripted, not to mention directed, scene on stage.

However, I think I must add here an important caveat: In these "scenic exercises" we must refrain from demanding, or even expecting, the scenic results we usually expect from a performed scene. We may not see clearly, or hear clearly, just what the actors are doing or saying. The event may not be at all interesting or dramatic. And it may have not a bit of the dramatic structure we have come to look for in a play or film. No matter! In these Scenic Exercises it is essential that we make no demands for scenic results. For if we make the actor conscious, much less the servant, of dramatic, directorial, or audience expectations, we will destroy the very freedom and involvement that we most desire of her. She must learn to Live on Stage for herself, first of all—and then for her character and her character's needs and goals. Only much later in the development of an actor, and of her character in rehearsal, might she be made aware of other obligations. Only then can she possibly comply with the scenic demands of the author, director, and audience without seriously impairing her very ability to achieve the convincing results they desire. Only then can she release the fullest flow of her talent and craft as she attempts the difficult, yet noble, task of Living on Stage.

But now I can pose the challenge of our next exercise. "We have built firm foundations of: 1) simple, familiar circumstances; 2) a series of arbitrary physical tasks; and 3) a minimum of shared actor's knowledge. Now we can profitably approach what I call 'Secrets.' Now we can pave the way to the beginnings of a contrapuntal, complementary inner life, or 'Subtext.' For next week, in addition to familiar circumstances, please bring three kinds of tasks—planned and seemingly unfamiliar, familiar and seemingly unplanned, and both seemingly unplanned and seemingly unfamiliar. Again, at least one shared and at least one done separately—and the shared task should be of a different category for each of you. In addition, I will ask you both to plant a *secret* in your imaginations. A secret about your partner that is occupying you and requires a decision of some kind. It may be pleasant or unpleasant—totally imaginary, yet plausible—that you do not share, but a secret that demands that you try to arrive at some course of action with regard to it. For example, if you, Lynne, have just heard of an opening for a young soprano in the Village Light Opera, should you tell Gaby of it, and so risk losing her as a scene partner? Or if you, Gaby, know that Lynne's husband has been courting one of your co-workers, should you tell Lynne and so plunge her life into turmoil? Exercise your imaginations, and we'll discover how this secret will affect your inner life as you continue to explore the paths to Living on Stage."

My students exchange a look of apparent confusion, but then gamely gather their props, put on their boots, their scarves, hats, coats, and gloves. They leave together. They have become scene partners! And—most importantly—without any scripted scene.

*   *   *

At our next session, Gaby waits in the reception area, having arrived twenty minutes before Lynne's private work is over. When Lynne and I have finished, I invite Gaby into the studio and am rewarded by seeing how delighted they are to see each other. Though they have only spent an hour or two together during the past two sessions, they embrace like old friends.

We warm up together on the carpet, brief physical relaxing stretches and a few moments of massaging one another's shoulders. Then they immediately set up their room together—a bed and the couch, and a few cubes serving as various small tables. They get their bags of props, the personal objects that each has brought. And they set to work—to live together as two roommates of an evening or on a weekend afternoon. Gaby on the sofa is working at writing something on a pad and is evidently having trouble. Clearly a planned and unfamiliar task. From time to time, she looks furtively at Lynne. Does she have a secret? Seems so. And while Lynne, lying on the bed, proceeds to open and peruse a stack of mail, she first studies Gaby in evident indecision. Another secret! Her task seems planned and familiar, until she discovers what seems to be a strange request in one of her letters. Puzzled, she finally decides to tear up these sheets to be discarded later. Again, unplanned and familiar.

In apparent frustration, Gaby gives up her writing and reaches for her book of arias. She starts to do a vocal warm-up. It appears quite familiar and seems unplanned. Lynne is intrigued and presently asks what in the world her roommate is up to. When she finds out, she admits that she had always wanted to study voice, but was afraid that her sound would put off any teacher. Gaby assures her that anyone who tries can do it; and then, at Lynne's urging, she proceeds to instruct her as she herself has been taught. So they enter into a vocal lesson, all the while Lynne laughing at the strange sounds she tries to repeat after Gaby. It is clearly unplanned for both, but familiar to Gaby and quite unfamiliar to Lynne.

I see clearly that the assigned, arbitrary tasks have been no problem for both. But what has happened to their secrets? Their attention to their physical tasks has quite chased whatever secret each may have had quite out of their minds. While now they seem to be enjoying this interaction, I think we have done enough for the exercise. I interrupt.

"Very good." And I enumerate the various tasks I perceived. The girls are pleased that they seem to have accomplished the exercise.

"But what about your secrets? I believe I saw that each of you had something on your minds at first, but as you got into your tasks, and then started the vocal lessons, what might have been secrets completely disappeared. Am I right?"

"Why—yes. I guess so," admits Gaby.

"I seem to have forgotten all about mine," adds Lynne.

"Well, Lynne, now tell us: what was your secret?"

"I just heard that Gaby's voice teacher had died. And I wondered if she knew and, if she didn't, whether or not I should tell her.

"And yours, Gaby?"

"That I had met her boyfriend and realized that he was going with another girl."

"I see. Secrets most pregnant. So, why didn't I see any signs of them after the very first moment?"

They cannot say, only that their attention to their physical tasks had chased their secrets right out of their imaginations.

"Well, let's find out. Lynne, when did you find out about Gaby's voice teacher?"

"Last week."

"I see. And when is Gaby due to report to her for her next lesson?"

"Why, next week."

"Well, suppose you just found out about it this morning. And suppose Gaby is due to go to her voice teacher directly from here—this afternoon? Might that not make it more immediate? And put it in the forefront of your mind?"

"Of course."

"It is a cardinal rule of acting that dramatic choices should be as immediate as possible. We must learn to raise the stakes for our lives on stage. And you, Gaby, when did you meet her boyfriend and realize he was also going with another girl?"

"The other evening."

"And when do you think she is due to meet him again?"

"This weekend."

"Well, suppose you just found out last night, and that tonight she has a date with him and is expecting him to propose to her? Wouldn't that make it more pressing?"

"Certainly."

"Well, let's continue, and see if you can rearrange your circumstances so that the problems of your secrets are much more immediate."

They think this over and gradually continue the voice lessons. But now, it is clear that something else is on their minds, something unspoken and troubling, and they have some difficulty continuing with the lessons. They have evidently created an inner preoccupation that is disturbing the easy flow of their outer tasks. Something else is occupying them. I don't know what, but I am quite curious as to what it is.

"Excellent! You have planted something alive and demanding in your imaginations. Something kinetic—a Subtext that persists in occupying your attention—of an entirely different hue. Remember this when you must create your given circumstances on stage!

"And now we can move on to a vital new problem—that extremely important element of 'With Whom?'

"For our next class, I'll start you on the problem of *Relationship*—one of the most rewarding considerations for the actor. Again, a familiar time and place, and three tasks—any of the various kinds we have touched upon. One to be shared, and one to be done separately. But, in addition, you are to relate to your partner As If she were someone else in your life. First, as someone you enjoy being with, and then as someone whom you would not like to be with. That person may be old or young, male or female, but someone with whom you have, or have had, a strong relationship. Parent, sibling, teacher, friend, whomever. And think of your chosen relationships before you agree on the mutual time and place and the task you will share. And as these relationships will be secret, it will help if you refrain from addressing each other by proper names. All clear?"

They nod. But they are also somewhat perplexed by the assignment. I assure them that they will surely profit by this next step. And so they leave together—misery in company.

❊   ❊   ❊

At our next session, immediately after our warm-ups, they proceed to set up another roommate scene. Together, they move the sofa onto the stage area, bring out the desk and a chair, and then the daybed onto the carpet. They are evidently looking forward to this exercise, for it is clear that both have interesting secrets in store. I interject.

"Now, as you are setting up, preparing the physical elements of your situation, begin to prepare your imaginations. Choose either of the two relationships you have chosen for this exercise and start to relate to your partner as one of those two different people in your life. Think about that other person and perhaps specific experiences you have shared with him or her. Now find that she or he is here with you—either that someone you enjoy being with or the other you'd rather avoid. And go on to your tasks."

Lynne sits at the vanity table and starts to brush her hair. Gaby checks the clothes she has packed in her valise. (I know that she is planning to take the train to Philadelphia after class for an important audition.) Lynne, while trying to arrange a new hair-do, compliments Gaby on her new outfit. Gaby seems cool, answering Lynne in monosyllables. It is clear that she is reluctant to enter into any conversation. She brings out a new dress and holds it up to herself for inspection. But when Lynne compliments her on the dress, Gaby turns away and quickly drops the dress onto her valise. Lynne chatters on, explaining that she's preparing for a "funky" party, and wants to try a new hair-do. She asks Gaby to help her, but Gaby seems quite reluctant to assist her in any way and instead starts on her own makeup. Since it is clear that Lynne has cast Gaby as someone she enjoys being with, and Gaby has cast Lynne as someone she wants to get away from, I think I can safely interject.

"Excellent. Now Lynne, change your relationship to Gaby—but Gaby, continue with the relationship you've already established."

There is an immediate drop in the temperature of the room. Lynne falls silent, continuing to braid her strands of hair, while Gaby continues to concentrate on her makeup. There is a very loud silence. Again, I see a very clear change in the relationship.

"Fine. Now, Gaby, why don't you go to the second relationship that you've prepared for Lynne? And Lynne, continue with the relationship to Gaby you are already working with."

Now Gaby, all smiles, stops putting on her makeup. "Here, let me help you with that." And she crosses to Lynne and starts assisting in her braiding. But Lynne pulls away.

"Oh, go fold up your dress! Better folded any which way than sitting in your lap!"

Gaby recoils, then gently resumes her braiding of Lynne's hair.

Lynne jerks her head away. She interjects sharply, "Watch what you're doing!" When Gaby continues more gingerly, Lynne submits silently.

Gaby tries to mollify Lynne, "I think you'll really look great—good and funky!"

No response from Lynne. Again, their relationship is quite clear.

"And now, Lynne, try resuming your original relationship to Gaby."

Immediately Lynne softens and cooperates with Gaby, as they both work in tandem on Lynne's new braids. I am quite pleased.

"All right! Let's stop for a bit and see what we've discovered." And while the girls relax, I identify the tasks I have seen and the kinds of relationships, both pleasant and unpleasant, that each has brought to the exercise.

"Lynne, now tell us: what were your relationships?"

"Well, first an old roommate I liked very much, and then one I couldn't stand."

"Quite apparent. And Gaby—yours?"

"Also, at first an old roommate I had to endure in college. And then my best friend."

"Also, quite clear. Very good, both of you. Now I think you can begin to understand just how important Relationships are on stage. And how valuable are your store of memories that can serve to change the psychic temperature of these Relationships so vividly. Along with the other questions we have been exploring until now—"Where am I? When? and Why?"—this "With Whom?" is one of the most powerful tools for the actor. And the last crucial question, "What am I trying to accomplish?" is best explored after the previous four have been asked and answered. In fact, the problem, goal, or intention is very often discovered in the answers to these first four questions. For they make up all the elements of the Given Circumstances; they reveal the main acting challenges in the *Dramatic Situation*.

"But let me also draw your attention to an element that I missed in this exercise. At each change of your relationship—depending on whomever you projected onto your partner—you each must have sensed a profound change. But I didn't quite see your recognition of this change and the surprise and readjustment this would logically entail. Moreover, you both drew on former roommates or friends for these relationships. They seemed somewhat limited—and rather literal to me. Why?"

Lynne breaks in. "I was going to use my husband—when he's fun, and also when I can't stand him. But I was afraid to—I thought it might not fit."

"Not at all. We must not be too literal in these areas. Why deprive your-selves of the strong relationships you have had in parents, teachers, siblings, of either sex or any age? And why not reach back to your childhood? Such strong relationships abound when we are children! Or, exercise your imaginations. After all, your imagined relationships are always completely private. No one else can, or should, know what you are using to stimulate your imaginations. So don't limit yourselves! Don't fall into the trap of being too literal to the text—to the apparent relationships of the given scene. So many talented actors fail to avail themselves of the powerful, imaginative colors they could bring to the stage and restrict their choices to a mere literal fidelity to the text!

"Now let's continue. But try completely new relationships for each other. Again, one of someone you enjoy being with, and the other just the opposite. Think for a few moments, and we'll pick up where we left off."

And so the improvisation continues. Lynne gets a curling iron to fix her hair, while Gaby immediately moves to the other side of the room to continue her makeup. Silence. Gaby glances at Lynne, sees her difficulty with the iron, and finally offers to help. Lynne retorts angrily,

"Don't talk to me!"

Gaby is confused. "Are you all right?" she asks.

Lynne ignores her. So Gaby does the same to Lynne. I sense a very icy emo-tional temperature.

"Fine. Now Lynne, switch your relationship. Maintain yours, Gaby."

Lynne turns to Gaby, holding her curling iron out in misery. "Won't you help me—please?"

Gaby buries herself in her valise, rearranging her packed clothing. Again, silence.

"Excellent! Now Gaby, change your relationship to Lynne, please."

And Gaby softens and quickly drops her packing and goes to help Lynne. They now work on the braiding together, exchanging the curling iron as they both enter into the game of creating a funky new hairdo. They are actually enjoying this activity, laughing at their combined efforts.

"Try changing your relationship once more, Lynne!"

And Lynne immediately cools toward Gaby. She pulls her head away curtly. "Never mind! I'll do it!"

Again Gaby seems hurt. And confused. She moves away slowly, sits, and watches Lynne in some disappointment. It is quite enough.

"Very good! Tell me, now—what were your relationships this time, Lynne?"

"First my grandmother—who can do no wrong. And then my husband when I'm mad at him."

"Excellent! And yours, Gaby?"

"My uncle—our family embarrassment. And then my best friend from childhood."

"Fine! You seem to understand the possibilities of these relationships so much better now." The girls glow in pride.

"So now I think we can move on to an actual scene. All of our work is really a preparation for the demands of the playwright. But I won't tell you what the scene is, or from what play. Nor will I give you any dialogue—the text. Not just yet. But here are the elements:

"Two sisters. One older, the town beauty, but not too brainy. The 'pretty one,' their mother calls her. And the other, the younger, very bright, college material in fact, but perhaps in reaction to a very pretty older sister, the town tomboy. Her mother calls her 'the smart one.' The scene is the girls' bedroom, the time, just before an important party—perhaps the end-of-the-year high school prom. Our older sister has a date to go with her beau, the son of the richest man in town. And our younger sister couldn't care less—or so it seems. Your intentions and physical tasks I'll leave to you. Just know there is a size-able dose of sibling rivalry between these sisters. And prepare to enter into both roles in turn. For we'll do the exercise twice—reversing the roles each time."

They seem confused and turn to look at each other. I realize I must clarify a bit.

"Yes, I realize that neither of you actually has a sister. But you have brothers. You must know plenty of girls who have sisters. And you have had friends and roommates. So just trust the work you've done today, and in our past exercises. Enter into the Given Circumstances through the doors of your imaginations and try out various relationships. I can guarantee you that you won't be disappointed. Finally—there is no need to discuss anything together! Just remember—the most potent stimulants for the actor's imagination are usually the most private!

"And so—we'll meet again next week. That's when we'll arrive at a major turning point in our training: a 'Scenic Exercise—From the Inside Out.'"

CHAPTER 12

Scenic Improvisations from the Other Perspective

At our next session, though my two students, following my instructions, have not consulted each other, they immediately seem to know how to prepare. As soon as I have assigned the roles for this first improvisation, they set up a bedroom with the daybed, the chest of drawers and the vanity table and bench. They then proceed to strew personal objects around the furniture and onto the carpet. Our studio stage becomes a veritable roommates' or sisters' bedroom. And they settle in to live in the space they have created.

Lynne, as the older sister, immediately sits at the vanity table and starts to arrange her hair, consulting a fashion magazine as she tries out various hair-dos. She examines the effect of each variation in the mirror. Gaby, as the younger sister, brings a thick book and a notebook and pencil, and, sitting on the daybed, immerses herself in what seems to be a serious problem. Silence, as each is involved in her individual tasks. Finally, Lynne speaks.

"Whatever are you doing there?"

Gaby doesn't bother to raise her head, but merely answers curtly. "Math."

"Why don't you get ready for the dance?"

"Why should I? I'm not going."

"Why not? It would do you good."

"Says who?"

Lynne shrugs and starts to choose from the pile of makeup she has arranged on the vanity table. She begins to make up her face, carefully appraising the results in the mirror. Again, silence. Gaby falls back on the bed, and bringing the book to her face, covertly sneaks a look at Lynne's preparations. When Lynne rises to get into an evening dress she has hung nearby, Gaby quickly returns to her book. Lynne pulls the dress over her head and turns to Gaby.

"How do I look?"

"Stupid."

Lynne merely laughs and sits again at the vanity table. It is clear that each girl has managed to enter into the roles I have assigned. I decide to interrupt.

"Very good. Now let's reverse the roles. Party time for you, Gaby. And whatever else you like, Lynne."

The two young women immediately change places. But now Lynne gets out a baseball glove and ball and hovers over Gaby at the vanity table. As Gaby proceeds to fix her hair and makeup, Lynne keeps tossing the ball into the air and catching it—noisily, as if to annoy her sister.

And yes, now Gaby is annoyed. "Now, what?"

"Nothing. Just warming up this old glove. Spring practice, you know."

"No, I don't know. And I wish you would get out of my light."

Pleased to get a rise out of Gaby, Lynne lies on the bed and keeps tossing the baseball ever higher and more noisily. She laughs loudly, as she continues to enjoy baiting her sister. Gaby looks to heaven, shakes her head at having to endure such a burden of a sister, and focuses more intently on her makeup. Again, it is clear that both have found successful adjustments to the new roles. Now, I think we can explore the ingredients.

"Excellent, both of you! Lynne, whom did you choose to create those different relationships with Gaby?"

"Two different old roommates. One from college—a real grind who would never join in any fun, and then one from high school who always thought she was the best-looking girl in the class. Both of them gave me a pain."

"And you were able to relate accordingly to Gaby as each in turn?"

"I think so." And Lynne seems pleasantly surprised at how readily she was able to apply the lessons of our last class.

"And you, Gaby? You also seemed quite able to relate to Lynne correctly each time."

"Yes. First I chose a stuck-up cousin of mine; she was always showing off how pretty she thought she was and bragging about all the boys running after her. And then, a cabin-mate at camp who was the best athlete and never let us forget it. She was really a pest!"

"Excellent. You see how valuable your personal choices of relationships can be. You don't have to change yourself so much for each new role: it's mainly the relationship with your partner, what she means to you, that leads to such different results. Now let me add a few adjustments to your acting scores to bring you closer to the situation in the actual scene we are preparing.

"For this first Scenic Improvisation, I thought it best to set up the normal, everyday relationship of these young women as we are led to believe it existed before the events of the play. I have found such explorations into the Prior Life of the characters to be extremely valuable in laying the foundations for the new Dramatic Situation presented during the action of the play. Such scenes as you just improvised might well have happened a year before the play begins. By living through them in rehearsal, you will better appreciate, and thus be better able to suggest, the changes that the actual play demands.

"For the day of his play, our author has heightened the dramatic circumstances, and we must adjust. Let me add a few more complications for you to bring to our next session.

"It is a year later. The older sister—'the pretty one'—and I think that now we can call her by her actual name, Madge—has been going with her boyfriend Alan all summer. He is about to return to college, and Madge's mother has been urging her to solidify their relationship. It may well be Madge's last chance to escape from her dead-end life. But Madge has been having doubts; she doesn't feel comfortable with Alan's college friends and is hardly excited by Alan. She is really confused about her future; she feels she is just marking time.

"Millie, the tomboy younger sister, 'the smart one,' has suddenly found a date! She has been asked to go to the party with Alan's sexy fraternity brother, Hal, the drifter who dropped out of college to become a Hollywood star. Defeated and broke, he has arrived in town only this morning, hoping to land a job with Alan's father. So now the situation for the two sisters is quite reversed. Madge seems almost reluctant to attend the party with Alan, while Millie is both excited to be Hal's date and afraid that her social ineptitude will lead to disaster. And the only source of help for her now is the older sister she has always fought with and dismissed as brainless. So new ingredients are demanded for this scene; and you may well have to bring other analogies into your circumstances to help make these new realities alive for you both. Any questions?"

Of course there are questions, big ones. My scene partners again look to each other, apparently at a loss. But I know that over the coming week, as these new elements germinate in their imaginations, they will find fresh moments in their memories that will help them connect with these new developments. And I feel sure that they cannot help but discover the stage realities for which the scene now calls.

❊ ❊ ❊

At our next session, the young women again set up their "bedroom." While the scene in the actual play takes place on the front porch, I encourage their continued use of this indoor space. It seems more logical, and it also provides opportunities for many more helpful objects and personal tasks. Indeed, it probably was located here in the film version, for it is quite likely that only the conventions of the one-set play led to its original outdoor setting on stage. But now it is Gaby, as Millie, who sits at the vanity table, while Lynne, armed with her fashion magazines, lies almost listlessly on the bed. Gaby immediately starts to query Lynne.

"How should I do my hair?" No answer. "Madge, help me please! What can I do with my hair?"

"Oh, just put it up." Lynne continues to leaf through her magazine.

Gaby pins her hair up and turns to Lynne. "How's this?"

"Fine." Though it is clear that she hardly thinks it is fine.

Gaby is not convinced. "I'm not so sure. Well, then what makeup do I use?"

"Not mine!"

"But I've got a date! Madge, please! I don't know what goes on first."

Lynne just throws the fashion magazine at her and turns over on the bed. Gaby grabs the magazine and studies the parade of glamorous models, page by page. And furtively, she starts to try on Lynne's array of makeup scattered on the table. Both girls have clearly adjusted to the new circumstances. Still, something seems missing. They appear to have plenty of time to prepare for this party. How much? I think I had best interrupt.

"Gaby, what are you doing?"

"Trying to get ready for my date."

"And he's coming to pick you up? When?"

"In a couple of hours."

"I see. And Lynne, what are you up to?"

"I really don't feel much like getting ready for tonight."

"How much time do you have?"

"Oh, a few more hours."

"Well, it seems clear that your circumstances are different now. But perhaps you haven't made them quite pressing enough. Let's suppose you both had much less time to prepare for this party—let's say that your dates will be here in half an hour. Wouldn't that make it much more immediate? So, just continue, but with this new adjustment."

This has an instant effect. Lynne goes to Gaby and takes the makeup from her.

"Here—like this." She brushes Gaby's hair into an upswept style and pins it in place. Then she takes the makeup and begins on Gaby's face. "It's so easy, really. Just don't overdo it." And she hands the makeup to Gaby. Gaby continues, following Lynne's example. Meanwhile Lynne gets her party dress and holds it up in front of herself. She appraises the result in the mirror. It looks fine, but Lynne doesn't seem pleased.

"What's the matter, Lynne?" I ask.

"I don't know. Nothing seems right."

"Very good! I see the new immediacy has heightened your stakes. Excellent! Now let's reverse the roles."

And again they change roles. Lynne, now as Millie, tries to find a model for her makeup in the fashion magazine, at the same time trying out a simple dance step. And Gaby, now as Madge, sits on the bed, brushing her hair while lost in thought. She rouses herself and goes to the mirror, sitting down to finish her makeup, while Lynne now tries to copy her, leaning over her shoulder as she follows Gaby's process in the mirror.

"That's better," Gaby encourages her. "Just don't overdo it. You don't need much."

Satisfied with her own appearance, she rises and sits Lynne at the vanity table. "But your hair is a mess." And Gaby proceeds to brush and pin up Lynne's hair more acceptably.

"It's really not too difficult, if you try."

"I'll try," Lynne moans, "but I don't think I'll ever get it right." And she resumes her dance practice. Gaby shakes her head and starts to partner her sister in a more skillful dancing, Lynne all the while looking at their feet. I think they've gotten closer to the heightened circumstances. At the same time, it is clear to me just what additional adjustments are needed to bring their work closer still to the actual scene.

"Very good, ladies! We are on the very verge of the scene as written. So let me add a few more adjustments to your mix for our next session. Then, I think we'll be ready for the text itself. Millie is very insecure about her performance this evening in this new role. The dress and shoes Madge has lent her make her feel awkward; she particularly needs help in the secrets of social talk with boys on a date. Most of all, she is mortally afraid that she'll disgrace herself with this sexy college man just back from Hollywood. Madge has had to help her mother in the kitchen all afternoon preparing food for this community picnic-dance. Try to add these adjustments to the circumstances you've already made real to yourselves. Just remember—review your Analogies, your Relationships, and your 'As Ifs'—but no rehearsing!"

※　※　※

Lynne has already set up the sisters' bedroom when Gaby arrives for our next class. Now, while Gaby, as Millie, tries to make a tape-recorder play to help herself practice a basic dance step, Lynne, as Madge, lies down on the bed and closes her eyes. She seems truly tired and not at all wanting a scene with her sister. But Gaby, as Millie, evidently does.

"Have you got any batteries?" she asks Lynne. Lynne ignores her, maybe feigning sleep.

"I said, do you have any batteries?" Gaby is insistent

"Are you serious? No, I don't have any batteries!" And Lynne turns over on the bed.

Gaby thinks a moment. Then, more placating, she ventures, "I like the dress." Though it is not quite clear whether she means the one Lynne has hanging, ready to put on at the last moment, or the one her sister has lent her for this party. When she gets no answer from Lynne, Gaby tries another tack. She holds out a fashion magazine turned to a picture of a glamorous model. "I thought I'd try this hair-do. What do you think?"

Now Lynne sits up and takes the magazine. After a brief look, she shakes her head. "No way! Keep it simple." And she proceeds to look through the magazine herself.

Again spurned, Gaby now takes a few pieces of makeup out of a small bag she has brought. "It says you have to choose the right brush. But I don't know one brush from another." And she looks beseechingly to Lynne.

Lynne never raises her eyes from the pages of her glamour magazine. "If you'd have helped me earlier, maybe I could have helped you." She is evidently annoyed with her sister, or with something. Now Lynne sighs, and rises to get the evening dress hanging from the hat-rack by the bureau. She pulls the dress on over her head, and over her jeans and blouse as well. Is she trying it on? Or does she intend to go to the dance dressed this way? I make a note.

Gaby, apparently giving up trying to get her sister's help, tries to apply the makeup herself. As Lynne goes wearily to the vanity table, Gaby jumps up, now eager to let her sister sit at the mirror to begin her own makeup. With a practiced hand, Lynne wields various brushes, juggling lotions and powders of various shades, eyeliners, and even an eyelash curler. Gaby watches her enthralled and then tries to copy her technique. Finally Lynne seems to relent; she turns to her sister, takes the lipstick brush from her and carefully paints her lips for her. Madge is helping Millie at last!

I think we've had enough for now. So I query the girls: "Lynne, were you able to find a more meaningful Alan for yourself this time?"

Lynne nods in pain. "Yes, indeed. He was—"

"Keep it to yourself! And Gaby—were you able to find someone for Millie's new date who might excite you and also intimidate you? Remember it doesn't have to be a sexy guy. It could be a respected singer or actor you have never actually met—Plácido Domingo, say, or Maria Callas—or a new demanding role you've been asked to play. Don't limit your possibilities to literal analogies, or even to reasonable possibilities. For example, I know I would be both excited and intimidated at once if Stanislavsky walked into this class right now—though we all agree that his appearance is not very likely. Now let's explore the situation as we reverse the roles again.

Now Gaby sits pensively on the bed and takes up a notepad and pen, evidently preparing to write. But she has difficulty framing her thoughts, for after writing a few words, she scratches out what she has written and starts again. And again she gives up, dissatisfied.

Intrigued, I query her. "What are you doing, Gaby?"

"Trying to write to Alan."

"Why?"

"I'm not sure. I don't feel much like going to the party. Sometimes I think I want to break up with him. But then again I don't. I just don't know—or what to say to him."

She is sincerely troubled—a new color that adds an expressive new dimension to her situation. I nod appreciatively, as she tries again to find the right words to write.

Meanwhile, Lynne has gotten out of her formal "Madge" dress and sits at the vanity table, staring at herself in the mirror in frustration. She seems equally perplexed with her own new problem.

"Hair, makeup—I've got to get ready! Madge, aren't you going to help me?"

Gaby shakes her head. "You're the smart one—you've seen me do it."

"Just tell me where to begin."

"Try washing your face."

Rebuffed, Lynne examines each article of makeup she has brought in a small, zippered bag—evidently brand-new equipment. She tries the effect of each in applications to her face.

"Madge—which one?"

Gaby looks at her and shakes her head. "I'm busy. Just go and put some lotion on your face!"

Lynne spreads the cream over her face and goes to try on a pair of high-heeled shoes. She walks with difficulty and again appeals to Gaby. "What do you think, Madge? Please tell me!"

Sighing, Gaby puts down her paper and pen and goes to help Lynne. Perhaps glad to have an excuse to put off her letter-writing problem, she starts to correct Lynne's makeup with a practiced hand.

"Relax. You'll be fine."

As I review their improvisation, I tell my two students that I think they have gone far enough. They have made specific, personal adjustments to the circumstances of each sister's situation. The elements of the scene as written are all manifest on stage now. It only remains to rearrange them into the author's sequence and add his words to the actors' own inner lives and outer tasks. In other words, they are ready for the text! I take out the two typewritten pages I have already brought to my desk for this session.

"Now I can safely give you actual text of the scene. You have prepared to enter into the circumstances of each of these young women, adding necessary adjustments as I've thrown them at you. Now that you have found the inner and outer life of both Madge and Millie, you are quite ready for the author's words. So—here they are."

I hand each one the two typed pages: The opening scene of Act II from William Inge's *Picnic*.

"You will notice that there are no stage directions at all—just the words of the two sisters. Now, I don't think you should try to memorize these words. Eventually, they will 'memorize you.' But you can see the sequence of the events and the clues to their thoughts revealed in the dialogue. Again, do not rehearse together. Read over the scene to find the sequence, then try to adjust to the given sequence as you arrange each young woman's problems and tasks in your own minds. And when we meet next week, use your own words as well as any of these words that may seem appropriate. Don't worry about the details; our process involves shaping the Relationship, the Circumstances, and the Intentions of each of the characters. As we attend now to the Essential Elements that form the basic structure of the scene, you may rest assured that the fine points will come in due time!"

❊   ❊   ❊

At our next session, Lynne arrives first and proceeds immediately to arrange the Studio furniture to suggest the sisters' bedroom. The same daybed, mirrored vanity-table, and bench, and a cube to serve as a stool. She hangs the party dress she has brought on the hat-rack and scatters other objects around the "room": evening shoes, fashion magazines, and various articles of makeup in a small handbag. Then she gets out her script of the scene—the dialogue I had given her—and studies it. I see I must interrupt.

"What are you doing, Lynne?"

"Getting ready for our scene."

"And is that the text you are studying?"

"Yes—I'm not sure that I know it."

"You're not supposed to *know* it. I think I told you not to try to memorize the text. Didn't I?"

"Yes, but—I want to do it right."

"You had no problem 'doing it right' in our last sessions before you had the text. You had the Scenic Elements—the Given Circumstances, your Relationship with your sister, and the possible Intentions of each of the young women. And you were able to converse quite well, as I recall. Now you have the text, and it appears that concern for the proper words has usurped your attention! That is what generally happens; it's a major problem that I have tried to forestall. But before we address the problems that come with the text, I'd like to suggest a better preparation for you. As I think I have previously noted, I have found that while she is setting up the furniture and props for her scene, the actor should also 'set up' her imagination. Prepare your Inner Instrument as you prepare your stage furniture and properties: review your Circumstances and Relationships; go over in your mind what has happened previously this day; review your Analogies, your personal associations, and the problems you must confront. Prepare your Inner Life as you prepare for your Physical Life. And relax! Plant the germ of the scenic problem in your mind so that it will grow to occupy you and send you on stage to try to solve your character's Problems. You have done all the work you have been able to do until now; and the text will be here tomorrow, as it has been here for many yesterdays. But this fleeting moment will never come again. Prepare to enter into the Scenic Situation—and words will come. The good actor doesn't have to memorize the text; in time the text will memorize her!

Lynne tries to do as I suggest. She is relaxing on the daybed, but jumps up as Gaby appears. She is late and is apologetic. They greet each other warmly, and Gaby places her dress, shoes, and other personal objects in the "room" on stage. When she finishes, they both turn to me.

"All right. Let's start with you as Millie, Lynne, and you, Gaby, as Madge. Suppose Millie is alone in the room at the start, and Madge comes in from her afternoon chores in the kitchen. Whenever you're ready, ladies."

Lynne immediately sits at the vanity table and studies her face in the mirror. From a small zippered bag, she takes out a variety of articles and starts to apply her makeup. Gaby enters and goes directly to the daybed. She sits and pouts at Lynne.

GABY: "I don't know why you couldn't have helped us in the kitchen."

LYNNE: "I had to get dressed for the party."

GABY: "I had to make the eggs and hundreds of bread and butter sandwiches."

LYNNE: "I had to get ready." As Gaby doesn't reply, Lynne continues, "I feel kind of . . . funny."

GABY: "Did you clean out the bathtub?"

LYNNE: "Yes, I cleaned out the bathroom." She continues applying her makeup. It appears to be quite a familiar task, as if she had done this many times before. I make a note. She continues: "Madge, how do I look?"

GABY: "You look pretty."

LYNNE (continuing with her makeup): "I feel funny." She ponders, concentrating. Is she trying to remember the text? Suddenly she continues. "He's a big show-off. Alan took us to the High-Ho for cokes, and then Juanita Bolger came in with her gang, and when they saw him, she came over to me and said,

'Isn't he the cutest thing you ever saw?' The sentences come out as if by rote, as something she had just remembered.

GABY (staring at Lynne): "I never speak to Juanita *Badger*."

Silence. The girls seem to be lost in thought. They have stopped their physical activities and apparently are trying to remember the text. Lynne turns away from me and tries to control an outburst of nervous laughter. I think I must interrupt.

"So? What's going on?"

LYNNE, defensively: "I'm trying to get it right. I just forgot what comes next."

"What? The words of the scene? You had no trouble in our last sessions before you were given the text. What has happened?" I can hear the rising sharpness in my voice. No, I am not pleased.

The girls look crestfallen. I continue. "Has the text stopped your lives? You hardly seem to be connecting with the inner problems, as you did so well in our previous sessions. Lynne, are you familiar with makeup? You seem to be putting it on as if you'd done it many times before. Isn't that "Off Circumstances," as Uta Hagen would put it? And Gaby, you said you've come from working all afternoon in the kitchen, but I see no physical signs of it. Are you hot? Tired? Where in your body? What muscles are sore and may need massaging? And why, though you lay down on the daybed when you first entered, as soon as Gaby spoke to you, did you sit up to answer her? And then you continued to gaze at her, as if you had no other thought in your head. What happened to the problem you had with Alan? Were you waiting for the next line? And wondering if you both were saying the 'correct words?'"

My students are properly chastised. It is all too clear that this text has been a mixed blessing. Before, knowing just the Elements of the Relationship, the Circumstances, and the Intentions of each, they had no trouble conversing, while they continued their inner focus on their separate problems and their physical tasks in the situation. Now, the text and the fear of not remembering the words correctly have driven all connection to the Essential Elements out of their minds! They have been cut off suddenly from their Relationship, their Circumstances, and their Intentions! They have stopped Living on Stage!

Text can be a major hazard for the beginning actor. When the actors have the Scenic Elements to nourish their imagination and challenge their attention, they seem to have no problem. For these are the elements we have offstage, in our real lives. But as soon as they are given the text, they stop living and merely try to remember their lines. This is all too often the danger of the actor's focus on the author's words instead of on the Circumstances, Relationships, and Intentions. And my students weren't given the text until after they had made the elements their own. They had been behaving convincingly with these stimulating Elements. Now the text had reduced them to automatons—and it had replaced the human problems and tasks of these sisters with "What line comes next?" in the forefront of their attentions!

I see that I have given my students no hint of the way the text can work for them, no clues to breaking down the text and discovering how the words suggest inner thoughts and outer tasks. I see that I will have to give a lesson in a first reading of the scene before we conclude today's session. But now, I think I must give them another try. Perhaps my unusually stern lecture itself will have a positive effect.

"Let's reverse the roles. And let's forget the text. You'll remember enough of it. Or use your own words, as you had no trouble doing heretofore. Just reconnect to your individual problems and tasks—now you, Lynne, as Madge, and you, Gaby, as Millie."

They change positions. Gaby, as Millie, puts on her party dress and goes to the vanity table, where she starts to brush her hair. Lynne removes her own evening dress and goes off to the "kitchen" to prepare to enter.

LYNNE (entering in some annoyance) "I don't see why you couldn't have helped us in the kitchen!" She flops on the bed, kicks off her shoes and closes her eyes.

GABY (trying to arrange her hair on top of her head): "I had to bathe and dress for the ball and slip into my frock!"

LYNNE (caustic): "Did you clean out the bathtub?"

GABY (sighs): "Yes, I cleaned out the bathtub."

LYNNE begins to massage her feet. Gaby gives up trying to get her hair to stay "up" and brushes it down again. She stands up and turns to Lynne.

GABY (very hesitant): "Madge—how do I look?"

LYNNE turns to look at her a moment. "You look very nice." And she turns away again.

GABY: "I feel kind of funny."

LYNNE: "You can have the dress if you want it."

GABY: "Thanks." And she takes out a lipstick and begins to try to apply it. She seems quite inexperienced.

I am pleased. Now that their self-imposed obligation to the text of the scene is lifted, my students seem to have recovered their connections to their Relationship, Circumstances, and Intentions. Moreover, they seem to remember the words without any apparent problem. They continue through the scene, reconnecting with most of the problems and tasks they had found in previous sessions, as well as managing to converse in words very close to the actual text. We are making progress.

I let them proceed to the end of the scene as written. "Excellent! You seem to have come back to life. And when you forgot about remembering the words, the work you had already done apparently helped you to remember them. For you seemed to have little trouble in combining your Inner and Outer Life with a conversation very close to the actual text. But I think that before we part, we should try a First Reading exercise that I learned from Mr. Strasberg. In conventional training, as well as in usual rehearsals before a performance, you generally begin with the text. Here, in my training, as you have discovered, I start with the essential elements of the dramatic situation, and I follow this sequence for the next two Scenic Exercises. After that, I can trust my students to begin with the text and extract the essential elements for themselves, without falling into the problems you both did today.

"But now, for this reading exercise, just take the written scene, sit comfortably wherever you like and forget about any tasks. You will simply read to each other.

"When I say 'read,' I really mean talk and listen. Some helpful guidelines: relax; take plenty of time; try to look at your partner as she speaks to you, referring to the text in your hands only when it seems to be your turn to speak; and listen to each other carefully, so that you may discover a possible reason to reply. You may discover why certain lines are said, and why certain lines don't seem to respond to what your partner has said. And you will be stimulated to find what they suggest as you continue working at home. Most of all, you should discover many new thoughts—personal associations, analogies, and additional questions. For the actor, these are clues that will lead her to build a personal Subtext and a firm foundation to the Relationships, Circumstances, and Intentions of her character in the scene."

The girls get their two pages of text, without any stage directions, as I have typed it out for them, and sit comfortably facing each other. They seem more than willing to follow my suggestions in this new approach. They speak to each other calmly, taking time to think as they talk and listen.

GABY (as Madge): "I don't see why you couldn't have helped us in the kitchen."

LYNNE (as Millie, after thinking this over): "I had to dress for the ball."

GABY: "I had to make the potato salad and stuff the eggs and make three dozen bread-and-butter sandwiches."

LYNNE: "I had to bathe and dust my limbs with powder and slip into my frock."

GABY: "Did you clean out the bathtub?"

LYNNE: "Yes, I cleaned out the bathtub."

And they continue on until the end of the dialogue. I am very pleased, for they have done just what I wanted them to do. They have truly listened to each other; they have spoken simply, without any attempt to dramatize, but merely to contact their partner and open themselves to the possible event of the interaction.

"Fine. Reverse the roles and try it again!"

Remaining where they are, they begin the dialogue again, Lynne now as Madge and Gaby reading Millie. And again, they are able to talk and listen, to slow down to permit new thoughts and stimulate new questions. And I think they have sensed the value and the purpose of this simple exercise. I am pleased indeed, for now we have found a happier ending to our class.

And so, for our next session—and perhaps the last working on this scene—I ask Gaby and Lynne just to read over the text, separately. Again, no need to confer, much less to rehearse together. Their homework involves letting the text and their previously discovered Elements mingle in their imaginations; to ponder how the dialogue connects with their inner and outer tasks; and where silences may better express what may be happening.

❊   ❊   ❊

At our next session, after both have set up their room and their individual props, and while Gaby, as Millie, is changing into her formal dress, Lynne, as Madge, sits on the daybed offstage. She is watching Gaby, waiting for an appropriate moment to enter. I think she needs some prodding.

"What are you doing, Lynne?"

"Waiting for Gaby to get ready."

"And preparing?"

"Of course."

"Then you shouldn't be watching Gaby. Now is your opportunity to review your day, your inner problems and the outer expressions of your previous hours. You've had to work all afternoon in the kitchen, haven't you? Try to find in your body the symptoms of stress, of your afternoon preparing those eggs and sandwiches."

And Lynne goes out of the room to reconnect with her afternoon at work. After a moment—when Gaby, in her party dress, is seated at the vanity table and trying to brush her hair into a possible arrangement on top of her head—Lynne enters in some annoyance. She falls onto the daybed and covers her eyes with her arm. She seems worn out. After a moment, she almost snarls:

"I don't see why you couldn't have helped us in the kitchen." And she kicks off her shoes.

GABY (sweetly): "I had to dress for the ball."

LYNNE (still not looking at her, with some anger): "I had to stuff the eggs and make three dozen bread-and-butter sandwiches."

GABY (proudly): "I had to bathe, and dust my limbs with powder and slip into my frock."

LYNNE (caustic): "Did you clean out the bathtub?" She sits up and starts to massage her feet.

GABY (deflated): "Yes, I cleaned out the bathtub." Then, after a moment, she rises and turns to Lynne. She tries a friendly approach. "Madge—how do I look?"

LYNNE (looks over to Gaby in some annoyance; she appraises her sister): "You look very pretty." And she resumes massaging her feet.

GABY (pleased, sits again at the vanity table and immediately turns to Lynne): Madge—how do you talk to boys?" I wonder where this thought has come from and make a note.

LYNNE (curtly): "You just talk, silly."

GABY: "How do you think of things to say?"

LYNNE (annoyed): "You say whatever comes into your head."

GABY (forlorn): "Suppose nothing comes into my head?"

LYNNE (dismissing her): "You talked all right with him this morning."

GABY: "Yes, but now I have a date with him."

LYNNE: "You're crazy." She rises, gets a brush to do her hair and lies back down.

And they continue the scene, the dialogue almost word-for-word as in the text. They pursue their tasks, Gaby trying to arrange her hair while still very insecure, and Lynne, now apparently depressed, sitting on the daybed, her head in her hands, seemingly lost in thought. They continue the scene to the end, and I am impressed at how well they have managed to maintain their individual problems while continuing with the dialogue. They finish and turn to me.

"Fine. Very good, indeed. I see you had no problem with the text while you kept to your inner problems and outer tasks. Excellent progress! Lynne, did you change your adjustment to Gaby as Millie? You seemed to have a much sharper relationship with her today."

"Yes. I decided to use my brother this time. The one who always gets on my nerves."

"A very good choice! And Gaby, why did you ask Lynne 'How do you talk to boys?' when you did?"

Gaby is somewhat shamefaced. "I suddenly remembered it was my next line."

"Exactly. It came out of nowhere. Instead of from a problem that has been occupying you all afternoon—as well as some trepidation before you dare ask Lynne's advice. You must learn to resist the pull of the next words on the page until they have come from a thought. And in this case, a problem that has been growing in you for some time. But on the whole, very good work! Now, let's reverse roles and try it again."

And they quickly change clothing; Lynne into her formal gown and Gaby out of hers. Lynne, now as Millie, sits at the vanity table as Gaby, now as Madge, goes off to the "kitchen" to prepare.

Again, they seem to inhabit distinctly different attitudes toward the coming party. Lynne at first stares intently into the mirror, somewhat in despair; while

Gaby enters in something of a snit, goes immediately to the daybed, falls onto it and covers her eyes with her handkerchief, so that Lynne has to cross and remove it to gain her attention. And again, they seem to have no trouble with the text, conversing with the exact words throughout the scene. I notice two moments particularly worthy of comment.

"Lynne, whose makeup were you using there?"

"Madge's, of course. I don't have any."

"Really? The way you used that brush to paint your lips, you seemed quite familiar, not to say expert, with such things. Is that what you intended?"

"Not at all. I tried to make it seem unfamiliar."

"Well, unfortunately it seemed very familiar. Your own expertise 'bled through,' so to speak. You'd have to work more diligently on such tasks to create a seeming unfamiliarity. And Gaby, I noticed you had taken off your socks and were intent on massaging your feet when you said, 'I think I'll paint my toenails tonight and wear sandals.' It was an excellent use of a physical task to bring fresh justification to the text.

"Now let me sum up. I don't think we need to work on this scene any further. Not that it's finished, by any means. That's the director's job. When you have made the inner problems and the outer tasks your own, and you have connected them to the text in an appropriate sequence, you have accomplished most of the actor's work. The timing, the specific wedding of word to task, as well as the staging; this is the director's work. It is your job to bring the characters' relationship—their situation and concerns, their inner and outer problems and tasks—to immediate, personal life. Details of how these events and this dialogue are to be staged in time and space is best left to the overall eye of a director. And the director will help you connect your work on each scene to his view of the play as a whole.

"So now, if you're ready, as I think you are, and willing and able, we'll proceed to a second scene. We'll use the same approach that we have just followed—Essential Elements and Subtext before I give you the text. So that by our third scene, I think we can safely start with reading the text. I'll guide you through the process of identifying the clues to the actor's work that are inherent, but often hidden, in the lines. I'll help you dig out the Relationships, Circumstances, and Intentions. After our sessions working on this third scene, I feel confident that you can begin rehearsing a new role as is most customary—with the text. And I know you'll be well enough armed to avoid the lures of instant results and conventional outer forms. You'll be able to form your own Subtext from the Essential Elements in the scene. For you'll be habituated to working organically—from the inside out!"

PART VI

Raising Stakes: Exercising the Imagination

CHAPTER 13

Endowing: Recording and Projecting Sensory Images

"Ontogeny Recapitulates Phylogeny."

Ever since I first heard that phrase and thrashed out its meaning in my Biology classes at Cornell, this mantra reverberated in my memory like an unforgettable melody. What an unbelievable, yet scientifically unassailable, axiom it expressed: In the development of each individual organism, the evolution of that entire species is repeated in microcosm. Wow!

And this phenomenon came to influence many areas of my life and thinking. So that when I came to directing plays and actors, I found that, for myself at least, any proper process of rehearsal should encapsulate not only the author's conception and execution of his play, but the entire training and development of the actor as well. I soon found out that I was able to pinpoint the failings of various productions: This one failed to start at A, jumping immediately to F; that one skipped from C to K or from L to R; while another overlooked H to M entirely. My own failing, I usually discovered, was my habitual inability to arrange time enough to arrive at X-Y-Z.

Similarly, I also came to hold that the converse was true as well: Philogeny Forecasts Ontogeny. What I mean is that for me a proper training program for actors should presage a well-planned rehearsal process of any play. The same basic problems are recycled for each new staging. The same basic exercises form the tools with which we try to find fresh answers to more challenging artistic problems. Like our study of American History in successive years of our schooling, we review the same material in ever-growing depth and widening perspectives. At first, in my fifth- and sixth-grade classes at P.S. 6, we were introduced to the stirring story of our nation's founding. In our "departmental" years of the seventh- and eighth-grade classes, we surveyed that story from a somewhat different viewpoint. In High School, that history is perceived to have new, often darker colors. And if we study those same years in college, we most likely examine them from another perspective altogether.

So, as I developed my progression of actor-training exercises, I found similarly valid ways of recycling basic techniques. The first simple steps that helped my young actors to continue to "Live" on Stage proved equally productive as these actors grew more at home on stage and were encouraged to stretch their wings and fly.

Now that my students have embarked on scenic exercises with a partner in one of their weekly sessions (as described in the chapters above), their craft training continues with additional private sessions. These focus on more demanding monologues, as well as the new and important challenge of exercising and training the imagination. And while the imagination is perhaps the most valuable aspect of the actor's talent, its development has been confused and mishandled for far too long.

Stanislavsky was fascinated by this problem. For himself as an actor, for his colleagues in the Moscow Art Theatre, and for his students in the various studios his Theatre spawned, he continued to explore and develop exercises that would train the imagination. One of his most successful approaches he called "Working with Air." His student Richard Boleslavsky called it "Sense-Memory" when he introduced it to his students at his American Laboratory Theatre in New York in the mid-1920s. And Boleslavsky's classes inspired Harold Clurman and Lee Strasberg, who founded the Group Theatre in 1930, where they continued to develop Sense-Memory as an essential tool in their work. And so it has come down to us, primarily through Strasberg and his devotees.

When I studied with Lee in the early 1950s, we were plunged into these exercises without any preparation, and also without any indication of a proper sequence to follow. No "basic" to "advanced" for Lee's students! No, you attempted whatever Sense-Memory exercise took your fancy, brought it in to

Lee's technique sessions, and took your lumps, however they came. When I started my own classes, privately at first and later for Herbert Berghof and Uta Hagen at their HB Studio, I tried to follow Lee's regimen. But I soon discovered that these Sense-Memory exercises proved extremely difficult and frustrating for my young beginners. So I developed an introductory series of exercises. These also focused on remembering images of sensations, but not reproduced in class "with air," but projected onto appropriate, bland objects of a similar size and shape, much as a photographic image on a film is projected (though also much enlarged) onto the blank silver screen. These "Endowing" exercises subsequently proved both highly practical and also extremely effective in helping committed student actors refine and strengthen the power of their imaginations.

When we attempt to order our imagination, we encounter a peculiar problem. Unlike our basic simple tasks, which can be ordered at will, our imagination resists any command to function. It seems to act when we least drive it— when we are otherwise engaged, so to speak. As every artist needs to activate his imagination, perhaps the actor most consistently, this presents an immediate problem. For unlike voluntary tasks that can be ordered by will, the imagination cannot function on demand. When so ordered, it will only dispense tired old clichés. Moreover, a simple task when approached with a will, a clear and logical goal, and the solid support of a plausible purpose will succeed in relaxing us. But for our imagination to function, we must already be relaxed! Imagine a farmer, sowing his new crop with fertile seeds—but onto earth still hardened from last year's crop, not yet ploughed-up and furrowed to expose fresh nutrients to enrich the seeds with the help of sunshine and rain. No matter how rich the seeds, they will not take root; they will not sprout. And so it is with the seeds of inspiration with which the actor, together with the dramatist and the director, seeks to stimulate his own imagination; unless the field of his mind, body, and voice is relaxed and open, the most stimulating seeds will not sprout. They will not pervade and activate his instrument.

Therefore, in approaching these exercises that train our imagination, I insist on a fully relaxed body and a basic simplicity. When we "endow" someone or something in life, we are giving, bestowing a gift. This gift may be money, a bequest, or a treasure of some value. Just as often, unconsciously, we may "endow" a loved one with beauties or charms seen only in the eyes of the lover. Children endow constantly; they often lose interest in a specific new toy but continue to find renewed interest in the plain box in which it came. The box enlists the child's imagination, as he endows it with manifold new attributes. Similarly, the actor's age-old problem has been to bring immediate, personal value to the properties of the stage. By whatever means, the actor must learn to "endow," often with dramatic power, the prosaic elements that he encounters on stage. It is the actor's craft that transforms his objects and relationships to the required dramatic pitch.

Now, in my "endowing" series of exercises, I return to the simple cup or mug that was so helpful in our first exercise. It served then to divert the actor's attention from his own concern for his performance, as well as my evaluation of him; it helped to free him to continue to "Live on Stage." So now we return to a simple cup or glass of an ordinary drink with which we may best begin the process of "endowing," or exercising our imagination.

"For our first endowing exercise," I instruct my student, "I'll ask you to study two different drinks at home. Two drinks that you have fairly often — part of your daily diet, if possible. Orange juice, perhaps, milk, tea, or coffee — nothing extraordinary. Drinks that we generally take for granted, on which we focus only when they smell or taste unusual. Now when you approach each of these drinks, please take your time. For you will need to slow down to observe the sense images you encounter each step of the way. As a photographer using slow-motion, try to record in your imagination each successive sensory impression that you encounter as you approach and taste each drink. Try to remember the touch, taste, smell, and feeling each sensation evokes in succession. Then, when you come to class next week, I'll ask you to relax and start to project those images onto a glass of plain water. I'll guide you through the process, and I'm sure you won't find it difficult. Remember — we achieve results only when your observation at home is sharp and your relaxation in class is full. Until our next session!"

❊ ❊ ❊

At our following session, while the student relaxes in the easy chair on stage, with two small glasses of room-temperature water on the table before her, I gently prod, "Now, as you're relaxing . . . that's right, explore those tense muscles . . . as you're relaxing, does some image of a sense impression come gradually into focus? It may come first to your mind's eye — or nose — or tongue. It makes no difference . . . what do you sense?"

"A smell."

"Good. What kind of smell?"

"Sweet . . . citrus . . . orange, I think."

"Fine. Can you locate that smell around you? Perhaps coming from that glass on the table?"

The student leans over the glass. "Yes. It smells like orange juice."

"Can you see it? What color does it appear to be?"

"Orange. With bits of something."

"Is it clear, would you say?"

The student puts her fingers around the glass of water. "I can see the shadows of my fingers. So I guess it's—translucent?"

"Exactly. Does it have any temperature?"

"Cold."

"Any texture?"

She sticks the tip of a finger into the water, and smiles. "Pulpy."

"Would you like to taste it?"

"Okay." She takes a sip. She clearly likes it, as she smiles. "Yes—orange juice."

"Tropicana?"

"No, fresh. I just squeezed it." And she enjoys another sip.

"Can you sense it going down as you swallow it?"

"Yes . . . it's good."

"Have some more. You've earned it."

And so my student drinks some more "orange juice." Clearly, her memories of the sensations that she recorded as she examined and drank the juice at home have been well stored in her imagination; now they have been readily projected onto this glass of plain water. Her endowment is immediate and vivid. I congratulate her.

"Excellent! You've just endowed that ordinary glass of water as if it were the actual orange juice that you made and drank at home. Relax again, and we'll proceed to your second drink."

And we repeat the process with the second drink she has selected and explored at home. I start this series of Endowing Exercises with such simple objects, usually part of our daily lives, because we already have a clear image of the sensations they produce as we come in contact with them. And if the observation recorded at home has been detailed and specific, and the student is fully relaxed here in class, the imagined results are usually quick and strong.

From such a beginning, I developed a series of exercises with other liquids, then with solids like paper and cloth, and then on to simple objects of distinct sizes and shapes upon which the student can readily project a variety of personal Endowments. [See appendix B.] At first, all these objects will be chosen from the students' daily lives; they are also brought to class, so that I may test the accuracy of the recorded images. And, as her imagination is strengthened, I now will ask my student to put the various objects to use as they are endowed. For Endowing—giving a gift of a new reality to a bland, characterless prop—is what I call "actor work." It is done as preparation, offstage, in the dressing room, so to speak. The real test of the endowment is its ability to "Live on Stage"—to maintain its character in the throes of dramatic action. In common stage practice, we endow those objects that, first, are too rare or expensive for stage use — jewelry, precious metals and ermines of kings and queens, for example; second, too dangerous — actual poison, drugs or liquor, or bullets, knives, and daggers — objects that might unduly affect or control the actor, not only his character. Weapons that take their toll on the characters we play are commonly endowed properties. Most important, we endow objects that must be fraught with deep personal meanings — those "loaded" objects that, when contacted on stage, "go off," producing powerful emotional explosions. And, of course, the all-important relationships upon which the drama is built will often be constructed out of vivid personal endowments that the actor's trained and active imagination brings to his work on stage. So I approach this area gradually, moving from objects endowed from present daily life to those locked in our memories, and, finally, to whatever our imaginations may choose to conjure. As the imagination is sharpened, I also challenge my student with increasing problems of combining endowed and non-endowed objects in inter-action, as well as endowments from past life buttressed by fantasy.

Let me illustrate now with a climactic Endowment Exercise: Three objects are to be endowed and then used together in three different combinations. In each combination, one of the three objects — a different one each time — is not endowed in any way but is used in its own actual identity; while the other two objects are to be endowed in two different ways in each of two combinations. Though this sounds unduly complex, in practice it proves quite simple:

Today, Gloria has brought in three simple objects: a cardboard shoe box, an 8" x 11" notebook, and one short white sock. As she relaxes in the easy chair, she arranges and rearranges the three objects on the table in front of her. She now picks up the shoebox and examines it critically.

I nudge her lightly. "What do you have there, Gloria?"

She takes up the sock and carefully wipes down the box. "It's dusty. I just brought it down from my parents' closet." She handles the box delicately; it is apparently quite valuable. "My father made it from an old cigar box. He was a tobacconist for the May Company Department Store back in Cleveland. He was also a bit of an amateur craftsman. And he made this box for my Mom to keep her jewelry in. I just discovered it on an old shelf in their closet back home." She suddenly stifles a sob and continues to dust the box with the sock as she regains control.

"It's lovely. All shellacked in a high polish, red, like an oriental lacquered box. And covered with decals — a green dragon design, its mouth open, flashing eyes, yellow spots on the nose and tail, a comical look, one paw up and one down, the mouth open with a scaly tail . . . and it seems to be moving." She turns the box over. "Here, on the side, he put two modern clasps. Also more decals of flowers, all kinds—yellow, brown, purple, green, also shellacked to that same high polish. It's so pretty—but it's coming apart in spots." She rubs the edges gently. "I always loved it."

She handles the box with reverence. Clearly it is a treasured keepsake. And she continues to wipe it carefully with the sock. She now opens it slowly. "Inside he lined it with brown velvet . . . and . . . and I keep my private treasure in it!"

Now she takes out the notebook, positively glowing with pride and joy. She cradles it to her as if it were her dearest child. "It's hers—Marilyn's! Her very own script to *Some Like it Hot*! As I know Gloria is a fervent admirer of the late Marilyn Monroe, I can appreciate her extravagant glee.

"And how did you come to have it?

"Well! You remember that auction of her effects a year or so ago? Anna Strasberg was selling off all the things that Marilyn had bequeathed to Lee and herself. Well, I saw this script at the exhibition before the auction, and I wrote to Anna. I told her I was a student of yours, that you were to me as Lee had been to Marilyn, and I asked why her effects weren't going to the Lincoln Center Performing Arts Library. After all, they're national treasures! Marilyn had written her own notes all through the script—little private clues to help her perform, such as "like with Joe." Well, would you believe it, Anna did donate those effects to the Performing Arts Library—all except this script, which she sent to ME!"

And Gloria chortles in triumph. She is still cradling the notebook in her arms, her most beloved and adored child.

"Excellent, Gloria! We'll explore the specific ingredients of these endowments later. For now, just relax again and go on to your second arrangement."

Gloria stretches and relaxes her arms, neck, shoulders and her back. Again, she leans back in the easy chair and examines her three objects. The notebook goes back into the box, and the sock is now caressed with love.

"My first ballet slipper. How I loved it! So small, for a six-year-old. I'd forgotten that I'd saved it in this old box. Here's the elastic strap my Mom had sewn on. I used to think it was a magic slipper. How I begged for ballet lessons! You see, I had this friend, a neighbor who attended these Saturday morning ballet classes. Our mothers had taken us to see *The Nutcracker* that Christmas. What an experience! That fairy princess dancing in the snow, all those tutus twirling on their toes—I was transported! And I never let up on my mother. I remember visiting my friend, and she let me try on her own ballet slippers. They also put her stage makeup on me. And when it came time to leave, I wouldn't take off those slippers! I just hoped they wouldn't notice, and they did forget that I still had them on. But I knew! So I practically danced out the door and down the steps. Then my mother noticed. And she laughed at me and made me take them off . . . and . . . and I cried." Here Gloria suddenly begins to weep. Overcome, it's as if she cannot control herself. "And she made me go back and return them." She manages to control herself; she dries her eyes. "But she did enroll me in those Saturday morning classes. And this was one from the very first pair that she got for me." And she again caresses the sock, endowing it as that very precious first ballet slipper of her very own, holding it to her cheek in loving remembrance.

Now she opens the box and takes out the notebook reverently. "And this — this is the program from my first dance recital at the end of our first year — when I was Queen of the May! It was spring, 1951, I was six years old, I remember. There were three finalists for that spring recital — I was one of the three. And then the Queen was chosen — and that was me! I remember I sat on my throne with my crown on, and all the rest of the class danced round the maypole, holding the ends of the ribbons. And then they all sat and watched my solo. Oh, it was wonderful!" She is laughing and crying at the same time. But then she suddenly stops. "And that was the end of my dancing . . . for some reason, I didn't go back the next season. I don't remember why." And now, quite saddened, Gloria puts the notebook she has been treasuring and handling with extreme care back into the box, along with the sock. She sits quite still, lost in memories of a brief rainbow that disappeared all too soon, at seven years old.

I don't have to remind Gloria to relax once more. She immediately snaps out of her reverie and stretches her arms, neck, and shoulders. And she takes up the box with a new delight, standing it up on end.

"My steamer trunk for my Vogue Doll. See all the labels from foreign ships and hotels! It used to have the doll and all her clothes on a rack inside." She opens the box as if it were a miniature wardrobe trunk. "On one side were her outfits, and on the other, drawers full of her underwear and accessories. I remember a beautiful ski outfit." And here she takes out the sock, now folded into a miniature doll-size hat. "I only have the hat left." She tries the "hat" on her left fist, as if it were the doll. She admires it. "Yes, right in fashion. I must have been eight or nine. That Vogue Doll was the Barbie of her day." Now she takes the notebook and a pencil and searches the outside of the closed-up box. "I want to see if they still make it . . . I'd love to get one for my niece." She spies a trademark, some letters and numbers on the box. "Yes, 'Mattel, item 150X2353. USA 1953.'" And she carefully copies the serial number.

Having endowed her three objects in various guises, as well as putting them to use as so endowed, Gloria relaxes again and turns to me. She can tell I am very pleased.

"Excellent. Now tell me—what were your ingredients for this exercise? Which were based on fact, which embroidered somewhat, and which created out of whole cloth?"

"Well—there was actually a cigar box that my father made over for my mother as a jewel box I described. And I did think it was wonderful. But I don't know what happened to it. I lost it somehow after my parents' deaths. I would have liked to have it. And the script to *Some Like It Hot*—yes, I did see it on display at the exhibition of Marilyn's effects before the auction. And she did scribble her personal notes all over her scenes. But no, it was not given to me, I'm sorry to say—by Anna Strasberg or anyone else! But you surely know, that IF I had it—what a jewel for my collection!"

As I have seen Gloria's wall of Monroe memorabilia, I can appreciate what owning that script might mean to her. "What about the ballet slipper and the Mayday program?"

"Oh, yes, I was so in love with ballet as a kid. And that really happened— not wanting to take off my neighbor friend's slippers that day I tried them on at her house. And my mother did mock my infatuation, and she did make me cry and return those slippers. And I did attend those ballet classes for a year of Saturday mornings. I can't remember why they stopped all of a sudden . . . I did save my ballet slippers for some time. What became of them, I have no idea. As for the Queen of the May—well, I was indeed one of the three finalists. And there was a program, I remember, with all our names listed. But I was not chosen to be the Queen. I was sent back to the 'round-the-Maypole group. But I could have been Queen!" And so she now achieved that long-desired goal— today, here in the re-created history of her imagination—in her endowment.

"And your Vogue Doll and steamer trunk?"

"Again, based on fact. I did indeed have a Vogue Doll—and her steamer trunk with all her outfits. Including a very fashionable ski-suit. With a little hat, just like that. But I have no idea what happened to that doll, that trunk, or all her outfits. And no, I don't think my niece would want it now."

We review the various strands with which Gloria has fashioned this variety of meaningful, not to say "loaded," objects out of her endowment skills. We look at her childhood attachments, her devotion to the late Marilyn Monroe, and her flexible imagination that can transform third place into first, or lost treasures into found, and trigger past pleasures and pains as if very much alive and affective today. The actor's imagination, trained with stimulating exercises, will remain to replenish her instrument with ever-fresh emotional meaning and power.

In closing this chapter, I am reminded of perhaps the first recorded instance of this imaginative power and its practical application on stage. Only in this famous case, there was no Endowment as such. There was, indeed, a "Substitution," but the imaginative faculties only came into play much later. In the first performance of Sophocles' *Electra*, we are told, the actor who created that leading role was faced with a formidable acting problem. As one of the three actors, he played several different roles, women as well as men, with the aid of appropriate masks and costumes. And his role as Electra included a passionate outpouring of lamentation that challenged all his emotional powers.

When Electra is presented with the urn and told—as a test of her devotion—that it contains the ashes of her recently-deceased brother Orestes, she bursts into an aria of almost never-ending grief. The sole ray of hope for which she has been living is now gone, she believes, and her lamentation is extravagant in its suffering. Well, even in ancient Greece, this actor realized that he would somehow need to bring all his powers of expressing new heights of personal grief to this avalanche of emotion that Sophocles had written. And so what did he use to "force his soul to his own conceit"? In the property urn containing the supposed ashes of Electra's recently deceased brother, we are told that this actor had placed the actual ashes of his own recently deceased son. Talk about inhabiting a role on stage!

I extract two lessons from this amazing tale for my students: First, that the essential problems for the actor have always been, and will always be, the same—how to bring the role to life. How to bring the essential actual feeling, the required emotion, to the stipulated moment on stage. How to imbue the text with the appropriate passion that is always inevitable and yet always must appear spontaneous, so that the actor will truly appear to "inhabit" his role.

And second: that we do not need any such actually "loaded" objects to stir our souls to extravagant passion. The exercise of our imaginations, through the technique of Endowing, will serve quite well. And indeed, in his imaginative recall of potent past experiences, the actor will often release much more genuine feeling than he can remember having actually experienced in the stirring life moments now reviewed. When working with objects endowed with strong associations from his past, the actor often breaks down and gives way to a flood of overwhelming emotion. But when I question him about the actual object or event this endowment has recalled, the actor will generally deny any similar flow of feeling in the past. I can only conclude that the safety net of the studio or stage environment, the *imaginary* distress of his performance, frees the actor's emotions from the previous constraints and inhibitions of life. In other words, our habits and our culture may have led us to control our natural flow of feeling more than we know. But our craft—our training and technique—will liberate and channel all true expressions of emotion into our art on stage.

But this area will perhaps be more directly considered in my next series in training the imagination—in the actual Sense-Memory exercises, which will lead directly into the powerful trigger called "Affective Memory."

CHAPTER 14

Sense-Memory: Sequential Exercises "With Air"

"Relax . . . that's right. You've made a good habit of relaxing before attempting any endowment. Now try to maintain that habit when approaching Sense-Memory."

The student is sprawled in the relaxing chair on the carpet, his eyes closed. The mug he has been studying at home for this first Sense-Memory exercise sits on my desk. I have asked him only to select a cup or mug, one with a clear, simple pattern or design; he is to examine it carefully, touch it, lift it, and so begin to record in his memory the varying sensations he receives. Then he is to bring the mug to class, and I will guide him through the first exercise. Now I watch him relax. I wait a moment and then speak slowly, quietly.

"Now, as you're relaxing your muscles . . . yes, that's right . . . does an image of an object swim into focus in your mind's eye?"

"Yes. A mug."

"Can you describe it?"

"Green. With a curved shape."

"What shade of green? How curved?"

"Dark . . . forest? And it curves in at the bottom."

I check the mug on my desk. So far, he is correct. "Anything else?"

"Big letters—white, in script. U—C—F. Slanting up."

Correct again. "So you have a fairly clear image of this mug?"

"I think so."

"Fine. Now ask yourself: 'If that mug were out there—on the table in front of you—just where might it be?' Don't force—just ask, 'If . . . ?'"

The student opens his eyes and looks to the table. After a moment, he nods. "There."

"Can you visualize the letters? The white slanting script? And the sides curving out?"

"Yes. More clearly now."

"Fine. And, from where you're sitting, what does the texture does look like? Smooth or rough, for instance?"

"Smooth."

"Good. Would you say that it feels as smooth as it looks? Try and find out."

He stretches his hand out and hesitantly feels around the image of his mug. His fingers follow the shape; he finds where the handle is and moves round it. "Yes, it's smooth. Except for the letters. I can feel them—raised."

"And is it hard or soft? Cool or warm? Wet or dry?"

"Hard . . . cool . . . dry." His hands cup round the image of his mug —as if his cup were actually there on the table in front of him, not just the remembered feel of it projected into air.

"Good. And can you grasp the handle?" He does so, still recalling the image. "Would you say it has any weight—if you lift it by the handle?"

And he lifts it. "Not much. It's lighter than it looks." He weighs the imaginary cup as he holds it by the handle.

"And if you set it into the palm of your left hand, is the weight the same?"

He follows my suggestion. "Yes . . . I think so . . . no, not so much now."

"And how does the bottom of the mug feel in your hand?"

"Rough. With raised edges." And he raises the imaginary mug with his right hand to look at the bottom.

"Excellent. Can you put it against your cheek? Can you feel it touch your lips?"

He holds the imagined cup to his cheek and nods. "Very smooth . . . but the letters." And he moves it to his lips.

"Good. Now, does it have any sound?"

He taps it with a fingernail. "Not much."

"What about against your ear?"

And he cups it against his ear. He nods. "Yes—it sounds like a small ocean."

"Good. And now, can you rest it on your head—upside-down?"

Very gingerly he places his "mug" on top of his head, upside-down.

"Can you rest it there—taking your hand away? Hold your head up!"

Slowly, slowly, he straightens his head and removes his hand from the imaginary mug. He is totally focused on balancing this mug on his head.

"Good. Now, try to stand up, but don't let the mug fall! " He rises, very slowly. "And come over here to my desk." He moves slowly, carefully, his imaginary mug balanced ever-so-carefully. "Now, hold your hands out in front of you, palms up—yes, like that—and see if you can tip your head—and now catch the mug as it falls into your hands."

It is clear that he doesn't quite approve of this risky command. But he trusts me, and in a moment he does indeed tilt his head. As he "catches" his imaginary mug, I quickly rise to place the actual mug into his outstretched hands. He weighs the actual mug, testing it in his palm, against his cheek and lips, and finally upon his head.

"Is that what you sensed?"

"Yes. Very much so." He is somewhat surprised.

"And did you try all this at home?"

"Seeing and touching it, yes. Lifting it also. But not against my cheek or lips—or to my ear. And certainly not on top of my head."

"I wanted you to discover that when your observation has been sharp, and imprinted on your Sense-Memory, you're in no way limited only to what you had rehearsed. As with the actual object, you may experience it, use it, and deal with it in new ways, almost without limit."

"So I did it correctly?"

"Very correctly. Yes, indeed."

I use this first exercise with a simple mug to start my students onto a correct path to Sense-Memory. This supportive, gently questioning approach is a positive legacy of my training with Lee Strasberg. Building on Stanislavsky's work and his own experiments with the Group Theatre, Lee created, through Sense-Memory, that remarkable operation-room scene that was his brilliant high point of the Group's first success, *Men in White*. Lee found that the actor's imagination may be trained to an unusually high degree when it is exercised with pointed, specific questioning and a more conscious awareness of our daily sensations. Never demanding, always exploring with the "Magic IF," the actor can learn to recall the experience of his senses on demand—so they may be recreated at will. Thus, with talent and proper sensory exercises, the trained actor will readily be able to trigger his own sensations whenever needed. He will be magically able to experience and express on stage, both physically and emotionally, in his immediate performance, the imaginary inner life of his character.

In my years of trying to help my students make maximum use of these Sense-Memory exercises, I have developed an approach that is clearly structured, logical, sequential and accessible. The details of this sequence of Sense-Memory exercises can be found in an Appendix. Here I shall only outline the basic structure of my approach and illustrate it with a few vivid examples of memorable applications.

My first series of Sense-Memory exercises focus on eating and drinking. Simple varieties and combinations of foods that we daily see, smell, touch, and taste I have found to be both accessible and most helpful. Temperatures, textures and tastes changes as we bite, chew, and swallow; handling knives, forks, and spoons, and all the details of daily meals, make a very available and useful focus for basic sensory exploration. This series usually culminates in an exercise of contrasting, strongly flavored foods we can clearly call "loaded." When seen, smelled or tasted, they usually stimulate a powerful response.

My next series centers on muscular awareness and daily moments of bodily grooming. The student explores the sensory images of such tasks as washing hands and face, shaving, applying makeup, dressing and undressing, and, finally, the over-all bodily sensations of taking a shower or bath. To finish this close examination—and newly conscious recording—of daily sensory experiences, I ask for a selection of disparate sounds and smells. These are to be found in contemporary life and are also to be "loaded"—both pleasant and unpleasant. And I test the student's training by asking him to maintain images of contradictory sensations.

Now I guide my student as he begins to tap his store of remembered images. Until this point, our Sense-Memory experiences have been like scales for the pianist: training for the muscles as they prepare to play music we long to hear, music that requires agility as well as feeling. Our sensory exercises aim to sharpen the actor's ability to recall and re-experience recently explored daily-life experiences. But the larger aim of sensory recall is to equip the actor with a reliable access to the store of experience lodged in his memory. And we discover that releasing and then channeling this experience is perhaps the richest reward of honing our Sense-Memory skills.

I open this new path by way of a picture of some landscape, a view to be chosen, studied and visually recorded by the student—some impersonal view of a natural scene, countryside, village or town. And I ask that the student bring this photo, sketch or reprint to class so that I may check the accuracy of his visual memory when he projects this view onto a blank wall of the studio. If, as generally happens, the student has no difficulty in visualizing the details of this picture when projected, I know that now he will be able to tap into his memories. So next I ask for another exterior—but one that he knows from personal experience. This may be a house he has lived in or a building he associates with vivid memories. It doesn't matter whether he has an actual photograph of this building; I can trust that he will have it long implanted in his mind's eye. Thus we begin a first exploration of the powerful, often "loaded," memories that Sense-Memory training opens for us.

I start with visual memories. Then I question other sense images that might be associated with the remembered sight of that place: sounds, smells, temperatures, weather. We pursue a possible time of day and of year, and I challenge the actor to extend his view, to encourage him to evoke a 360-degree remembrance. Forgotten sounds and smells suddenly come to life: traffic, neighboring children, scents of autumn bonfires. Then he is to add tactile exploration—to "touch" various remembered objects as he moves closer to that special place—bushes, a fence, porch railing, flowers, perhaps—all now recalled as if at a particular time in the past as well.

If, as now often appears, the actor begins to experience feelings associated with that recalled image of a special place, I will ask him, for a next class session, to try to recall a particular room in that place—and at a particular time. He is to prepare to "enter" that room on stage. And while his conscious memory of specific details may be quite vague, our experience tells us that when he "walks into" that room on the particular, recalled occasion, much more detailed sensory images will be recovered. His step-by-step questioning of his shadowy memories will be like a torch throwing illuminating clarity on a succession of objects, now seen, heard, smelled, and touched.

I often remember one exercise that clearly revealed the power of such "loaded" sense images. Helene had brought memories of her former home in the Midwest to these exercises. She had left that home to come to New York to pursue a career in dance many years ago. In fact, she had been reluctant to return to that former small town home ever since she had had to clear out the house after her mother's death. Now, ten years since her last visit to that house, she was prepared to return—in this climactic Sense-Memory exercise. And she chose that painful visit after that family funeral. She had tried to forget the pains of that day; but now, in class, she wanted to take that trip again, to see what her training and technique could bring back to life, back to present experience.

Having chosen to explore her mother's bedroom for this exercise, now Helene relaxes at the side of the studio. There is no furniture whatever on the acting area. It is quite bare, so that Helene may fill it with the imaginary rooms of her memory. First she recalls specific images of that house. I have encouraged her to speak her thoughts aloud, in whatever fragments come to mind, both to remind her to focus on sense images and to encourage a fuller expression of her moment-by-moment sensations. Now she rises and moves to an imaginary door. She grasps an imaginary handle, turns it and opens a door to the past.

"Her bedroom." She seems reluctant to enter. But she does so, and then turns to regard the images she now recalls. "Her bed—that woven red-and-blue spread. Always neat." She moves her hand over "the bedspread." She turns. "And her desk, her filing cabinet." She goes to a "desk" and opens it, shakes her head as she gazes at it. "Always in perfect order." She closes the desk. She touches the filing cabinet. "No, I can't look in there." She notices a family photo standing on the cabinet; she takes it up and shakes her head.

"Mom and Dad, and my brother and myself." She looks at the photo a moment, then puts it back and stands reluctant, almost afraid, to continue.

I decide to prod her. "Her clothing, Helene? Is there a bureau? Or a closet?

"Yes. Her closet." She moves across the room and grasps a door handle. She opens the imaginary door. And suddenly she starts to cry. She is overcome. Her hands reach out and seem to caress an article of clothing hanging in that closet. She tries to control herself. After a moment of internal struggle, all she can say is, "Her uniform—her nurse's uniform—still hanging there."

She grasps the image of that uniform. "Already pressed, ready for her next shift." And she slumps against the back wall, clutching the image of her mother's uniform close to her, savoring its freshly-ironed scent, and brushing her cheek against the recalled starch of that dress. Those specific, remembered images—that she had apparently forgotten—have stirred a sudden outpouring of grief. She continues to weep. Finally, she restores that "uniform" to its place in the closet, and she "closes the closet door."

Helene's journey into the past has proven to be more powerful than she had expected. And when, in a few moments, Helene returns from her "trip" back to that painful occasion, to the present moment in the class, she is not at all sad. On the contrary, she is surprisingly exhilarated. For her perilous voyage has been rewarded. Powerful feelings that she doesn't remember experiencing at all, she is relieved to discover that she had all along—only unrecognized and unexpressed back then. And more important, she has found and charted a clear path to those, and similar, strong feelings, emotions that she now can evoke whenever she chooses, whenever her art requires.

It is clear that these Sense-Memory exercises bring us to the threshold of what the French psychologist Ribault called "Affective Memories." These are simply memories that, when properly recalled, will once again stimulate, or affect, our emotions. Thus, they are extremely useful for an actor called upon to "Feel" on cue, to "Express" often violent passions truly and fully, at the same planned moment of each performance, or in take after take of the filmed scene. The main technical difference I have been able to discern between such "three-dimensional" exercises as I have just described and the "Affective Memory" narrative is that the latter usually centers around some memorable event recorded in time as well as space. Therefore, the stimulating sensory images may be just as effectively recalled while the actor remains seated and relaxed. I have found that it matters little whether the student projects the objects outside of himself, using techniques of Sense-Memory, or connects with them only in his mind. So long as he slowly describes a sequence of "loaded" images, genuine feelings will usually be triggered.

Whenever I arrive at this crucial moment in Sense-Memory training, I con-sider whether I should embark on an Affective Memory exercise with each student, or proceed directly to a litany of physical conditions. As the aim of Affective Memory is to stir up and release strong emotions from the actor's own past, it is always a most delicate experience for both student and teacher. I am reminded of my own experience in doing my first—and only—Affective Memory back in the early 1950s, when I was a member of Lee Strasberg's private acting classes. The results were more vivid, the emotions more powerful, than in any other instance of this exercise I have since witnessed, either in Lee's or my own classes. So it may well serve here as an excellent example of the process and possibilities involved.

I had been training with Lee for several years and had heard him mention this special exercise called "Affective Memory." One or two of my classmates had attempted this exercise and achieved a somewhat distressing, painful state, but their results hadn't seemed to me to be particularly striking. Still, I was sufficiently stimulated by what Lee related of other student's attempts. And so when my turn was coming round, I bravely announced that I would like to try an "Affective Memory exercise." Fine, Lee said. I was to choose some memorable incident in my life that had occurred at least seven years ago. And that was all the preparation I should do. Lee would lead me through the exercise in class.

Without quite knowing what I was searching for, I chose my opening night performance as a gang-member called Innocence in the Damon Runyon comedy-melodrama, *A Slight Case of Murder*. Why did I choose that evening at Priscilla Beach Theatre some ten and a half years earlier?

In July 1942, I was a month shy of eighteen; it was my first summer stock experience. And it proved to be a major turning point for me. That round of applause on my exit that evening led me to choose a major in Speech and Drama when I returned to Cornell for my junior year. And it ultimately led me to a life in the theater. Perhaps I chose that experience for my Affective Memory because I remembered it as a happy event. I had even recorded the excitement of that performance in a postcard home. It seemed not at all fraught with pain, as were all the other exercises that I had seen in class. And it did fit Lee's time frame. So I came to class ready to relive, under Lee's guidance, my third-act scene in *A Slight Case of Murder* on that memorable opening night some ten years earlier.

I was sent up to the chair on stage in which students would relax before starting any exercise. I remained in the chair, relaxing, my eyes closed, while Lee quietly asked me questions to prod my memory and keep me focused on my moment-to-moment sensations. He particularly urged me to use the present tense in recalling the event. Since the exercise aims to bring the past to the immediate present, Lee explained that is a great help to speak as if each moment were happening now.

I first recall standing on the platform behind a door offstage, as if hiding upstairs, but also listening for my cue to enter. Lee focuses my attention on my clothing, and I begin to recall my shabby costume—baggy pants, old shoes, tight vest with worn shirt and tie—almost a Chaplin "little tramp" outfit. As I recover the tactile sensations of this getup, particularly the rope belt I have made to keep my trousers up, I begin to smile—to giggle, chortle, and then to laugh aloud. I become consumed with irrepressible, delighted glee. Infected by my laughter, the class begins to laugh as well, and it continues laughing more and more uncontrollably. As I "hear" my cue—a gunshot—I proceed to relive my precipitous entrance. I pull the door open and rush down the stairs onto the stage floor—all the while actually remaining seated and moving only in my memory, speaking out my flow of action as if now, in the present tense. My manic laughter continues to grow, as I relive my moments on stage. I come to a halt downstage center and stand frozen in a front-facing, hands-up, "don't shoot!" position. And I continue to hold that pose forever, it seems, while now still overcome with laughter. Then my fellow actors on stage finally take notice of me. They ask me who I am and what I am doing there. And I barely manage to say my lines. "Innocence, sir. I am Innocence."

Eventually, after the few lines of my fellow actors, I recall my final hasty exit offstage left. And all the while my outlandish, outrageous laughter continues. The class is in stitches. And then . . . then comes that strange sound from the place I have just left in my memory. I "hear" that audience applauding. The applause grows and grows. And the strangest thing happens. It was stranger still than my incredible laughter. I began to cry. And as I heard the applause echoing in my mind's ear, my crying grew—uncontrollably. The class grew silent, shocked. And I was embarrassed. I quickly tried to recover, to control myself. I had to stop the exercise.

I had never seen such full and contradictory expressions of both laughter and tears, or heard of anything like this, in an affective memory exercise. And neither the laughter nor the tears had occurred back at Priscilla Beach in 1942; neither had been part of the initial experience. From where had this glee and this pain come? And what did it all mean?

Since I was in therapy at the time, I immediately started to search for answers. I felt I had a need to apologize—almost to atone for such uncontrolled emotions. I had gotten into the habit of conquering feelings with intellect, so I began to search for the source of such strong emotion. Perhaps the outwardly "innocent" little boy was filled with secret glee at upstaging his brothers—and winning the audience's full attention. And then perhaps I felt the awful guilt and fear of being found out, of my upstaging being unmasked. For that audience so clearly and demonstratively *did* find out—and seemed to like it! Suddenly, Lee interrupted, "Don't analyze! Don't try to explain! Don't intellectualize!"

Distraught as I was, I was able to understand something of his message—that analysis of such strong emotions, though a most useful step in therapy, is anathema to the actor. The actor needs to maintain his connection with the entire keyboard of his emotional instrument. He must not diminish its full soundings with the soft pedal of intellectual dissection.

So I learned that a focus on the meaning of strong emotions often inhibits the actor's ready access to them. Such analyzing can prevent him from using this technique to recall, recreate and re-experience at will a strong flow of feelings triggered by some past experience.

It was an invaluable lesson. Ever since, I have approached this volatile area of "Affective Memories" with extreme caution. In teaching, only when I know a student extremely well, after at least two years' training, dare I introduce him to Affective Memory. And in directing, only when absolutely necessary, only when nothing else works.

CHAPTER 15

Conditions

Ben lies on the stage carpet, stretching his muscles and relaxing when I enter the studio. Having arrived at this new series of exercises, he has clearly learned to relax before attempting to order his imagination. And today we are starting on Conditions. He knows that this extension of our Sense-Memory work will require—and reward—the utmost relaxation. Now we can plunge right in.

"Good. I've told you only that we would be starting a new series of sensory work today on Conditions. And that our first focus will be on an overall bodily sensation, heat and then cold. I've found three different approaches to such conditions, and I'll try to introduce you to all three today. First of all, I believe I told you to recall two occasions when you can remember being unusually warm and then extremely cold. Were you able to select two such moments, Ben?"

"No problem."

"Good. Let's start with the heat. Some time when you were uncomfortably hot. Can you recall such an occasion now?"

"Oh, yes . . . I'm on the beach. Last summer at Sagaponack . . . Mid-August . . . and mid-afternoon. A very hot sun." And he begins to sense a growing warmth.

"Where on your body do you feel this heat?"

"On my face . . . and hands. I haven't got into my bathing suit yet. I just had to see what the beach was like. It's my first visit of the summer." He shields his face from an apparently uncomfortable sun. He rolls over on the carpet, then sits up and starts to remove his shoes and socks. "That's better."

"Can you feel this heat anywhere else? On what areas of your body?"

He squirms. "Under my arms." He loosens his shirt from his arms. "And in my crotch." And he loosens his belt. Now he unbuttons his shirt and removes it. "I can feel it on my shoulders. And now my back." He lies back down, stretching out. "Oh, yes, on my chest now. Good and warm."

"Excellent. You can sense the results of stimulating a particular condition by a remembered occasion. Your previous training in Sense-Memory has equipped you to resurrect a particular physical condition with little difficulty. Now try to continue this sensation and bring it here. I mean that the heat stimulated by your sense-memory of that day on the beach at Sagaponack is to be continued as you live—act and react—here and now, on stage. Try to maintain your condition and deal with it in whatever way seems appropriate."

Ben apparently has no difficulty understanding. For he rises, walks to the window, tests it for a more fresh flow of air, then finds the air-conditioner and switches it on. He continues to ease his clothing from his body; he exhibits all the symptoms of coping with an unusually hot space. Finally, he leans back on the daybed and gently fans his face. There appears to be no doubt that our studio has somehow got unaccountably hot. I think I can challenge him further.

"Excellent. Now let me suggest another problem. You have triggered this condition of heat by a remembered occasion; as you relax on the daybed now, try to stimulate a condition of cold by another such memory. You'll recall that I asked you to prepare for both conditions for today's exercise. Take your time, explore that other occasion . . . and again find memories of external objects that have made you cold."

Ben continues to relax. Then, slowly, he reaches for his shirt and puts it on. He rises and gets his socks and shoes, putting them on also. He seems to be cooling off. I query, "What's going on, Ben? What do you sense?"

"The heat's off again, in the middle of winter. Our lousy furnace is acting up, just when we need it most." He goes over to the radiator, feels it top to bottom, and now starts to rub his hands together, wrap his arms about his chest, and exhibits all the signs of an unwanted chill. He gets his jacket from the seats out front and puts it on; still chilled, he goes to the prop shelves and searches out a bedspread. He wraps it around his shoulders and folds his arms to hold the spread tightly about him. He is shivering now. He huddles on the daybed, trying to keep the warmth from escaping.

"Again, excellent. You seem to have no problem in stimulating these two conditions from remembered occasions. Now let me suggest a second approach. Continue the cold, as you seem to be experiencing now, but in addition to calling on details of remembered occasions that you may have experienced heat or cold, for example, you can also generate such conditions from what I call 'the here and now.' As you're huddled there, trying to relax, can you find one spot in your body that is somewhat warmer than the rest of you? Your feet, perhaps? Or under your arms? Wherever you can locate such a spot, just imagine that warmth growing; let it continue gradually to increase in temperature and spread over more of your body. Take your time."

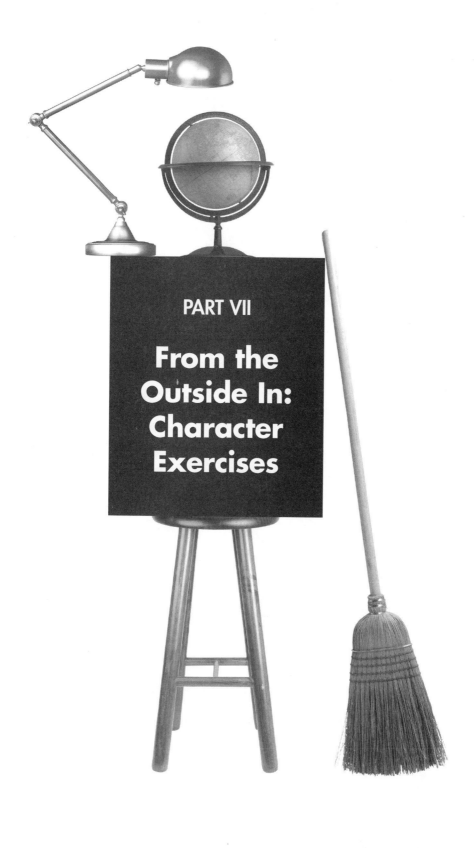

PART VII

From the Outside In: Character Exercises

CHAPTER 16

Character Elements: From Observation to Impersonation

The directive was clear: as Acting Mentor for "Purchase Six," I was challenged to devise a complete, four-year acting-training program. "Purchase Six" was the name given to the ambitiously-designated "Acting Company," which was in fact the entering Class of 1981—the sixth class since the founding of the new campus for the arts at the State University of New York at Purchase. It was now September 1977. This "Company" of thirty-two had been selected after a series of rigorous auditions held the previous spring. I had been hired somewhat later—during the summer, after interviews late that spring, and was told I could select one "alternate" member of the class. The others I met that first day of the fall term in the Dance Building at this Rockefeller monument of modernism.

Four state-of-the-art theatres had been built for $25,000,000, I had heard; but there was no building for instruction in Theatre. Music, Fine Art, and Dance each had its own distinctively designed, also state-of-the-art, building. But funds had run out before a building for Theatre could be built. So room was found in the Dance Building, which could accommodate many more than were presently enrolled in the Dance Program. Ample space provided that each "Acting Company" would have a dance studio to make over as its own "home" for the entire four-year program. And that each of the four Acting Mentors would have complete control over the course of acting training for the particular "Company" he or she taught.

The sequential training would be process-oriented during the first year and a half, leading to a full-scale performance of a play under the Acting Mentor's direction at the end of the second year. This would be followed by an increasing emphasis on performing in the final two years. Three plays, one by Shakespeare, with different directors, were to be scheduled for the junior year; and four, with a variety of stylistic demands, and with a variety of guest directors, in the final year. It was my first opportunity to chart the intensive training program for a group of thirty young, talented, and eager candidates for the BFA in Acting. And I welcomed the challenge. Our subsequent four years together proved to be always stimulating and rewarding. We developed a close, familial relationship that still endures more than twenty years after graduation. But in hindsight, I have come to feel that these students—twenty-two of the original thirty-two who graduated—were cheated of a college education. Ninety hours in theatre and only thirty in catch-as-catch-can other courses left wide cultural areas undernourished. Now I question the validity of such complete focus on acting for most young, beginning college students; now, whenever I am asked, I usually advise a liberal arts program at first, with intensive acting training deferred to later years.

By the end of our first year, meeting four afternoons each week, we had made significant progress from physical tasks to interactions in simple scenes, and from endowments to a full-range of sensory exercises. I arranged an impressive end-of-the-school-year, two-evening demonstration by the full Company that revealed a freedom and confidence in improvisation, as well as skillful interaction in a variety of scenic exercises. One of my colleagues commented that it appeared to him "the perfect demonstration of first-year work"; and several students from his own Company came to study with me in my summer classes, as well as later, at the HB Studio in New York's West Village. But for our second year, I now felt the need to devise a new set of exercises for my Purchase students—to prepare them for character roles.

I had carefully chosen the scenes that students had tackled in their first year—all were of young people, caught up in problems familiar, or understandable, in light of their own experiences. By the following spring, we were to mount a full production of an American classic with a wider range of roles under my own direction. I was already considering Sidney Howard's *Yellow Jack*, a large-cast, epic drama of the conquest of yellow fever in Cuba at the turn of the century, as well as three of Thornton Wilder's imaginative one-acts from 1930. These were original experiments in space and time that centered on his panoply of American archetypes. Eventually, as it turned out, we did both projects: *Yellow Jack*, though it provided a fully rewarding challenge for the men of the company, had only one woman's role. *The Happy Journey, The Long Christmas Dinner*, and *Pullman Car Hiawatha* were presented as *Three Trips in*

Space-Time. And for all these projects, some work in characterization would be decidedly helpful, if not essential.

Again I planned a sequence of exercises, starting as close to the students' personal lives as possible, but now, going "from the outside in." I had to discover if the first year's intensive training, always from the inside out, as it were, would now prove sturdy enough that my students could accept external input without being pulled away from their centers.

"For our first character exercise, I ask you to focus on someone in your own lives whom you think of as 'a character.' He, or she, may be old or young, near and dear to you, or further removed, but someone with very clear characteristics. Study him or her, and at our next class, I'll ask you first to describe that person in detail—to explain why you think he or she may seem to be a "character" and just why you think that he or she behaves in such a fashion. Then I will ask you to demonstrate some specific characteristic behavior."

The students are immediately turned on by this assignment; perhaps they had been longing to get further away from themselves on stage for a year now!

And yes, the exercises are tackled with vivid results: Grandparents, maiden aunts, high-school teachers, baby or neurotic relatives, all are vividly described. I ask that they ascribe logical reasons for what often seems to be outlandish behavior; and only then do I ask them to enter into that character, so to speak, and suggest him or her in voice and movement. Canes, umbrellas, toys, and sporting equipment are brought into play; eyeglasses, hats, purses with intimate contents are used. It seems clear that this demonstration of "characters" known in our students' own lives is channeling new, specific, and useful areas of my students' talents. I am encouraged; I think I am on the right track.

Next, I ask for another such "character" from my students' own lives. This time, the choices are even more daring, stretching further from their own centers to wider ranges of age and gender, and exploring the varieties of voice, speech, and bodily adjustments appropriate to these observed "characters."

And now I ask them to bring in elements of a public figure, one they probably do not know personally, but about whom they have read and heard much, or observed on television, and, again, one with clearly recognizable character elements. The students respond eagerly with political or performing personalities, TV hosts, popular idols, star singers, or athletes.

And as these "characters" are well known to most of the class, now they can meet, improvise, and interchange these roles with one another. We discover a roomful of these characters, interacting and connecting, and then exchanging ages, sexes, and habits with a full freedom, sharp observation, and attention to detail that would have seemed impossible six months earlier.

From here, it is only a detour to the library to explore characters in history or in fiction. I pointedly exclude characters in drama; these are to be held in reserve for the forthcoming character roles in the plays slated for production next term and in the following two years.

For further character work, in addition to the full productions now scheduled, I turn next to animals. I arrange a day at the Bronx Zoo. The class is charged to choose a specific animal, study it, and, at our next session, "inhabit" the chosen animal as accurately as possible. Domestic pets are also an excellent source of inspiration and have the advantage of providing repeated study. Our next class finds a menagerie of crawling, loping, hopping creatures; of growls, caws, and roars, a jungle of sounds; and a slithering of anthropomorphic animals. From these impersonations, as close to the perceived animal behavior as possible, I now ask the students to develop human characters based on these animal characteristics. Lee Strasberg had also led us into these exercises, which challenge the actor's observation and his imagination and demand new physical and vocal extensions. Now I am rewarded with remarkably original conceptions and astonishing transformation. A purring pussycat becomes a sleek streetwalker; a foraging squirrel grows into a meticulous shoplifter. Again, in a class situation, the actors can exchange animals, discovering individual variations as they find fresh stimuli in each other's physical alterations.

Finally, I turn our source material to painting and sculpture. I arrange a class trip to the Frick Collection, that elegant private mansion on Fifth Avenue filled with masterworks. I ask each student to select a portrait, study the pose, and bring his or her interpretation, along with a postcard reproduction, to the next class. First, the problem is to reproduce, in exact detail, the pose of the artist's subject; next to justify that moment, improvise the prior life leading up to that particular instant, and then to continue a follow-through to a possible resolution. When these were presented to my satisfaction, I then asked for groupings of two or three figures in scenes of interaction. Further trips to museums, or to art books, and the stimulation of these masterworks, again prove a revelation. How many different interpretations these groupings afford! The three muscular blacksmiths in Goya's powerful painting, *The Forge*, clashed in social as well as physical sparks; while a subtle study of a Degas couple merely avoiding eye contact provide five different character-relationships and situations, and I am convinced by each version and able to avow that each seems eminently possible.

I have since refined these character exercises in my current private training. Now my students will tackle them at the end of the second year, or the start of the third. But I adhere strongly to the sequential "from the inside out" for these "from the outside in" efforts at impersonation. I invariably start with family members, friends or intimate associates from the student's own life: first description, then some analysis of possible causes of specific characteristics, and last, an impersonation, entering inside the mind, voice, speech, body, and movement of this character. The results in class usually encourage us to move to other well-observed "characters" of the students' lives.

When we next come to observe public figures, seen on television, photographed and written of in the daily press, the student must first build a "public persona"—after all, it is all we can know from observation, and that generally of programmed, performance-like moments on the public stage. So I ask my students to imagine and improvise a private moment as well—before or after this famous figure appears in public—preparing or recovering from the role he or she has attempted, or learned, to play. Often we discover unusual and revealing differences between the public and the private. I have found these exercises to be excellent preparation for the many subtle degrees of revelation that our great dramas from Shakespeare to Chekhov demand of the actor-character.

After present-day public figures, I challenge the student with notables of the past, only known usually in history or biography. Now research into habits, manners, and customs of bygone times is in order. The new problems are stimulating: to make personal the different ways of behaving and speaking that historical fashions and manners demand. And lastly, figures vividly characterized in literature provide challenging and rewarding character studies.

Next come the forays into the animal kingdom—both domestic and as wild as a modern zoo permits. Again, the first demand is to recreate, as accurately as possible, the representation of the animal selected in terms of the actor's own body, movement, and sound. Next comes the challenge to develop a human being with whatever specific animal characteristics the student chooses to adapt. Literal fidelity may provide a starting point, but further extensions will bring out more subtle adjustments that often throw hitherto hidden lights on a particular character.

To conclude this sequence of character work, I enlist the great painters and sculptures in a "justify this pose" exercise. Again, precise embodiment of the pose is the starting-point; then an improvised situation that naturally, but seemingly inevitably, precipitates the pose; and finally, a resolution or exit from the moment caught and frozen in time by the artist. After two or three such exercises, a final series explores the stimulating possibilities of a twosome or small group. Needless to add, the larger the group, the more, and the more unusual, will be the various interpretations.

By the time my students are ready to tackle these character exercises, making fresh demands on their observation and imagination, as well as greater physical and vocal extensions, their inner technique has grown strong enough so that the pull "from the outside in" will not strain that technique unduly. Most often it will complement and stretch their instrument and their craft. In addition, quite often, they will be rehearsing and performing in various workshop projects on New York and out-of-town stages. I have found this character work to be an excellent preparation for the performing demands of new playwrights and directors. These exercises will then complement and enhance the skills the actor needs when charged with solving challenging new problems, as he moves out of the studio and onto the performing stage.

Finally, I must add that some of the most stimulating clues to creating fresh characters are often found in a variety of outer objects. In a notable example of this creative voyage, Stanislavsky charts for us, in the second volume of his training regimen, *Building a Character*, the remarkable discovery by his alter ego, the student "Kostya," of the unusual character of his own inner Critic. In Chapter Two, "Dressing a Character," the narrator, Kostya, recounts how frustrated he becomes when he and his fellow students are charged to find a fresh character and array him in appropriate costume and makeup.

Without quite knowing what character he is dressing, Kostya chooses an old morning coat, faded and "covered with spots and dust mixed with ashes." He finishes with a hat, gloves, dusty foot gear, and a wig and makeup in the same color and tones—"all grayish, yellowish, greenish." But for the life of him, he cannot identify the character he is costuming in this manner. Days of frustration and sleepless nights pass as Kostya searches vainly for this character that his unconscious has somehow suggested. Finally, on the day when the students are to present their characters to Stanislavsky himself as the teacher, "Tortsov," Kostya sits at the makeup table in the dressing room in despair. The other students go on stage to present their characters, and Kostya, in a fit of frustration, decides he can't possibly go on. He starts to remove his makeup with some cream on the table of a "horrid looking greenish hue." But as he rubs the cream fiercely over his face, smearing all his features to a greenish-grayish-yellowish pallor, he is suddenly inspired to spread this muck onto his false beard and mustache, and even over his wig as well. And from some depths of insight, he finally realizes what character he is preparing. His toes turn inward, his legs bend askew, he grabs a cane and a quill pen to hold in his lips; he narrows his mouth into a straight, angry line; and with an uncertain, uneven gait he goes to the stage to confront his teacher—suddenly in the thrall of this new character.

TORTSOV exclaims: "What's that? Who is that? Kostya? No, it isn't . . . who are you?"

KOSTYA: "I am the Critic!"

TORTSOV: "The Critic? . . . what Critic are you? Critic of what?"

KOSTYA (rasping): "Of the person I live with."

TORTSOV: "Who is that?"

KOSTYA: "Kostya!"

TORTSOV (immediately understanding, cueing him on): "Have you gotten under his skin?"

KOSTYA: "Indeed, yes!"

TORTSOV: "Who let you do it?"

KOSTYA (with a squeaking, choking laugh): "He did!"

And a further improvised interaction erupts between the teacher, Tortsov, and this outrageous, perverse new character that Kostya now embodies. That jaundiced, carping critic that lay within him, always ready to find fault and damn his every creative effort—this fantastic character emerged fully-formed out of an impulsive combination of costume and makeup. Needless to add, Stanislavsky-Tortsov is immensely pleased; he gives his student an impulsive hug—thereby getting some of that awful, smeared makeup on his own clothes. And young Stanislavsky-Kostya is elated; he runs offstage, filled with a joy stemming from this impulse of creativity—this new, spontaneously discovered artistic achievement.

Laurence Olivier, perhaps the greatest actor of his generation, avowed how often it was the nose that led him to the character he sought. He would experiment at his makeup table, shaping various putty noses until he found one that somehow seemed to him to be right for whatever new character he was contemplating. And then his inspiration flowed: that nose would lead him to the inner soul of that character, and manifold outer character elements would follow. One of his most memorable characters was Richard III (fortunately recorded for us in his unusual film), the signature role of so many leading Shakespearean actors of the English-speaking stage. And Olivier said that he found the right nose in a combination of two very unpleasant "characters" of his own experience. One was that of the Big Bad Wolf in the Disney *Three Little Pigs* cartoon; the other was that of the notoriously demanding and imperious Broadway producer-director, Jed Harris. Olivier had suffered under his demonic direction in his first New York role in *The Green Bay Tree*, and, though the play was a signal success and made Olivier a star of the American stage, Harris' torments had left an indelible mark. But Laurence Olivier was able to recycle this painful experience with the alchemy of his talent and his putty nose when that elongated "Wolf-Harris" nose led him to his remarkable Richard III.

Finally, Uta Hagen, one of our most astonishing actresses and a unique treasure of our theatre, told me that when she had first attempted the role of Joan of Arc in Shaw's *St. Joan* on Broadway, she felt distant from Joan. And she discovered that not until she had removed her shoes and stockings, and her bare feet could connect with the bare floor, could she make contact with the essence of Joan, the peasant girl, who became Joan the warrior, and, five centuries later, St. Joan.

In my own recent experience, returning to acting after four decades of focusing on directing and teaching, I remember a most unusual and revealing experience in finding a character. For my one-man program, culled from the lyrics of W. S. Gilbert, *Innocent Merriment*, or *Gilbert without Sullivan*. I was challenged by a self-explanatory lyric of a very unpleasant character—King Gama from *Princess Ida*. He is traditionally portrayed as a nagging, complaining, snooping creature, who is altogether nasty, but who cannot understand why everyone says he's such a disagreeable man. (You may see and hear just such a portrayal in the Mike Leigh film *Topsy-Turvy*.) My director, also a Gilbert and Sullivan addict, kept reminding me how disagreeable this character was. She recalled how the last performer she had seen in a traditional British production, a relic of Gilbert's own staging, had succeeded in the role with his extremely nasty, obviously disagreeable demeanor. Somehow, this traditional interpretation didn't seem right for me, and I was convinced I could find a fresh interpretation to which I could connect. But all my efforts were fruitless. Finally I gave up on this elusive character and turned my attention to others I seemed to have less difficulty in connecting with. I remember that I went to a local costume house one afternoon in search of an admiral's hat for Sir Joseph Porter, the "Ruler of the Queen's Navee" from *H.M.S. Pinafore*. And while I didn't find any hat suitable for Sir Joseph, I did notice another, quite remarkable hat on a high shelf that immediately attracted me.

It was a tan, unusually round, bowl-like hat that somehow caught my fancy. It immediately reminded of the hat worn by the boy in a famous advertisement of my childhood for Buster Brown shoes. He was a rather chubby youngster, with an appealing dog beside him, and he smiled a rapturous, self-satisfied smile as he proclaimed the delights of wearing those shoes. And along with that long-buried memory came another image—that of the boy movie actor, Jackie Searle. He was always cast as that smirking, stuck-up smarty, who challenged the regular-boy hero, often Jackie Cooper, and who was always reduced to a flood of tears of failure—if not beaten to a pulp—by our hero at the satisfying conclusion. Yes—this was the Buster Brown hat of that sissy, smarty-pants, and this suggested a smiling, smug, know-it-all character for my disagreeable man!

I immediately bought the hat and raced home to try out this new character. I searched out an old ankle-length raincoat from my closet, put it on buttoned up to the neck, and tried out King Gama's lyric in the new, high-pitched voice that somehow came out of me along with the costume. Did Jackie Searle speak this way? I couldn't quite remember. But it seemed to belong to this new character. Immediately it all seemed right—the words, the hat and raincoat, and the voice; and though I'm not sure that my director was as pleased as I was, she agreed that it certainly worked for me much better than our former efforts at the more conventional interpretation. And so it proved. I enjoyed playing this self-satisfied tattletale, as he seemed to enjoy himself, and he proved quite a hit with our audiences. My young "King Gama" proved one of the most successful of my twenty-five Gilbertian characters.

I am reminded of another character I had discovered with another outer object—many years earlier, long before I had learned to act, I must admit. Trading on talent alone, my first acting efforts were somehow often applauded. Indeed, as I have recounted in an earlier chapter, such applause had led me to my life's vocation in the theatre. But I still had no technique, no craft—so that I often found it difficult, if not impossible, to maintain and repeat such haphazard successes. One memorable such experience remains a most painful, yet very instructive, memory. I was cast as the Prince of Aragon in a modern-dress Off-Broadway mounting of *The Merchant of Venice*. It was a one-scene role, but I found an immediate affinity for this fool of a suitor for Portia's hand. And it was my eyeglasses that led me into an interesting interpretation. Perhaps because this Prince is a victim of self-deception, his perceptions quite disordered, I found myself removing and replacing my eyeglasses in apparent confusion as I bent to read the inscriptions on the various caskets that contained the clue to the prize, the heiress Portia. This Prince seemed not to know whether he was near- or far-sighted.

As is customary in productions of Shakespeare's multi-plot dramas, we rehearsed our several scenes separately. After two weeks of such preparation of the diverse scenes, the entire cast came together for a first rough run-through of the play. None of us had seen any of the scenes in which we didn't appear; certainly none but our Portia and Nerissa had witnessed my one scene. The assembled cast now sat against the walls of this classroom we used for rehearsal at the Lenox Hill Neighborhood House in the East Seventies, getting up as needed to play the successive scenes. And after I performed my one scene as the Prince of Aragon, the rest of the company burst into applause. I had never before experienced, or had even heard of, such a response in any rehearsal. Needless to say, I was pleased indeed. Apparently I had created an original and successful character. And the director seemed highly pleased as well. Though, as he was playing Shylock, in addition to directing, I thought he might also be a bit jealous of my success.

However, my characterization, inspired by my eyeglasses, somehow did not continue to please in succeeding rehearsals. I seemed unable to capture, much less repeat, that successful first interpretation; and by our dress rehearsal, two weeks later, our director was reduced to yelling at me. "Witcover—pick it up! Why so slow? It's boring! Why aren't you funny any more?"

It was disastrous. I was beside myself. But try as I could, I could not rediscover that illusive link that had made my Prince so freshly ridiculous at that first run-through. I tried every trick with my eyeglasses, all to no avail. Because I had no craft, no inkling of an acting score, no clue as to my sequence of intentions, I was lost. I groped mechanically for the missing link; I searched for some conscious logic to my seemingly spontaneous removing and replacing the glasses.

But it had gone, never to return. The secret formula of justification that could be followed consciously, and yet seem so spontaneous, was not to be found for many years—only after I had finally learned to act.

Happily I now can reap some benefit from this most unpleasant experience: I learned that talent alone will not an actor make. And a happy inspiration from specific outer objects can only serve to build a character when such an inspiration is supported by a solid technique. Only the training that will develop a conscious craft will support the discoveries of talent and inspiration. And enable them to be repeated—and often enhanced—in succeeding rehearsals and performances.

PART VIII

Dramatic Extensions: Extravagant Expression

CHAPTER 17

My "Seven-Step Sonnet Solution" for Poetry and Song

When we survey the spectrum of contemporary American actor training, we find a devoutly-held belief. On the one hand, it is generally acknowledged that a Stanislavsky-derived "Method," or organic approach, has proven its value in building dynamic performances in dramas from Chekhov through Eugene O'Neill and Clifford Odets to Tennessee Williams and Arthur Miller. It is accepted to be most appropriate when portraying characters that inhabit our contemporary world and express themselves in contemporary, natural-sounding, life-like speech. But such an approach should in no way be followed in tackling the great roles of classic stature! Certainly not the overwhelming Greek tragedies, Shakespeare, and Moliere; and of course not modern symbolist, expressionist and "absurdist" works. For these "larger than life" dramas, it is assumed, a much more choreographed, outwardly body-and-voice approach is demanded. And certainly we shouldn't dream of using our basic "I am" training in the passionate extravagances of music drama—in that inherently unrealistic, contradictory, yet marvelous form we know as opera.

It was precisely this notion that I was determined to challenge when I undertook my "Experiments in Theatrical Opera" in the Directors Unit of the Actors Studio, led by Lee Strasberg, from the fall of 1965 through the spring of 1969. At the rate of about one act per year, my students and I set ourselves to explore the problems of acting in opera with a fresh, organic approach; we sought to bring inner truth and expressive human behavior to Verdi's *La Traviata*. If our fresh approaches could bring such intense new life to modern prose drama, I thought, what new miracles of truthful passion might it bring to classics, even in music? Granted that *Traviata* was based on a most realistic play, pioneering a fresh, realistic approach to a decadent society. Dumas' *La Dame aux Camelias* may seem melodramatic to us today, a hundred and fifty years later, but in its own day it was a truly shocking, revolutionary revelation. In the event, I found that the "Method" approaches to personal, intimate human behavior, stripped of stylized and often empty operatic conventions, succeeded to a degree none of us had anticipated—they served marvelously to intensify the dramatic experience. We also discovered fresh and vitally new stage forms that were immediately expressive of the music.

From that experience grew our Masterworks Laboratory Theatre, which for the past thirty-five years has been the nurturing home of my exploratory work in classics of opera, drama, song, poetry, and literature. My training studios have often prepared young artists for the creative work of these projects; and the work of these projects has in turn nourished my training approaches. Now, my experience has led to my conviction that while an inner, organic approach is most helpful in modern realistic drama, it is even more helpful—indeed, essential—in approaching classic and poetic drama and opera. I have found that the more extravagant the form and the language, the more heightened and removed from realistic drama and our daily speech, the more valuable is a process that centers the actor in his own persona. I find it essential to encourage him to build his performance on the sturdy supports of his own analogies; to bring intimate, personal experience to the Relationships, given Circumstances, and Intentions outlined for the actor in these extravagant dramatic situations. Hence, I have developed a step-by-step approach to help the actor chart his way to a living performance of such highly-charged material. I call it my "Seven-Step Sonnet Solution."

I discovered this approach by necessity, as it were, when trying to help those of my students who came from the world of opera. Thrust into tackling poetically charged material with, at best, only the rudiments of any acting technique, they were also often hampered by destructive formulae in performing lyric works from habits developed in "Opera Workshops." Unfortunately, these experiences, which usually demand immediate results in traditional forms, as well as the dominance of musical obligations, too often succeed only in leading young singers to a stifling convention of outer "emoting," demonstrating and indicating. The "Seven-Step Solution" that I developed as I tried to help release these often self-conscious, restricted young singers, has proven an effective remedy for such habits. Subsequently, I found that this process admirably serves all actors as they approach complex dramatic material. Let me now try to explain the workings of this "Solution" in more detail.

In order to find a path, we must first know where we are heading. We first need a clear goal, an objective. In charting our way to performing poetry, it is essential that we understand the special poetic language, even in the most prosaic way. Naturally, the meaning of the poet is hardly expressed in a prose translation; but however much it leaves to be filled in later, I have found that an essential first step is to Paraphrase the Text.

This is not the same as personalizing, finding substitutions or analogies — these come later. At first, it is important that we clearly understand the simple meaning of the words of our author. This process is hardly original — I am sure that most of us have been dragged through this rough-translation step in scholastic encounters with the Bard. And I was very pleased to discover, at an open demonstration of their work with Shakespearean text on a visit here a few seasons ago, that the actors of the Royal Shakespeare Company initiate the start of each fresh rehearsal period with just this simple step. They read and paraphrase every line, or phrase, in turn, to make sure that the poet's meaning is clearly understood. Of course, fine poetry does not reveal all its riches at a first reading — meanings, often contradictory, will proliferate with study. Moreover, paraphrasing a passage of Shakespeare is a much simpler process for an experienced classical actor than for young actors venturing for the first time into these dangerous waters. But the teacher or director will only encounter unwanted and, often, difficult problems later on, if he fails to lead his actors through this necessary first step.

When the meaning is clear, it is now possible to extract the essential elements. This is the second step. Only then do I choose a possible analogy with which to enter into the spirit of the verse. I must now find an appropriate personal experience that may bring new life to the text. If this third step proves productive, I may proceed to the successive ones as I return to the poem, now imbedded with a personal subtext — as meaningful to me as was the poet's when he first created his poem. I think I can best clarify what I mean by applying this seven-step process to a specific piece of poetry. So — let's light on Shakespeare's painful assessment of his love in his:

SONNET 57

Being your slave, what should I do but tend
Upon the hours and times of your desire? (1)
I have no precious time at all to spend,
Nor services to do, till you require. (2)

Nor dare I chide the world-without-end hour
Whilst I, my sovereign, watch the clock for you, (3)
Nor think the bitterness of absence sour
When you have bid your servant once adieu. (4)
Nor dare I question with my jealous thought
Where you may be, or your affairs suppose, (5)
But, like a sad slave, stay and think of nought
Save where you are how happy you make those. (6)
    So true a fool is love, that in your Will,
    Though you do anything, he thinks no ill. (7)

First, to paraphrase the text:

1. Since I am your property, what else can I do but wait to do whatever you wish?

2. I can do nothing but wait for your orders.

3. I must not even complain when waiting anxiously for you,

4. Or permit myself any pain when you have gone from me.

5. I cannot presume to wonder where you are or what you're up to;

6. I can only remain alone and fret that your other companions are so lucky.

7. My love has made me so crazy that whatever you do, still I can't blame you.

Next: to extract the essential elements:

First, an immoderate love, on my part, that is overwhelming for my beloved; second, a beloved that seems unaware of my pain at being ignored, and my jealousy that I may not even express; and third, my recognition that despite my beloved's insensitivity, I still forgive him/her and remain committed to my love.

With these three elements, I can now proceed to the third step, to select, or imagine, an appropriate analogy.

I let my experiences in love waft through me and find myself remembering a time when I felt similar sentiments for one who took my love for granted, so to speak; one whose feelings for me in no way matched my own fervor. This analogy need not be a love closely paralleling the poet's own, or even a human being; it may range far afield to a love for a respected role model or a precious object, to an art, to a part of nature, loved but unaware and unresponsive. It only needs to match in fervor the immoderate, all-serving love expressed in the text. But since I can relate it to a similar personal experience, I can try to make use of it here.

Now, fourth, it is my task to set up an appropriate situation in which I can improvise on this analogy. I recall a time when I was preparing a dinner for the young friend with whom I was in love, waiting impatiently for him with increasing pain and frustration. I set up the dinner table in my former small apartment near the university, specifying the time and place in detail. I set out the dishes, check the dinner cooking on the stove, allow my impatience and my anguished thoughts to be expressed, voicing my inner monologue. I give vent to feelings that I had, but perhaps never expressed. I experience all the subtext of the first twelve lines of the sonnet. Finally, when I recognize that my actual experience at the time hardly resolved into the forgiveness found in the final couplet, I search my memory for another moment when my loving feelings were able to forgive him and forget his taking me so lightly. Now I remake the actual remembered experience with an imagined resolution, grafted from quite another occasion. And so I am able to live through the sequence of inner events — pain at my subservient position, frustration at having my love taken for granted, jealousy of his other companions, and final acceptance without rancor. I acknowledge that such pain inevitably accompanies love, and that whatever he does, I cannot hold it against him.

Fifth, now I will try to shape my analogy to the form of the text. I redo my inner monologue so that my voiced thoughts follow more closely the three quatrains and final couplet of the poem. As I follow this process, I find I am unconsciously learning the text of the sonnet. It now has an organic unity that ties my feeling-thoughts to the specific form of the text.

Sixth, I will now mix and match my own improvised thoughts with the phrases of the text, sometimes voicing my analogy as well as the words of the sonnet, sometimes letting my feelings pour directly into the text itself.

And seventh, and lastly, I can now return to the text with my own personal feelings firmly imbedded. I have found and processed a solid subtext, one that will arise in me whenever I come to the sequence of the sonnet. The very words of the poem will remind me of my frustrating love, and at each recital I will relive the pain and then the rueful acceptance that the sonnet expresses.

And so this seven-step process has brought me into the soul of the sonnet; not only do I understand it, now I experience it anew each time as I speak it. The poem has captured my own experience, and this personal experience now informs the poem with immediate, personal feeling. I can now bring the essential personal involvement as subtext to fill the text with the necessary inner life: by bringing the sonnet to myself and myself to the sonnet, I am able to embody the poet's experience in my own terms. Thus I can bring the poem to performing life.

To sum up: My "Seven-Step Sonnet Solution" is a practical approach to heightened or difficult material—poetic, lyrical, or operatic. It offers a clear solution to problems that often embroil the performer in conventional, generalized, indicated "emoting." Such external performing engages neither the performer nor his audience. I have found this "Sonnet Solution" to be rich in liberating rewards for the performer who is willing to follow it. To reprise: the seven steps of this process are:

1. Read and paraphrase the text.

2. Extract the Essential Ingredients.

3. Choose a possible personal Analogy (preferably from experience, or else from the actor's own imagination) that will engage the main ingredients.

4. Improvise on this Analogy, setting up the circumstances and intentions, and maintaining a flow of the inner-monologue if alone; or to an endowed listener if in company. (If this improvised analogy proves appropriate, embodying and expressing the Essential Elements, then proceed to step 5. If it fails to provide the necessary connections, reconsider the choice of Analogy. Revisit the now steps 3 and 4.)

5. Now try to repeat the improvised analogy, restructuring its format closer to the size and shape of the text. This might well take several repetitions.

6. Again repeat the improvised analogy, now structured quite closely to the text, while mixing and matching improvised spoken thoughts with phrases of the actual text.

7. Finally, recite the entire text. The personal subtext should now be firmly embedded in the size, shape, and actual words of the text.

This sequence of attack has proved to be highly effective in scenes from Shakespeare for my advanced students, as well as in both contemporary and classical songs for performers in musical theatre. And for opera singers, this technique has proved extremely liberating: they have consistently found that this approach brings them immediately into the intense personal involvement so essential to music-drama.

I tried to follow this process when preparing to perform my "Parlor Programs" of poetic material. And I have recently found that my own performances of verse have inspired some of my students. In exploring possible new theatrical values for themselves, they are adapting the formats and the processes I have developed over my years of training actors and singers. And often we are also searching for new forms for poetic material that may never have been intended for the stage.

For example, after four years of training with me, Brian, a devoted student, now ventures to bring new life to some of his favorite, once-popular poems. Too often nowadays, these venerable relics of amateur recitation are ridiculed; now they are usually regarded as overripe food for satire. But the challenge to rediscover the original vitality of such poems is enticing, and I encourage my mature student to go for it! He now brings to class Tennyson's famous ode of 1864, commemorating the ill-fated British cavalry unit that made a suicidal attack on Balaclava during the Crimean War, ten years earlier:

THE CHARGE OF THE LIGHT BRIGADE

Half a league, half a league,
Half a league onward,
All in the valley of Death
   Rode the six hundred.
   "Forward, the Light Brigade!
Charge for the guns!" he said.
Into the valley of Death
   Rode the six hundred.

"Forward, the Light Brigade!"
Was there a man dismayed?
Not though the soldier knew
   Some one had blundered.
Theirs not to make reply,
Theirs not to reason why,
Theirs but to do and die.
Into the valley of Death
   Rode the six hundred.

Cannon to right of them,
Cannon to left of them,
Cannon in front of them
   Volleyed and thundered;
Stormed at with shot and shell,
Boldly they rode and well,
Into the jaws of Death,
Into the mouth of Hell
   Rode the six hundred.

Flashed all the sabres bare,
Flashed as they turned in air
Sabring the gunners there,
Charging an army, while
    All the world wondered:
Plunged in the battery-smoke
Right down the line they broke;
All that was left of them,
Cossack and Russian
Reeled from the sabre-stroke
    Shattered and sundered.
Then they rode back, but not,
    Rode the six hundred.

Cannon to right of them,
Cannon to left of them,
Cannon behind them
    Volleyed and thundered;
Stormed at with shot and shell,
While horse and hero fell,
They that had fought so well
Came through the jaws of Death,
Back from the mouth of Hell,
    Left of six hundred.

When can their glory fade?
O the wild charge they made!
    All the world wondered.
Honor the charge they made!
Honor the Light Brigade,
    Noble six hundred!

At our first session, Brian, by now familiar with our process, simply reads and paraphrases the poem, line by line. Though I know he admires the poem, for both its compelling tempo/rhythm and its fervent salute to these heroes, he restrains the inherent pull toward declamation so often linked to such "poetical" verse. We agree this is an admirable choice for both a fresh viewpoint and the devotion of organically-trained Brian to express its fervid, not to say florid, sentiments with fresh skill and insight. And so Brian goes home inspired to work; he will follow my "Seven-Step Sonnet Solution" in preparing this challenging poem.

※   ※   ※

At our next session, Brian again relaxes in the armchair facing me on stage and now recites:

> *"Seventy miles, seventy miles,*
> *Seventy miles to the target!"*
> *On to the Chosen Reservoir*
> > *Attacked the First Marines Division.*
> > *"Marines, Forward!" MacArthur ordered.*
> *"On to the Chosen Reservoir!" he ordered.*
> *Far above the 38th Parallel*
> > *Charged the First Marines.*
> *"Forward, the First Marines!"*
> *And they wondered*
> *They wondered what had happened—*
> > *Did MacArthur screw up?*
> *Was he mistaken?*
> *No time to think then.*
> *No choice but to follow,*
> *Just shoot their way in*
> > *And shoot their way out.*
> *Mortars to left of them,*
> *Machine guns to the right of them,*
> > *Cross fire all covered them.*
> *Boldly they went forward.*
> *Straight to the Chosen Reservoir,*
> *Just as they'd trained to do,*
> *Attacked the overwhelming Chinese*
> > *The Marines First Division.*
> Etc., etc.

It is a remarkable analogy—this account of the attack ordered by General MacArthur during the Korean War, for the First Marine Division to cross the 38th Parallel and advance seventy miles into North Korea to secure the Chosen Reservoir in the face of the overwhelming force of the Chinese. And couched in a shape uncannily close to the format of Tennyson's poem.

I find that my response to Brian's work is strangely mixed: I admire his apparent skill in finding a modern analogy that seems to relate to the poem so directly; but I am also somewhat chagrined. He seems largely uninvolved; and an important element seems missing. Has he really touched all the steps in this approach, or is something seriously adrift? Since he has been away for several weeks, I wonder if I am confused about the sequence of his work.

"You read and paraphrased the poem at our last session, I recall?"

"Oh, yes."

"And now, you are working on which step?"

"Well, I thought I would apply the analogy today."

"Yes, that seemed clear. But—what analogy? I don't remember your extracting the essential elements and then finding an analogy suggested by these elements—much less improvising on it. So let's see if we can't get back on track. Where did you find this analogy, by the way, this battle from the Korean War?"

"Well, my brother had been in the Marines, and I remember his telling me about that battle of the First Marine Division at the Inchon landing. It was just across the border, and they thought it would clinch a victory right at the start if they could control the Chosen Reservoir. But they were so outnumbered by the new Chinese Communist troops, they had to retreat and lost a lot of men. And it became known as a major defeat for us."

"I see. But shouldn't we first back up a bit? Let's review the steps to our "Seven-Step Solution" to get us back on track. I remember quite well your reading and paraphrasing. But today it seemed you not only went directly to your analogy, but you were already shaping that analogy to the form of the poem—the fifth step of our sequence. Let's go back now to the second step. Did you extract the essential elements of Tennyson's poem? What are they?"

"Well, first of all—a group of soldiers—professionals, trained to do their duty."

"Certainly."

"Then a much larger, more powerful force."

"Indeed, yes."

"And the defeat. So many lives lost. Though they fought very bravely."

"Quite so. Anything else?"

"I guess the reaction to their fight. They became known as heroes—even though they didn't succeed."

"Yes. That seems to be four essential elements. Anything else?"

Brian ponders. "I don't think so."

"Which explains why I missed an important ingredient in your work today. And why we must remind ourselves not to skip over any of the steps in this process. I think there is another, very essential element in this poem. Tell me, Brian—was the command to the Marines to seize the Chosen reservoir a mistake?"

"Not at all. It was a terrific idea—to control it would have been a major victory. They just had no suspicion that the Chinese would be so many and so strong."

"But don't you think it important that Tennyson reminds us that the charge at Balaclava was a colossal blunder? And that everyone—that is, all but the officer who gave the command—everyone knew it? And the men charged anyway. They were trained to obey, not to question, and so they obeyed. That mistake of an order seems to me a most necessary element in the poem. Isn't the poet also, perhaps, calling attention to the ineptitude of the British command? The rigid class system dictating only aristocratic, often incompetent, officers? As well as saluting the heroic men who obeyed without question, fought bravely in such a clearly impossible and suicidal charge?"

"Of course. But didn't I include that?"

"Apparently the order to the Marines to make a dash for the reservoir was not at all a mistake—you tell me that it seemed a very smart decision at the time."

"I see. So what do I do now?"

"Well, if the analogy you have selected turns out not to include all the essential elements, it seems to me you have two choices. Either you substitute quite another command for the sensible order to your Marines to capture that reservoir in Korea; you exchange the fact of an intelligent decision to make the attack with one from some other source in quite another situation—another such command that was clearly a "blunder." Which may be quite a problem. The other possibility is to choose another analogy altogether—one not so close to the specific details of the poem. We have to remind ourselves that a not uncommon obstacle to finding helpful analogies is the limitation of being too literal in our choices. That is why listing the essential elements in a more general way can open up your imagination to a much wider variety of choices for possible analogies. And these may indeed turn out to be much closer in spirit to the elements of the poem than a more literal analogy may be.

"Suppose we put it this way: Tennyson's main ingredients are: first, a small group of people—or even, perhaps, a single person—under orders to obey blindly, without question; second, an adversary clearly overwhelming; third an order to that small group—or person—to attack (or oppose) the larger— an order that everyone perceives to be a huge mistake; fourth, the obedient, obviously outclassed small group—or person—following the suicidal order blindly, bravely, in the line of duty, but at immense cost; and fifth and last, the reaction of the rest of us—to honor their bravery, but perhaps also effect a change in a system that leads to such incompetent, not to say immoral, leadership. If we put it this way, doesn't the range of possible analogies grow much wider? Doesn't this view of the essential elements suggest not only a military battle against such clear odds—but to a variety of other, clearly mistaken, albeit dutiful, and eventually heroic actions? Try to explore your own personal life, members of your family, your social or religious group, or larger elements of our society. And I think you may well find a more compelling analogy that will engage you more personally, as well as all the essential elements of the poem. What do you say?"

Though a bit crestfallen, Brian is game. "All right—I'll try." And we are both curious as to what our next session will bring.

❊ ❊ ❊

At our next session, Brian arrives with another analogy. He has found one that he thinks will incorporate all the five essential elements of Tennyson's poem. I ask him to tell me of it simply, making no attempt to couch it in the format of the poem—so that we may clearly test the analogy to see if it touches on all the required elements.

BRIAN: "Well, in 1876, the U.S. Cavalry, under General George Custer, ordered what turned out to be a suicidal attack on the assembled tribes of Indians at Little Big Horn. Under orders to rid the area of the local Indian tribe, Custer sent his Indian scout to ascertain the number of the enemy and report back to him. Custer had no idea that the Sioux, the Cheyennes, and other tribes had banded together to oppose him and that now their camp numbered about five thousand. When Custer asked his returning scout how many Indians were now opposing him, the scout pointed to the nearest tree. He indicated there were as many assembled Indian warriors as there were leaves on that tree."

"Then Custer decided to split up his force of six hundred soldiers into three groups—about two hundred each. Each group would attack from a different direction and thus surprise and overwhelm the assembled tribes. Custer's officers saw that this was a very risky plan, and they begged him not to do it. But the General was headstrong—in the Civil War he had been known for his often rash, peremptory commands. He wouldn't listen to his men. He insisted on his plan—and so his two hundred soldiers attacked five thousand Indians. Before the other groups could join them, Custer's men retreated and found themselves surrounded by several thousand of the Indians. It became a massacre, that famous—or shall we say infamous—annihilation. The men were all killed, while Custer continued fighting to the end. Some say he committed suicide. His other two groups, about four hundred men, found cover and managed to hold off the Indians until they retreated. I think this contains all five of the essential elements, doesn't it?"

We review the five: A small group of men; a vastly superior opposing force;

a clearly untenable plan of attack; the group dutifully obeying the order and fighting fiercely to the death; and the general reaction of horror to their annihilation, as well as awe, respect and honor for their heroic efforts. Yes, this analogy does encompass all the essential elements.

But I am still unsatisfied. This analogy seems to me too similar to Brian's initial attempt—a bit too impersonal and a bit too literal. But I refrain from sharing these thoughts with him now. Instead, I question Brian further. What suggested "Custer's Last Stand" to him? Aren't there any possible analogies that might be closer to him personally? And again, one not so literal, not necessarily of a military nature, another battle of a small force against an army. Why not perhaps one single person foolishly attacking a group?

This sets Brian to ruminating.

"Well, when I was a nurse at Pilgrim (a state hospital for the mentally ill), there were many times when staff members were assaulted by some of the more violent patients. I remember when we were "working short," as they called it— when some of the staff were off sick, and only a couple were left to deal with a bunch that were out of control. That was clearly against regulations. And those guys got beaten up pretty badly. Once I even had to bathe and shave fourteen men in the unstable ward. That was something else! And once a woman socked me right in the eye!"

Clearly, Brian has had a more personal experience with the essential elements of Tennyson's poem! And he begins to get my message. I intimate that perhaps a more personal, and less literal, analogy—further from the letter, yet closer to the spirit—of the original, may prove more compelling for him. I urge him to consider such encounters in the coming week; I am confident that he will find in this area of his own life an analogy that might engage him more deeply. But as to his assignment, since we want to move forward, trying to follow this sequence of steps, I make it plain that Brian has a clear choice. He may select another, more personal analogy, probably from his experiences as a nurse at Pilgrim; or he may continue with his "Custer's Last Stand" analogy— which does contain all the essential ingredients. The ball is in his court. And we part, both of us curious as to what he will bring forth next week.

※　　※　　※

At our next session, I first review the previous work Brian has done on the Tennyson poem: his initial choice of a literal analogy; then skipping some intermediate steps to a semi-improvised analogy, one already sized and shaped to the original. Then we discover that a major element is missing. We review the sequence of steps and realize we must proceed more slowly, bringing from some other area the missing ingredient, or else, finding another analogy altogether. Next, Brian found another fairly close analogy in Custer's famous "Last Stand" at Little Big Horn in 1876. I note that while this time all the necessary ingredients are present, it is again a fairly literal analogy. I suggest that a more personal analogy might prove more nourishing, and Brian is reminded of his experiences when he was a nurse in a State psychiatric hospital. I encourage him to explore this area but leave it to him to choose his next step. Either to continue with General Custer or explore this new area of personal experience.

Now Brian goes out of the studio; in a moment he returns in his topcoat, a small tape-recorder in his hand; he looks carefully around the room, evidently searching the space for something. He begins to speak his thoughts aloud as he looks about.

BRIAN: "May 23, 2003. One hundred and twenty-seven years after the Battle . . . yes, here's the marker (apparently reading from a marker) — "General George C. Custer . . . etc., etc. June 21, 1876 . . . six hundred men rode out . . . five thousand Sioux, Cheyenne and Sandhoques . . . etc., etc. (Now he speaks into the recorder, evidently reporting his findings). The main monument seems dry and intact . . . could use a little sandblasting and cleaning. (He looks around.) Most of the graves need work . . . get rid of all this overgrown brush . . . power-washing or blasting to see some of the names more clearly . . . all in all, yes, it seems quite doable."

Brian now sits on a bench and ruminates, recalling the bravery of Custer's men, outnumbered twenty-five to one, imagining their cries. He murmurs, "What a shame!" and speaks again into his recorder.

"Still a good possibility we can get this work done before the anniversary, one month from today." And he puts the recorder back in his pocket and strides off.

We examine the improvisation. Brian has imagined that there might be a scheduled memorial a month from today on the anniversary of "Custer's Last Stand." He has created a government official who has come to the site to report on whatever restoration work is needed and to estimate what chance there may be to get the site ready for a commemorative ceremony a month from today.

It seems a reasonable analogy to the poem, but again I am not satisfied.

"Yes, I think you have all the elements in this new analogy. But again I think something is missing. How did you arrive at this analogy?"

"Well, I tried to find various ways to get closer to recalling the event. I thought of an archeologist contracted to explore the place; then I remembered a movie I saw on television where the heroine stopped at the site of a National Monument. And it seemed a logical connection for me."

"Yes, I would agree. You were able to cover all the bases. But still, isn't there a major difference between your improvised thoughts today and Tennyson's poem? What would you say is clearly missing?"

"The rhyming and the repetition?"

"That comes later—as we size and shape your material to the poet's format. No, I think it is a matter of what we call Tone. All your thoughts in this analogy today were logical and to the point. You were reasonable, respectful, even reverent—but almost detached. And we could hardly say that of Tennyson. What we cannot ignore in his "Charge . . ." is the passion, the energy, the sweep that seems to capture the excitement of that event. This highly-charged energy permeates his reciting of the facts, as well as his salute to the self-sacrificing heroes."

"But I—"

"Yes, I realize this is a work-in-progress. And you could very well build to a much more heightened involvement that could approach the tone of Tennyson. But I must return to your own personal recollections of your experience as a nurse in the psychiatric wards at that state hospital. Even when you first shared it with me, you seemed to connect to some of the energy and strong reactions you had felt at the time—because it was your own experience! I strongly suggest that you explore an analogy based on those experiences. For no matter how detailed is your research on the Marines at the Chosen Reservoir in the Korean War—or Custer's Last Stand—it still will not have the vibrant tone, the vivid color of a personal experience. And if you need to research history for an analogy, why not research the very event Tennyson celebrates? If we have to build a play from historical facts, why create another play altogether?"

"Only a personally experienced or observed analogy can provide the immediate emotional involvement that we seek. Yes, I can hear Stella Adler and Sanford Meisner stoutly proclaiming that the sole source of feeling for the actor is the text:

'It's all in the text! Look to the text!'

"But it is the conviction of my teacher, Lee Strasberg, as well as my own experience, that while a first-rate text can often provide the necessary inspiration, just as often, it may not. Research will deepen our knowledge of the event and our understanding of the text—but we still have to create the inner life that will make that text our own. It still requires our personal emotional involvement. And for that essential ingredient, what Lee called "personalization" and Uta Hagen called "substitution," I rely on an analogy. Whatever we call it, it remains the quickest and surest way to provide the actor's personal involvement that alone can bring immediate life to any text."

My conclusion is inevitable: An orderly, organic path to Living on Stage can be learned in a structured, sequential training process. This process will enable the actor to select and accomplish expressive stage tasks; it will enable him to communicate truthfully, as if for the very first time; and it will teach him to bring life to the text with his own immediate, personal involvement. The resulting sequence of vital dramatic problems can be charted in an Acting Score that can be repeated with dynamic truth and effective spontaneity. Through this conscious process, imaginative realities created by the actor, author, director, designers, and composer working together can be made manifest in convincing, compelling performances on stage or screen.

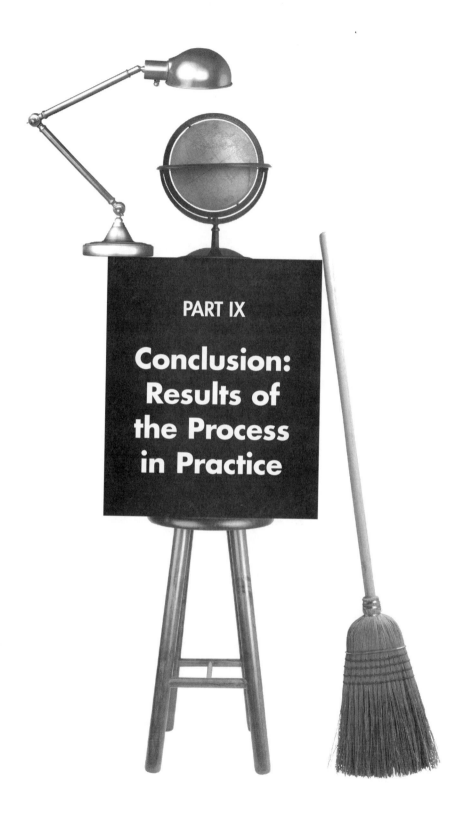

PART IX

**Conclusion:
Results of
the Process
in Practice**

CHAPTER 18

Former Students Performing

September 1999

Dear Fellow "Witcoverian":

You will be pleased to know that Walt is finally writing his book. Yes, that one he's been talking about for years—and that's remained stuck in his head all this time.

Last year we challenged him. We offered to help him into moving his book ideas out of his head and his daily teaching in his studio—and help get them "from the stage onto the page." Where they could be spread around, "encouraging young things to grow."

And we've been doing that. Walt's already compiled an introductory memoir detailing his formative years, as he became an actor, a director, and a teacher. But the book on his process, as it developed over his years of teaching, is proving more difficult. It's to be called LIVING ON STAGE. It sounds like a winner and could make an important contribution.

Now we need your help. Walt maintains that the true authors of this book should be ourselves—his former students. We hope you'll agree. And agree to help—by sharing your experiences in acquiring and using Walt's training. Your specific examples and personal particulars will be most valuable.

Please send your answers to the enclosed questionnaire by December 1st if you can. And don't be stingy with your reminiscences! Send your replies by U.S. Mail or email.

And if you have any questions or suggestions, don't hesitate to mention them. All our thanks.

The "Witcoverian" Committee

Thus my eight committed former students, banding together in the fall of 1999, sent out the following questionnaire to a hundred fellow former students:

Witcover *Living on Stage* Questionnaire

1. When and where did you train with Walt Witcover? Did you have any previous training? How long did you work with Walt? Did you perform in any of his projects? Which?

2. What were some of the most memorable moments of your work with Walt?

3. What other experiences did you share in, or witness, that might typify Walt's approaches?

4. What were the particulars that you would say distinguish Walt's processes from those of other teachers and/or directors with whom you have worked?

5. Has Walt's training influenced your career? How have you applied it in your work on stage or screen? In other areas of your life? — When and where? In what ways?

Please add any further relevant memories or comments.

THANK YOU!

By the winter of 2000, when I actually got around to starting this book, some thirty-five had responded. Another dozen contributed their experiences through tape-recorded interviews. Now, four years later, I can think of no better conclusion for this account of my training process than these responses. Herewith, then, excepting those answers specifically about my directing (saved for my next book!), are some of the memories and comments of these former students:

※　※　※

"Among the teachers I've learned from, Walt Witcover has been a major influence. His teaching is inspired, comprehensive and thorough . . . Walt was very demanding—he wouldn't let a thing go by. You couldn't cheat. It's all about being in the moment—being honest. And it works. Walt taught me always to examine. Where is this character coming from, and where is she going? What does she want, and what's the obstacle? And the most important question, 'What would you do, as the character, if you weren't doing this scene?' Later, I would go to him for coaching, for help in my auditions. And he was a great coach—wonderful."

—BARBARA BARRIE,
Actress, Writer

"I was tied up in cerebral knots with [a famous teacher] when I discovered Walt. His sense memory exercises freed me. I had thought I was taking too much time, that I was boring, but Walt said, 'Take your time.' It was very liberating. Another aspect of Walt's teaching that helps me so much—he taught us that whatever part you play, no matter how small, the play or movie is about *You*.

"I remember working with Walter Matthau in a small scene in a film. He comes to my office, and my task is to stop him from getting in. A simple scene, but I was with the star, so I was somewhat uptight. I remembered Walt's teaching and gave myself things to do at my desk, so I felt I lived there, it was my turf, and I wouldn't anticipate. After our reading the scene, he began to improvise. When I told him the person he came to see wasn't in, he said, 'I'll just wait.' That wasn't in the script at all, so I responded, and we went on from there, each of us trying to outwit the other. We did this four or five times, each time differently, and I met whatever excuse he would give me—I countered him every time. So then, when we filmed the scene as written, it was no problem at all, and it was fresh every take. Walt had helped me to trust myself, to feel that I had a right to be there, even with Walter Matthau—and to play each moment for itself.

"I found I was trusted to work with stars. Another interesting scene was in a film with Dennis Quaid. I played a homeless woman who found the missing cufflinks by the river. Again, I created a life for this character: it was November and we were shooting outside; so, waiting for the take, I wandered about in costume, connecting with a possible prior life for my character. I used all the work I'd done with Walt. And I worked well with Dennis Quaid. He kept asking challenging questions of me, and I responded in character.

"In film, the camera is so close, you don't have to act at all. I connect with the character, her relationships, circumstances and what she wants. I go back to Walt's basic technique—I try simply to talk and listen to my partner and to live in the moment—not to plan results. And one of Walt's basic principles is so helpful on the set: you have a right to be there, the movie is about *You*. When I go on a movie set, I'm nobody. They want me to be real; and my job is to create the conditions that allow me to be real. Walt's technique connects me with the character elements in myself. And then, I simply go moment-to-moment. Only if you're Walter Matthau or Dennis Quaid do you get all you want on a movie set. The rest of us have to bring what we need. And that's where Walt's techniques are such a help."

—PRUDENCE BARRY,
Actress, Director, Writer, Teacher

"I learned from Walt that there is a technique to acting. A crafted way to approach a text. That you don't just memorize a bunch of words, put on a nice dress, and stumble onto the stage 'saying your lines.' I learned what it takes to become an actor. After the first three months with Walt, I landed my first off-Broadway role. While I remained Walt's student for the next two years, not missing a single class, I went from one Off-Broadway role to another. By the time I stopped class, I'd become an original member of 'The Electric Company,' the Children Television Workshop's PBS show. I was making a living as an actor! I even won a Grammy I shared with Bill Cosby and Rita Moreno.

"Walt helped me understand where truth resides on stage or screen: not in saying the words, but in the emotional exploration required to give the words, any words, flesh, blood, and bone. Walt is thorough. He encouraged me to be thorough, and I've never allowed myself to be otherwise. I've had a thirty-year career as a working actor on stage, in television, on tape and film and on the big screen. I was even nominated for an Emmy! Thoroughness is the key, and I learned that from Walt Witcover.

"Walt's technique lays a solid foundation. It enables me to return time after time to the basic premise he insisted on: be specific. That exhortation has never failed me. I hold on to it always and particularly when I'm unsure of how to approach a particularly big acting challenge. Walt is a cornerstone of my professional life. I always know what I'm doing when I approach a role because Walt taught me how to go about it. I've also used his technique to help others. It simply can't be beat."

—LEE CHAMBERLIN,
Actress, Writer, Teacher

"Walt's training is about trying to use yourself as fully as possible. Own up to how you feel, acknowledge and accept it, and then use it. His process helped me out as much as a person as it did as an actor. Being alive on stage is no different than being alive inside. I now know how to make the quick choices needed in television and still fulfill a character the way Walt trained me—when and where, what and why and who.

"Once I was playing a defense attorney on *Law and Order*. The first day I have to sum up the case, but I haven't met any of the cast yet. I hadn't met the rape victim or the guy I'm defending, the rapist. I had never met the star, Sam Waterston. Everybody is new to me, and I have to face the jury and sum up this case. And I don't know anybody! I've been in this situation before, so I know how to relax myself and tune into relationship, circumstances and intention. Never having met Sam Waterston, the only relationship I could go on was Sam Waterston the actor, not the lawyer he is playing. He is an accomplished actor who has a very successful TV show. Now he's my opposition in the drama—that's our relationship. All I can go on is how I actually feel about him. That is some of the work that Walt has helped me understand and use. Maybe this defense attorney I'm playing is of low status compared to this prosecutor who works for the state—and maybe that's how I actually feel about Sam, someone who is much more successful than me. He has a TV show, he does movies. I'm just back in New York from Hollywood, I'm up-and-coming. There is no talking to Sam about relationship, no talking to the director about relationships. It's got to be right there—right away. So the most immediate thing I could access, the most appropriate circumstantially and emotionally, was *my actual relationship with Sam Waterston*. So that's where I started. The situation is I want to win the case. Sam also wants to win the case. So then I manipulate a little more—I want to show Sam I can beat him. I don't care if he has a hit TV show, I don't care if he's doing movies. I can damn well do that too. I'm going to beat him. So I tried to use that kind of actual, immediate stuff. And it worked.

"With Walt's training, you can take whatever is coming at you and then figure out how to use it and make the adjustments. In the TV world where I've been for the past fifteen years, I've had to adjust to whatever was thrown at me.

"Another example of how Walt's training came to my aid in the pinch on the set was when I did one scene in a movie with Marlon Brando. I was called to replace another actor who hadn't seemed strong enough to confront Brando. I was sent the script, and on the plane to Montreal I thought and thought. Nothing could possibly make me feel equal to Marlon Brando. My role is that of a mobster, sent to collect monies owing to my boss from another mobster, Brando. My character is hardly afraid of the Brando character—but how can I, Robert Clohessy get to feel more powerful than this other mobster, Marlon Brando? Feeling about him the way I do, there's absolutely no way I can stand up to Marlon Brando. I am so intimidated!

"But my training with Walt comes to my aid. I first admit this problem to myself. In my innermost self, Marlon Brando is definitely more powerful that I am. How can I possibly stand up to him, exert power over him? I just thought about the problem. On the set the next day, I meet Marlon Brando. The director briefly explains the scene to us. When he has left, Marlon takes me aside and re-directs the entire scene, line by line, telling me just how he wants it to be played. Now Marlon Brando is controlling the scene, taking over the direction as well! He's manipulating me! So my problem is still there, only worse.

"Well, while they're setting the lights and we're sitting around waiting, I continue thinking. And this is where Walt's training comes in. I realize I have to find a way to get over my own actual awe of my scene partner. For the relationship in the scene to work, I must feel equal to, or even better than, Marlon Brando. How can I possibly do that? And then I remember what I've heard about his life and his difficulties as a father—how his daughter committed suicide and his son is in jail for drugs. And I realize that I seem to be succeeding as a father. My boys are thriving, they're at the top of their classes and teams, growing up just great. And now I have a right handle to the relationship in the scene. I found the path to make me feel bigger than even Marlon Brando!

"It's defining the same problems Walt taught us—relationship, circumstance, intention. Always to question. And always the same acting problem— *to make it real to myself.* Not just knowing the answers, that's intellectual. But it's got to live inside of me. Also, as Walt taught us, you must then be totally relaxed. So you're open to follow your impulses. You trust them to take you wherever they go. And whatever happens then is real and alive."

—ROBERT CLOHESSY, Actor

"Barbara Barrie first pointed me in Walt's direction after she and I had worked together at the American Shakespeare Festival at Stratford, Connecticut. Taking her advice was one of the best things I've ever done. I cannot tell to what extent Walt's talent has profoundly influenced my life. Everything about my perceptions of the human condition and the ways that painters, poets, actors and musicians express themselves has been affected by Walt's gentle yet laser-like intuition about all of it.

I have had the good fortune to be nominated by the London critics for their Best Actor Award along with Albert Finney and Christopher Plummer. That was a very nice thing. However my experience with Walt was even better. He helped me to believe that I was truly an actor worthy of the title. He taught me how to get to the core of the human and the essence of the moment. He helped to make it possible for me to earn a living as an actor for forty years".

—ALEX CORD, Actor,
Academy Award–winner

"I had a good singing voice and a good personality, so I got to work in local dinner theatres in my home town, Charlotte, North Carolina. But something in me knew that I didn't know what I was doing, that something was amiss when I sang on stage. If something went wrong, I didn't know how to make it better. And the director of whatever school or community theatre show I had performed in couldn't help me. Now, the New York professionals I worked with in the dinner theatres told me I'd have to go to New York or L.A. to learn to act and pursue a career. But I didn't know where to go for training. On my first day in New York I happened to go to the HB Studio. I audited three teachers and I found that Walt Witcover was different. Walt was a revelation. To hear him talk with each student after the exercise or scene was so to the point. He articulated so clearly, it made so much sense. It was intimidating, but inspiring.

"His method is so deliciously step-by-step. What was so extraordinary about his technique class, when you did an exercise it was yours. Walt never asked, 'How do you think you did?' But 'What were you trying to do?' He then might say, 'I didn't see it.' Not 'You didn't do it.' He made me see clearly what I had to do. I learned how to work, how to talk about acting intelligently, to define the tasks and the steps. And Walt was very respectful of my privacy. He didn't force me to reveal what personal memories or imaginings I was using. He respected everything that made me different, that made me *me*.

"I went back home and helped out local talent in summer theatres. I was too late to audition for roles, but I said I could teach an acting class. Was there one for me? So the director formed a class for me to teach. I was scared and called Walt for help. He encouraged me—'Just stay one step ahead of the students,' he said. I was terrified. But I'd learned how to teach from being Walt's student for ten years. I used his method. He taught me how to stay out of the way— not to impose on the student my interpretation or how I thought the scene should go. And I was successful—my students got better. They still keep in touch, and one even keeps calling from L.A. for my guidance.

"Walt gave me confidence, the ability to approach a part. I learned how to start with the words and music and build to a living performance. I found I could act. I know how to work. Sometimes I've had to do 'instant performing,' and I'd go to Walt and say, 'I'm terrified about this role (or song) I have to perform in three days.' And he'd help me conquer my fears—by focusing on what I could do in the time I had—and to be there in the moment."

—LENORE FUERSTMAN,
Singer, Actress

"I'm an opera singer who was always interested in the drama of opera. But I didn't know how to channel my dramatic instincts on stage. So when I met Walt I was looking for some place to explore acting. It was most fortuitous timing. I started training in his private acting classes, then in both Basic Technique and Scene Technique when he moved to the HB Studio in 1960, and I continued for many years. I was very stimulated by his logical questions, his not demanding immediate results, his take-your-time, organic process. Then he started a class for musical theatre—for singing actors or actor-singers. And that was very exciting for me. I was ready to continue the logical organic approaches Walt espoused in his non-singing classes and now apply them to songs and arias, to opera. We found lots of clues to acting in the music as well as the word.

"Our ground-breaking, four-year 'Experiment in Lyric Theatre,' the Actors Studio *La Traviata* that Walt directed, grew out of my work on the role of Violetta in his HB Musical Theatre classes. We never intended to tackle the entire Act I, much less stage the full four-act opera, when we began; we were just trying to solve artistic problems that excited us and that were not addressed in opera as it was usually presented. Now I can help young singers in this role, as well as many others, because of the exciting work I did with Walt.

He inspired me to stretch my abilities and tap facets of my talent that were dormant, to release fears and inhibitions, and to free my imagination and my will as a performer. My work as an operatic stage director and teacher of acting for singers has been helped immeasurably, and the work with Walt set the foundation for the success I enjoy with my own students.

"I began teaching at Princeton, and I brought what I'd learned from Walt. His training is so well structured that I felt able to start teaching with his process. I grew in confidence; so then I started a workshop for acting in opera with another classical singer, my colleague Peter Schlosser, also a student of Walt. We had worked together in several of Walt's musical theatre projects at Masterworks Laboratory Theatre. Later I taught at SUNY–Purchase, again an Opera Workshop/Acting for Singers. I continued to adapt Walt's training exercises for young singers, and they proved extremely helpful. I presented an evening of operatic scenes with my students, and it made quite an impression; so next I directed a full-scale production of *Madama Butterly*. This was a tremendous success, the College President saying it was the best opera he'd ever seen. And we'd achieved such fine results by applying Walt's process, finding a truthful moment-to-moment logic of behavior suggested in the play and the music. Now opera singers come to me for help on a particular new role — Harolyn Blackwell, for one. I help them find a logical lifeline, as I learned to do with Walt. And it helps them as it helped me.

"Walt has had a profound influence on me. I've grown artistically, and I find teaching young singers very fulfilling. When I began teaching Acting for Singers, I felt I didn't know enough to teach voice, that it was too great a responsibility. Now I teach voice. I'm able to pinpoint precise vocal problems and instill a correct technique, as well as productive ways to approach a role. And I send my students who have dramatic potential to Walt—where they greatly benefit, as I did, from his inspiring and immensely practical training."

—LEYNA GABRIELE,
Opera Singer, Stage Director, Teacher

"Working with Walt in *Salon-Comédie* was an outstanding learning as well as pleasurable experience. It was the play in which I lost my stage fright. Thanks to the exercises and scenes we had been doing in class, my attention was very much on what I was doing on stage.

Walt's training has also been an integral part of my approach to the songs that I sing. When I begin working a new song, I first analyze the music. Then I read the poetry, put the characters in a specific place and time and give them a history. Only then can I begin to work on the ultimate interpretation. I believe this is a legitimate outgrowth of my training with Walt. And that training combined with my own musical talent has made my career rich."

—CAROLYN BOSTON GEER, Singer

"Only after Walt directed me [in *Maedchen in Uniform* off-Broadway] did I study with him at HB Studios. There is no one I have worked with before or since, either as teacher or director, who allowed me the absolute freedom to 'investigate' (Walt's pet word) characters in action. Nor can I clearly distinguish between his directorial and teaching skills, as they always seemed to me part and parcel of the same process. In rehearsal, after Walt had offered me nothing by way of criticism or praise for two weeks, one day I approached him: 'Won't you tell me how I'm doing? If I'm okay, I mean?' He answered, 'Just keep on working.' I was twenty. I didn't know it then, but Walt was teaching me the habits of art. After performing on tour and on Broadway [in *Jane Eyre*], I returned as his student, and those habits were reinforced. I had prepared a scene as Sonia in Chekhov's *Uncle Vanya*. Walt asked afterward, 'What were you doing?' 'That's the whole problem,' I admitted. 'I don't know what I'm doing in this scene!' To which he posed a series of questions involving Sonia's relationships. Anxious as always to show myself an interesting, intelligent person, I began promptly to answer. At which Walt's hand shot up with his habitual command: 'Don't make any decisions!' An immediate verbal response might serve an academic, but not an artistic purpose. Walt's questions were meant to be thought about and around, then mulled over; the answers were to be played out in our scenes."

—CAROL HEBALD,
Actress, Writer, Teacher

"As a beginning student I marveled at how Walt could analyze a scene and pinpoint the way in which the student was stuck, in such a way that the person could correct it. I now understand how much Walt was influenced by psychoanalysis. However, the most important thing I learned from Walt involved the way I approached singing a song. I always tried to understand the intention of the 'character' singing the song. No matter how archaic or florid the text, I tried to find 'the reality of the scene.' Though the sound may not always be perfect, when the action of the 'scene' makes internal sense, the ultimate result will be much more profound."

—HELEN TROWBRIDGE HOFFMAN,
Singer, Psychotherapist

"I met Walt at my audition for his Masterworks Laboratory Theatre production of *The Gondoliers*. As I was singing my audition piece, Walt got out of his chair, grabbed a big pillow, and began moving around the room playing catch with me. Certainly, it was one of the more releasing and relaxing audition experiences I have had. I was cast as one of the leads. As Marco, singing 'Take a pair of sparkling eyes,' Walt would not allow me to deliver the song without understanding what Marco is going through, why he was singing it.

Once we discovered that the song was about Marco's loneliness, and the possibility that he might not see his wife for months or years, the lyrics took on a special meaning which was far more real to me. I was also involved with the physical reality of the moment, and the action of wiping down all the chairs and swabbing the floor while singing grounded me in the action of the scene. The physical task was an expressive tool that helped me punctuate my singing.

Walt weds the music to the life of the actor on stage. He analyzes the script and music with his actors, then sets about to create the physical life in which these characters exist. And then he asks his actors to experience and experiment with the movement of a scene.

Walt's training has been of great help in all my singing work. For over twenty-five years, his work on finding the humanity in any song in any style has been with me. Even when performing recitals without any staging, I have felt Walt's influence. I create character situations for all the songs; I analyze the music to see if the composer has offered dramatic hints. This was particularly important in performances of Schubert's song cycles in which a character must be sustained through more then twenty songs, and through a wide range of physical and emotional experiences.

I now am encouraging students of my own, in both music and theatre programs, to begin to find the inner life of everything they sing. If I can help some of them the way Walt helped me, I will be fortunate indeed."

—MICHAEL HUME, Singer, Actor,
Musical Director, Teacher

"My acting work was so enriched by Walt Witcover's technique. It's a technique I still incorporate in my work, even in my singing . . . One of my all-time favorite pieces of my acting work was done in Walt's class. In Chekhov's *Marriage Proposal*, for the first time I was totally able to use my Mother's compulsive cleaning habits and set up the obstacles that made the character's situation real, a moment-to-moment happening and tragically funny. When I'm working on music, I look at the words, listen to the music, and let my imagination roam until it comes up with an idea of who and where. Since Walt's technique of acting is part of my technique, Walt is with me every day that I am singing or acting."

—ANNETTE HUNT,
Actress, Singer

"Walt cast me in his Alfred de Musset project, *Salon-Comédie*. It was a turning point for me. Walt's approach was slower and deeper than any I'd had before. I'd heard of a more 'process' approach, but never experienced it. Now I found that process so helpful in enabling me to find a much richer character. For the first time I felt, and was, part of the creative process. Walt taught me to explore in rehearsal—and also to continue that exploring process ever after, even in performance.

I carried Walt's approach on to commercial performing on Broadway—in *Me and My Girl*, *The Rothschilds*, *Cats*, *Grand Hotel*, *Lost in Yonkers*. I keep it fresh by 'tinkering.' Fellow actors marvel how I keep developing the role during the run. I mean in small details. You must stay true to staging demands, words and music, particular moments in time and space; I must continue to give security to my fellow actors in previously determined stage patterns. But the approaches to them can be fresh.

I give credit to Walt's inspiration for my ability to keep it fresh—to give myself permission to do that. He opened me to the possibility of discarding the discoveries of yesterday, to come, in the next performance, to the same problems of situation, relationships and intentions—and find fresh solutions. Walt teaches a structure that deconstructs artifice. It's a way of getting there by throwing yesterday's results away. It helps me stay fresh and continue to be creative during rehearsals and also performances, especially in a long run—like two-and-a-half years in *Beauty and the Beast*.

I'm a working actor, I think, largely because of my natural gifts. But Walt Witcover took me to another level. He crow-barred me out of my cave so I could find something I realized was much better. And I never went back."

—TIM JEROME, Actor,
Singer, Producer

"My most memorable acting moment for me in Walt's class was when I found a pencil my partner must accidentally have dropped. This accident and how I reacted to it, how it fueled me and created readings of lines that were completely fresh made the scene take off. And I got into the Actors Studio from that scene. And I got my first agent at the Actors Studio. And it was because Walt taught us the importance of the unplanned event, and how to use it.

Walt's patience always amazed me. People would come into a class and think they knew how to act or how to play a scene, and Walt would almost never tell them otherwise. He would let them learn this on their own through his guidance. I was one of these examples, and looking back I laugh at my *hubris*. But I am grateful to Walt for his gentleness and his commitment. He would never give up on anyone, no matter how off the track they might appear.

Walt gave me a system of how to create a character. There was a format to find and create a character out of one's own experience—real or imagined. It was specific and easy to follow. Maybe not easy to do, but easy to follow. I use it to this day.

I recently did a film in which I play a man who has a complete breakdown. I mean just sobbing, unable to stand up or speak. I was so scared of this scene when I read the script that I didn't care if I was hired because I didn't know if I could do it. And even if I did, I didn't know if I could repeat it the way you need to be able to do in a film. I remembered Walt telling back in class about 'putting it in the oven early in the day,' 'keep it simmering.' I did so, and on the first take I broke like a child. The director and everyone was so happy, but I stayed separate and focused because I knew I needed to stay with what was happening to me. Sure enough there was a problem with the camera, and they didn't get the shot. The director was furious, I was upset, and now a delay happened of half an hour. Now my emotion felt gone, but I knew from my training with Walt that it was still there; I just needed to relax and trust that it would come back. It did, not on the next take, but the one after. I think this was the hardest scene for me that I had ever done, and I would not have been able to do it without Walt's training. Walt would never tell you what to do. He would support you, encourage you and guide you, but when you got it—it felt like you did it all by yourself. And you knew you could do it again. For an actor this is essential."

—ROBERT KERBECK, Actor

"In order to better understand the actor's process, I took a year and a half of Walt's acting classes concurrently with his Directing Workshops. I was overwhelmed with what I didn't know! This was as enlightening as the classes in directing. I feel it has made me a better, more sensitive director, who is also less easily led astray when actors go off track. Walt stressed process above all else, stating that any focus on results too early will prevent discovery. I have found that he is absolutely right. And in comedy, to forget trying to be funny— that is the author's job. The straighter you play the scene, the funnier it will be. He also made us aware that good acting is so invisible that the audience should feel a slight sting of embarrassment that they are eavesdropping on real lives. And this could only be achieved when the actor internalized the character, when every word and action organically became the actor's own.

Walt taught me the 'right food' to nourish the actor with. Beginning directors often starved, stuffed, or malnourished their actors with unnecessary junk food. And I learned how important it was to provide an encouraging, safe, nonjudgmental environment in which actors can experiment, make mistakes, even fall on their faces, in the search for better work."

—BOB KISS, Photographer,
Director, Teacher

"After having studied with Walt for about a year and a half, I had graduated to working on monologues of my own choice. It really gives me pause to think that I had been requiring my college acting students to work on a monologue after only about two weeks worth of study. Hermione's public defense from *The Winter's Tale* was my choice. She is defending herself against her husband's false accusation that she has betrayed him with his old friend. I had been working on this piece for about three weeks without much progress. Then, one evening Walt asked me to endow any student in the class as someone in my life who had wrongfully accused me of something—and then to respond to that person. There was no time to plan: I had to react quickly. At that time in my life I was going through a grueling divorce, so my ex-husband came immediately to my mind.

About four years earlier my husband and I had adopted our infant daughter from Poland. It was, of course, particularly challenging raising a child as a professional woman. In addition to being a wife and a mother, I'm a professor of theatre, chair of the college's Arts and Humanities division, as well as founder, producer, and artistic director of a professional, Equity theatre-in-residence at the college. I'm also an actor and a student of acting, studying with Walt. Of course, I was vulnerable and on the edge of feeling guilty about not being an at-home mom.

So without thinking, only feeling, I dove into a confrontation. I approached a guy in class who reminded me of my ex. Cautiously, as I had done so often, I began with, 'Excuse me, Doc, can I talk with you a minute?' I didn't have any idea what I was holding back. I tried to be calm and logical without being emotional, but the floodgates had been opened. Immediately I was transported to my husband's study, trying not to cry, trying to explain to him that his accusation that I was a 'lousy mother' was untrue and hurtful.

This was only the beginning. Throughout the rest of this encounter I was taken on a moment-by-moment ride of what seemed an unending roller coaster of emotion. At no time in my experience as an actor had I ever been pulled so deeply into the vast ocean of my emotions and had them so available to me to ride. The whole experience—from anger to fear to rage to guilt to pain to vengeance to regret to pride to the edge of desperation and back—it felt like a rapidly swelling tide that I just couldn't hold back. As though I had grabbed onto the tail of a frenzied shark and was being pulled about frantically as it thrashed about. The flood was so overwhelming that I just let it swirl around me. And by allowing the flood to sweep me along, I was now letting it take me to some kind of emotional resolution.

What an amazing experience as an actor this was for me. Walt had, over time, by his keenly crafted process, brought me to the moment when I could use my developing endowment skills to take me to a place I had never been before. A place where I could be completely in the moment and discover the wealth of emotional depth that I had never before tapped as an actor.

At the end of this amazing ride, Walt said to me, 'Now, suppose you are Hermione. Or Hermione is you. Your husband has unjustly accused you of betrayal. What are you going to say to him?' I really believe that this was the most pivotal moment in my life as an actor. Using Shakespeare's words, I grabbed that shark's tail again, allowing it to take me where it would. I began to live as Hermione, pouring my own emotions into the text.

As a teacher of acting, I began to look at my task differently after this experience. Rather than ask my students to dive into script analysis and character development immediately, I start them on simple tasks—honest moments they can believe and live. One of the most important things I've learned from Walt is that living happens moment by moment, as should acting, for in the end they are the same thing."

—VALERIE LASH,
Actress, Teacher, Producer

"Before my recent concert [at the Weill Recital Hall at Carnegie Hall], I was fighting a severe allergy attack which caused a constant irritation in my throat. I did not want to give this concert up, and I decided that whatever voice comes out of my throat, I am going to make art, and be honest in my intentions no matter what.

And the tools that I learned from you carried me through and were a tremendous help. I really would like to thank you for all the great things that I learned from you. You really taught me how to connect a certain text with an inner, most intimate and meaningful picture and situations, so that the emotions can be re-Lived on Stage. Thank you so much!"

—BAVAT MAROM,
Opera Singer

"During my first year training with Walt, I had stopped doing theatre. I really wanted to learn something about this craft of acting. After the first year or so, I happened to be at a theatre that I had helped get on its feet. The night was an open call for auditions for all the theatres in Baltimore. I decided to watch the auditions. After an hour or so, there was a break. By then, I'd decided that there were a lot of new people, including new directors, and that maybe I should audition. I also wanted to show that I had (hopefully) improved during my self-imposed exile from performing. I asked the man running things if I could audition right after the break. 'Sure,' he said, then began telling people to get back in their seats. I borrowed his lighter and fumbled for a cigarette. Walking out on stage as people were still talking, I pulled out the lighter, lit my cigarette, looked up for a second, caught the eye of someone in the fourth row, smiled, and said, 'Yes, I have tricks in my pocket . . .'"

I nailed the piece! As I ended with 'I think the rest of the play will explain itself,' I pointed to the stage and began to walk out past the seats toward the door. The entire theatre broke out into applause. One director leaned over as I passed and said, 'Wow. I really thought you were talking to us—about some theatre business, until you were several lines into it.' I laughed and said, 'That was the idea.' And went home. I had nailed the piece—so I really had learned from Walt. This stuff really was working for me."

—MARTY McDONOUGH, Actor

"Walt's training saved me when I first did a film and had to re-shoot some scenes for the close-ups of my face supposedly from over my partner's shoulder. But there was no partner there now—What could I do? A star can ask or demand that his partner be there, and some generous stars will often be there for the younger supporting player. But there was no one there for me then. So I remembered Walt's sense memory exercises where I'd learned to recall and project an absent image. This training came to my aid, and I was able to imagine and relate to my non-existent partner for that close-up just fine.

In Walt's classes, I kept a journal of the exercises, the better to remember them and for future use when I might be away from Walt. And it served me well when I was in rehearsal—it helped remind me of processes to find a solution whenever I had an acting problem. And in film, shot way out of sequence, I keep a journal to remind myself where I am in the character's life on each day of shooting . . .

I also learned from Walt to keep my personal images and analogies to myself. Walt would say, 'I don't want to know what you're thinking, your own subtext. But if you share what you're searching for, I'll help you to find an appropriate analogy. But you must choose it. And keep it private.' And he was so right . . .

My first television show called on several of Walt's techniques. I wanted the leading role, a juvenile delinquent, a creep, a hoodlum. Even though it was summer, I picked a heavy leather jacket to wear to the audition. And I took out my brace of front teeth. I prepared to live as the character, even on the bus going uptown. In the outer office I played this character for the receptionist, smiling to show my front-toothed gap, and speaking as my character might. I had to wait for three hours to read, and I stayed 'in character' the whole time. But I got the part!

Another problem came up in playing this hoodlum who terrorizes a subway car of innocent victims. Walt had taught me the danger of letting the author's point of view influence my acting choices. While I, Tony Musante, fervently agreed with the message of the drama, that this was an awful kid who needed help—I realized I couldn't play the part unless I could find my character's viewpoint. I couldn't look *at* my character, but *with* him. I had to find his own values that justified such behavior that we think is deplorable. Walt had taught me I had to find in him something that might make him a hero in his own eyes. Finally I reasoned that he was trying to protect, and then revenge, his buddy. As my character, I was right and all the others were wrong. Everything I did was justified by my code. I found a point of view that was not the author's or my own, or intended for the audience, but for my character. And it worked. I was successful. And I got the role in the film, *Incident*, made of that TV show, *Ride with Terror*. And from that came the successful TV series, *Toma*, and my busy acting career on stage, TV, and in films, both here and in Italy, ever since.

—TONY MUSANTE, Actor

"What most distinguishes Walt's processes from those others I've worked with is his clarity of intent. Any process of Walt's is expertly crafted to facilitate the discovery of facts and circumstances of the character's life and times that might ignite the actor's imagination and feed his sense of truth. And, while most of the directors I've worked with are more or less eager to get blocking and performances 'set,' Walt encourages the process of experimentation and discovery to continue even on into performance.

Walt's training has been invaluable in all my acting experiences. It has provided me with the foundation necessary to succeed in this business."

—CRAIG NOBLE, Actor

"The true value of Walt's training showed when I went from his technique and scene classes out into the real world of theatre and films. I'm a member of Equity, SAG and AFTRA and have worked off-Broadway and in movies and TV. I had a nice role in Madonna's first film, *Desperately Seeking Susan*. In every area I worked in and in every production, there was not a single time when I did not use what I learned from Walt. He helped me to be independent and self-reliant; yet his technique also enabled me to work in complete harmony with others, whatever their training or background."

—D. J. O'NEILL, Actor

"In a university where teaching styles were conflicted and widely varied, Walt's class was distinctive. It stood apart from the others in that it focused on learning and process, and not on performing and results. [The college] described and presented itself as a school offering 'progressive' or 'avant-garde' theatre. But it offered no method for an actor. Most teachers simply demanded that an actor be emotionally uninhibited. Walt provided each actor the right environment and a clear method to assist with achieving emotional freedom. It helped me realize how, as an actor, I am the *instrument* and that I must acknowledge this when preparing a role. I always use what I learned from him. It is useful when solving any creative problem to have a clear method that marks the path to a creative solution."

—BRETT REED, Actor

"I was trained as a classical singer. I was impressed when Walt played the piano himself for my audition, as well as by his unconventional ideas. I studied six or seven years with Walt—in his HB Studio basic technique and scene classes, and then in his musical theatre and his directing classes. He gave me an insight into what opera could be.

All my work is influenced by Walt. I credit Walt for my concern for truthful behavior. The only drawback is that it makes it very hard to watch traditional productions of opera.

Walt asked me to join his Actors Studio *Traviata* project. I loved it. The work we did—the improvisations, exploring the life that happens offstage, trying to justify the music as well as the words. It's never thought of in any other opera company. It started me thinking in new ways that I tried to carry out in my own later work. I found it very effective. It really came to the fore when I started teaching and directing.

With my new acting skills, I now found many more performing opportunities. I sang in *Jesus Christ Superstar* on Broadway, leaving after six months (what more could I learn after six months, anyway?) to go into a new project of Walt's and explore fresh ways of performing song cycles, as well as scenes from opera. I later performed in Andre Serban's *Agamemnon* at Lincoln Center and in the Liz Swados cantata, *Oh, Jerusalem*, that she staged at La Mama.

While I continued to teach singing, Leyna Gabriele and I started an MLT Opera Workshop. We took Walt's exercises and shaped them particularly to singers. Later, I took over Leyna's classes in Acting for Singers at SUNY–Purchase, and then I began teaching acting at the City University of New York. Now I teach Walt's technique to non-singers as well as singers. We even created 'guerilla theatre'—staging seemingly spontaneous dramas in the cafeteria, say, during lunch hour.

I began directing opera for small companies all over New York, trying to apply Walt's processes. It was very hard to get conventional opera singers to act naturally. When performing in Liz Swados' *Haggadah*, I met a fellow performer, Ira Siff, who was then starting his parody opera company, *La Gran Scena Opera*. He asked me to direct Act IV of *Traviata* for him, and I jumped at the chance. I've now been directing for *Gran Scena* for twenty years. I was able to work the way I'd learned with Walt—taking plenty of time, improvising, getting the singers to behave truthfully, even in parody. Other stage directors from established, professional opera companies were impressed and wanted to use my techniques. I said to one of them, 'But this is parody opera.' He rejoined, 'I saw more truth in your parody Act from *Traviata* than in whole operas in regular opera houses.'

All the work I do, directing and teaching, is Walt-based. Because it works — for the actor, the play or opera, and for the audience. And new generations are passing the torch. One of my Purchase students wrote me, 'I want you to know that all the exercises I studied with you I am now teaching my own students.'

—PETER SCHLOSSER, Singer, Actor,
Stage Director, Teacher

"I studied with Walt on and off for ten years and performed in his production of *The Misanthrope*. Walt gave me the foundation I have as an actor, teacher, writer. Last summer I was teaching scene study to two hundred children of various ages in a performing workshop. I spent several days on Walt's 'Well Scene.' It's the clearest way to learn Circumstances, Relationship, and Intention and the difference between 'stage behavior' and real behavior.

It was this scene [of Walt's] that taught me what Living on Stage was. As long as I know where I am, what's going on, who I am in relation to the other person, and what I want, I'm okay. When I forget these basics, my performance suffers. Like many other actors, I want to chew scenery. I want to show. But my strength as an actor, and what I learned from Walt, is to just live within the world of Circumstances, Relationship, and Intention. Without these, I'm not serving the play, I'm serving myself and therefore not acting.

Other teachers I've had have remarked how wonderfully I've been trained. That's Walt they're talking about. What I learned from Walt informs my work. It's what makes me Live on Stage."

—JACQUELINE SYDNEY,
Actress, Teacher, Writer

"I first met Walt at HB Studios in 1967. I took his scene class for two or three terms. From the very beginning, I was 'hooked.' His sensitivity and ability to delve into the creative depths of his pupils was awesome.

Years passed, and I found myself acting and then directing community theatre. I believe that my time with Walt made me a far more sensitive actress — less technical, more real. Now I wanted to study directing. So, back to HB to find Walt. So, here it is — I think 1996 or '97 — I'm at HB, Walt isn't there, but I sit in on a directing class. I said, 'Thanks, but no thanks,' and I looked up Walt, a man with a wealth of information to impart and the zeal of a missionary to share it.

His technique of simple tasks was my most valuable learning experience. It was merely an execution of real life. I learned to ask questions—who, what, where, when, why—what's the history, how does it relate to the present?—the future?

Never stop questioning!

I have used what I have learned whenever I've directed. I hear Walt's words in my head. He has been and continues to be an inspiration."

—SUSANNE TRAUB, Director,
Clinical Social Worker

"I had the great good luck to become Walt's student. I responded immediately to his unique blend of idealism, knowledge, and ability to cultivate the best in a young actor. I joined his acting classes at HB and soon became his helper on projects he was staging with his students, at first at HB and later at the Actors Studio. My interest in design developed, as Walt's creative process seemed right to me. And tackling new problems suits me—what I haven't yet done is most interesting to me, as it is for Walt.

Walt found the studio workshop conditions that would permit and encourage creative discoveries. This is a very slow process, not possible in the commercial arena. But it prepares his students to work in any other area. It's an approach of questioning precisely that I bring to all my design work. It comes right from Walt's creative process that I learned working with him at HB, at the Actors Studio, off-Broadway, and in his fresh stagings of musical classics for MLT. I have worked on many projects with Walt and have never failed to benefit as an artist. Today, when I'm in trouble working on a design problem, I apply Walt's process and find a right answer.

Walt has had a huge influence on me. He taught me nothing about design, but everything about art. And I was able to take his values and his process to the world of stage and film design.

I am not unique in my debt to him—many across the country in all aspects of the entertainment industry first found their place in the theatre under his tutelage."

—PATRIZIA VON BRANDENSTEIN,
Designer, Art Director, Academy Award Winner

"What I got from Walt Witcover wasn't only a creative technique that I learned. Basically I learned to have confidence in my choices and to always be aware of what is happening around me—to listen on stage without judging and to respect and value the differences I see.

A breakthrough came in class in my training with Walt at HB. It was an emotional breakthrough—of finding a way to connect to and use deep, hidden pain. I was able to free myself from it, as a burden, and to use it creatively.

Later, in his professional classes, Walt suggested that another actor and I work on scenes from Moliere's *The Misanthrope*. Working as we had been trained, from ourselves and from our own lives today, we found we were able to connect with these perverse 17th-century lovers in a fresh, immediate way. Walt was excited, and from our work in class he developed his unusual '1930s Hollywood' production of the play, in which I played the same leading role of Celimene (now 'Sally Mayne').

My training and subsequent work in many of Walt's MLT projects that grew out of the collaborative work we did as a group was a rare and precious experience.

While I don't expect to find it often, I am able to work full time as a professional actor—off-Broadway, on TV soap operas, doing background work in films.

I am now learning to use Walt's training in a new way, as I take my first steps into the world of directing. I had just been asked to direct a one-woman piece and I was indecisive. But with Walt's encouraging words I took the challenge and found a new world open up to me. What once seemed too enormous a task now seems possible, thanks to Walt."

—JOANN WAHL, Actress

Appendices

APPENDIX A: GLOSSARY

"Affective Memory": A memory that, when recalled, brings significant emotions. For the actor, a technique that helps him bring immediate expression from past experiences.

Analogy: "A likeness, or correspondence, between the relations of things to one another." For the actor, a vivid means of bringing his character's problems close to himself; a personal translation of an element of character, relationship, circumstances, event, or intention in the actor's role. See Personalization and Substitution.

Endow (Endowing, Endowment): "To furnish, as with some gift, faculty, or quality." For the actor, to give an additional imaginary meaning, usually personal and/or charged, to the actual object or person on stage; to elevate a mundane element to dramatic significance.

"The Howsies": A habit of concern with preconceived, usually conventional, manners of behaving; an addiction to clichés of character and general stereotypes of the ways certain actions, scenes, or plays should be performed. Also known as

"Imagitis": An advanced case of "the Howsies." Adherence, often unconscious, to predetermined patterns of scenic results that obligates the actor to rigid forms of behavior and prohibits any spontaneous, fresh expression.

Improvise (Improvisation): To perform extemporaneously, without a prepared or memorized text; various elements of Circumstances, Relationships, or Intentions may be given or prepared, but dialogue is generally spontaneous. (See Structured Improvisation)

"Loaded": As with a firearm, prepared with a charge or bullet to explode when triggered; for the actor, any object or experience that has been so charged by life or craft; a powerful source of strong emotions to be released on contact.

"Method Acting": A loose, generic term for any structured process of organic acting that seeks expressive realism by the actor's identification with his role. An American version of Stanislavsky's "System" (see below) as interpreted by members of the Group Theatre, particularly by Lee Strasberg, Stella Adler, Sanford Meisner, and Elia Kazan, and their followers; taught at the Actors Studio.

Particularize (Particularizing, Particularization): To identify specific details of an object or person, time or place, in seeking stronger, more immediate dramatic responses.

"Partneritis": A group of symptoms that often afflicts two actors rehearsing together while preparing a scene for an acting class: greater anticipation, directing each other, a concern for specific results (the "Howsies"), and sharing intentions, subtexts, or personal images that would much better be kept private.

Personalize (Personalizing, Personalization): An actor's means of bringing himself closer to his role and his role closer to himself by use of private personal analogies, recalled or imagined; any such individual attempt to interpret or translate the text, Relationships, Circumstances, or Intentions; the term used and promulgated by Lee Strasberg.

"Public Privacy": One of the paradoxical conditions of most acting in western civilization: while the actor on stage is always performing in public, the character he enacts is usually in private. Thus the actor, while actually in public, must appear to behave as if in private, to live and function, while performing in this contradictory, imaginary state. Identified by Stanislavsky as the source of major acting problems.

Sense-Memory: A technique, developed by Stanislavsky, of recalling the details of sight, sound, smell, touch, and taste of outer objects or stimuli, as well as inner bodily sensing, so that the actor may appear actually to be experiencing such sensations.

"The Stanislavsky System": A generalized reference to the sum of discoveries, techniques and values of Stanislavsky's work at the Moscow Art Theatre from its founding in 1898 until his death in 1938; a misnomer, as Stanislavsky himself maintained—a "System" implies something set, whereas his work, his searching for better approaches to greater truth on stage and new expressiveness for the actor, was constantly evolving.

Structured Improvisation : A spontaneous interaction, unrehearsed, with extemporized dialogue, based on pre-determined circumstantial elements of time and place, relationships, and basic intentions.

Substitution: The term used and promulgated by Uta Hagen to refer to the actor's substituting his own images to make any scenic element stimulate the same response from himself as those in the play draw from his character. (see Personalization and Analogy)

"Witcoverian": Students of Walt Witcover who have trained with him for a significant period, who follow his precepts and make use of his techniques and processes in their work on stage or screen, in drama, opera, concert, or cabaret, and in the studio or classroom.

APPENDIX B: SEQUENCES OF SENSORY EXERCISES

I—Endowments:

- Two common drinks onto a glass of room-temperature water

- Two common liquids, non-drinkable

- One drink and one non-drinkable liquid

- Two clear pictures (e.g., greeting card) onto one or two blank pieces of paper of similar size(s); the pictures brought to class to check accuracy

- Two different textiles onto a plain white common textile of a similar size(s); the textiles brought to class to check accuracy

- Any bland object endowed as each of two different objects of similar size and shape, then put to use as endowed; all objects brought to class to test accuracy

- Two objects, one endowed successively in three different ways, the other remaining as it is, the two then used together; one or two of the objects brought to class, the other one or two from memories

- Two objects, A and B: first time A endowed, B not; second time B endowed, A not; third time, both A and B endowed in new ways, (four endowments); all endowments from memories; and used together each time

- Two objects, both endowed from memories that may be mixed with fantasy in three different ways each (six endowments), and used together each time

- Three objects, A, B, and C: first time A and B endowed, C not; second time, A and C endowed, B not; third time B and C endowed, A not (six endowments). A, B, and C to be used together each time; the endowments to be based either on memories with added elements of fantasy, or solely on fantasy

Students prepare for the first six exercises by examining the chosen objects closely at home. Endowments that are general or vague should be repeated. Exercises nine and ten may be done in two or three successive lessons.

II—Sense-Memory:

- Cup or Mug

- Same cup or mug with tea or coffee in it. Drinking and inner sensing.

- Last two or three steps in preparing hot drink of the previous exercise

- Large container of cold drink and glass. Compare sight, touch, temperature, smell, and weight of each. Then pour liquid into glass, testing seeing and hearing, change of weight, temperature, smell, and taste. Inner sensing.

- Soup or cereal and spoon. Hot or cold liquid with solids, eating.

- Soup or cereal, whichever not chosen in previous exercise.

- Making a sandwich, testing and tasting each ingredient in the process in turn; using knife, eating, sensing the mix of ingredients changing in the mouth.

- A salad of various ingredients; using knife and fork.

- A mix of foods: hot, cold, wet, and dry.

- Four "loaded" foods, not usually eaten together (viz., lemon, onion, liquor, candy)

- Weights: Dumbbells and barbells; OR a pail filled with three or four levels of water; OR a suitcase successively filled with three or four increasingly heavy loads of books; lifting, carrying, setting down the various weights

- Women: putting on makeup (on either left or right half of the face)

- Washing hands

- Washing hands and face with washcloth

- Men: shaving (either left or right half of the face)

- Washing an article of clothing

- Dressing and/or undressing

- Taking a bath or shower

- Two sounds and two smells that can be explored outside of class, one pleasant and one unpleasant of each; in class sensing each separately, then in combinations—pleasant sound with unpleasant smell, etc. Responding either toward or away from each spontaneously.

- Picture of exterior scene, studied to fix a visual sense memory, brought to class to check accuracy as image is projected onto a wall of the studio

- Another picture of a personal exterior; if not physically available, then from the student's memory; adding other senses of time and place, season, weather, possible sounds and smells, visualizing beyond the picture limits

- Going closer to the building; touching external parts, entering

- A room selected from that building for personal associations

- Another room (if helpful for more "loaded" memories)

- A particular time remembered in one of these rooms

This brings the sequence to the threshold of Affective Memory. If desired and appropriate, the student may then either recall and explore a memorable time and place, using all previous learned sense-memories projected in air, or else relive the event solely in his inner senses, as he relaxes in an easy chair and is guided by the teacher.

III—Conditions:

- Overall heat and cold

- Bodily pains actually experienced (headache, toothache, sprained ankle, etc.)

- Bodily pains transferred to different parts of the body

- Bodily pains never actually experienced

- Overall bodily distress (nausea, dizziness, exhaustion, drunkenness, etc.)

- Outer sensory conditions (dark, bright, noisy, smelly, smoke, wind, rain, etc.)

- Circumstantial conditions (hurry, quiet, problems, good or bad news, etc.)

Exercises continue combining various conditions as progressive obstacles to carrying out simple tasks in familiar circumstances. Tasks should be repeated, first with one condition, then another, and then a combination. Additional new conditions should be added singly before attempting combinations.

APPENDIX C: BASIC MONOLOGUES AND SCENES

MONOLOGUES:

For both MEN and WOMEN:
 The Glass Menagerie: Tom's opening narration
 I am a Camera: Christopher's opening monologue
 Dream Girl: Georgina's opening monologue (cutting radio)

For MEN, after the above:
 The Matchmaker: Vandergelder, Act I
        Cornelius, Act II
        Malachi, Act III
 The Seagull: Treplef, Act I, to Sorin
      Trigorin, Act II, to Nina
 A View from the Bridge: Alfieri
 Our Town: Stage Manager

For WOMEN, after the above:
 The Skin of Our Teeth: Sabina, Act I
         Fortune Teller, Act II
         Mrs. Antrobus, Act II
 Uncle Vanya: Sonia, Act II
 The Seagull: Masha, Act III, to Trigorin
 The Matchmaker: Mrs. Levi, Act IV
 This Property Has Been Condemned: Willie

BASIC SHAKESPEARE:
 Romeo and Juliet: Prologue
 Sonnets

SCENES:

For Two MEN:
 The Glass Menagerie: Tom and Jim, Act II
 Death of a Salesman: Biff and Happy, Act I
 Come Blow Your Horn: Buddy and Alan, Act I
 All My Sons: Joe and Chris, Act I
 Career: Sam and Maury
 A View from the Bridge: Alfieri and Eddie
 The Odd Couple: Oscar and Felix, Act II

For Two WOMEN:

Picnic: Millie and Madge, Act II

Middle of the Night: Betty and Marilyn

The Children's Hour: Martha and Karen, Act I

All My Sons: Ann and Sue

A View from the Bridge: Beatrice and Catherine

The Glass Menagerie: Amanda and Laura, Scene 2; Scene 7

The Young and Fair: All Two-Women Scenes

For One MAN and One WOMAN:

Career: Sam and Shirley, Act I

       Sam and Barbara, Act I

I am a Camera: Sally and Chris, Acts I, II, III

Middle of the Night: Betty and George

Waiting for Lefty: Joe and Edna

Golden Boy: Joe and Lorna

The Glass Menagerie: Tom and Amanda; Tom and Laura; Jim and Laura

A View from the Bridge: Eddie and Beatrice

       Eddie and Catherine

       Catherine and Rudolf

ABOUT THE AUTHOR

An actor for sixty years, a director for fifty-five years, a teacher of acting for fifty years—Walt Witcover appears to have spent several lives in the theatre.

Born and bred in New York City, he soon became addicted to concerts, opera, and theatre-going with his widowed mother, who was a popular lecturer on current books and plays. He was also a secret movie-addict, dosing up weekly on the musical romances of Deanna Durbin and the lush Jeannette MacDonald-Nelson Eddy operettas. He attended Townsend Harris High School and Cornell University, where—after two-and-a-half years' time out for Field Artillery service during World War II—he received his BA in Speech and Drama and his MA in Dramatic Production.

Returning to New York, he first trained in the professional program of the American Theatre Wing, studying acting with Curt Conway and Herbert Berghof, dance with Martha Graham, voice with Marian Rich, and directing with Lee Strasberg. He also began performing off-Broadway in Equity Library Theatre projects, in National Theatre Conference showcases, at the Cherry Lane and with the New York City Theatre Company, while touring with the Children's World Theatre. Summers he spent stage-managing and lighting for the Barter Theatre of Virginia, and as a Junior Artist-in-Residence in acting at Stanford University. New performing problems led him to seek out Mr. Strasberg for more intensive acting training over the next three years. At the same time he was directing community theatre in Westchester. When a sudden casting replacement opened the directing slot in the Long Island summer theatre in which he was performing, he was able to jump in and direct his first professional production. Its unusual success led to his directing the rest of the season.

He found his first New York directing job staging the 1954 Equity Library-Equity Community production of *The Hasty Heart*. It proved a major success, and won him a position directing the summer "package" of the play starring Farley Granger. Now he was firmly committed to a directing career; over the next twelve years he became known as an "up-and-coming" director of talent, as his productions were recognized for their originality, taste and sensitive skill. They reaped many awards: his Equity Library *Maedchen in Uniform*, O'Casey's *Red Roses for Me* at the Stella Adler Studio, the Obie-Award production of Joyce's *Exiles*, the American premiere of Yukio Mishima's *Modern Noh Plays*, and the Lola d'Annunzio prize production of Jerome Max's *The Exhaustion of Our Son's Love*. His talents were also recognized by his mentor, Lee Strasberg, who now invited him to join his Directors Unit at the Actors Studio.

He also started teaching acting—albeit reluctantly. The cast of his ELT *Hasty Heart* wanted to continue working with him the following season; it took but a few months conducting weekly sessions of exercises and scene work to reveal his talent for teaching. New students came, he found he had to rent a larger space for two evenings weekly, and his reputation as a supportive, honest and perceptive teacher grew. He found that in addition to helping "support his habit" of directing, these classes proved to be stimulating and rewarding. He refined his processes, seeking to find a clearer structure and process; and when Herbert Berghof invited him to join the faculty at his new HB Studio on Bank Street in the West Village, he agreed. For the next twenty-five years, from 1960 to 1985, he taught weekly classes in basic technique, scene technique and directing, later adding musical theatre, poetry for the actor, and a classics workshop.

Meanwhile at the Actors Studio, under the inspiration of Lee Strasberg, he began to experiment directing classic and musical material. So often excited by what he heard in opera and on the classic stage, but just as often so disappointed by what he saw, he now found the conditions of the Studio Directors Unit conducive to an "experiment in lyric theatre." Over five years, his influential, one-act-per-year "mod" project of Verdi's *La Traviata* (which won the 1968 Actors Studio "Total Theatre" Award), and his first half of Sheridan's *The Rivals* proved that modern "Method" techniques could lead to new staging and performing riches in lyric classics. So rewarding did he find this kind of directorial process, that with his closest collaborators, he was moved to create a theatre laboratory where similar problems could be fully explored and the results shared. And so, quite without realizing it, Walt Witcover turned away from the commercial career he had been pursuing to take up the challenge of bringing classic drama and opera to fresh performing life in his Masterworks Laboratory Theatre. There he and his colleagues also widened their scope to include literature and music not intended for the stage — poetry, short stories, and song-cycles.

With his reputation growing as a master acting teacher, he was sought out in academic theatre departments: as a guest director with a fresh approach to classics by Syracuse University, the University of Maryland, and Virginia Tech; and as a full-time Professor of Theatre Arts and Acting Mentor in the BFA training program of the State University of New York College at Purchase, and then at the University of Maryland, Baltimore County. In all of these venues, he continued to refine his approaches to the training of actors and directors, constantly seeking a clearer, more sequential process that would prove its worth in practice. He now teaches exclusively at the Witcover Acting Studio in mid-Manhattan, offering private training and coaching for actors and singers.

Recently he has resumed performing; after sixty years, he maintains, he "has finally learned how to do it." Perhaps, he also wants to show his students that he can, and does, practice what he preaches. His recent "Parlor Programs" are proving increasingly popular: in high schools and colleges, for retirement communities and private parties, he continues to perform his one-man arrangement of one of MLT's most unusual and successful projects, *A Serving of Verse*, as well as a fifty-minute version of his own *Innocent Merriment*, or *Gilbert without Sullivan*. A new program of Chekhov short stories is in rehearsal to mark the 100th anniversary of Chekhov's death.

He has two more books in preparation: *A Road Less Traveled* examines why and how he became an actor and a director; and *Dissecting Directing* is an account of his organic process in approaching specific new works and classics, both spoken and sung, as well as poetry, song, and story-theatre projects. After thirty-five years, Walt Witcover and his Masterworks Laboratory Theatre are still exploring fresh approaches to Living on Stage.